Treachery and Retribution

England's Dukes, Marquesses and Earls
1066–1707

Andrew Rawson

Pen & Sword
MILITARY

First published in Great Britain in 2017 by
PEN AND SWORD MILITARY
an imprint of
Pen and Sword Books Ltd
47 Church Street
Barnsley
South Yorkshire S70 2AS

ISBN 978 1 47387 624 8

Printed and bound in Malta by
Gutenberg Press Ltd, Gudja Road, Tarxien GXQ 2902

Typeset in Times by CHIC GRAPHICS

Pen & Sword Books Ltd incorporates the imprints of
Archaeology, Atlas, Aviation, Battleground, Discovery,
Family History, History, Maritime, Military, Naval, Politics,
Railways, Select, Social History, Transport, True Crime,
Claymore Press, Frontline Books, Leo Cooper, Praetorian Press,
Remember When, Seaforth Publishing and Wharncliffe.

For a complete list of Pen and Sword titles please contact
Pen and Sword Books Limited
47 Church Street, Barnsley, South Yorkshire, S70 2AS, England
E-mail: enquiries@pen-and-sword.co.uk
Website: www.pen-and-sword.co.uk

Contents

Introduction

This is the history of England during its formative years, told through the stories of a select class of people: its nobility. Plenty has been written and said about the kings and queens who ruled the kingdom; their strengths and weaknesses, their conquests and defeats. But these are the stories of the men and women who ran the country and served their monarch, sometimes loyally and sometimes treacherously. It is told in short stories, in the form of news summaries of a particular event, a family or a group of earls. This means we can see how a single person, or group of people, developed their motives and how their actions played out, either in court, on their estates, or on campaign.

The original noble of the kingdom of England was the earl. Earls owned the area associated with their title, administering it on behalf of the crown. Titles were awarded for a range of reasons: loyalty, good diplomacy, victorious campaigning or friendship. Edward III introduced the new rank of Duke of Cornwall for his son Edward of Woodstock (later known as the Black Prince) in 1337 and this dukedom is still associated with the monarch's eldest son. Five royal relatives were created dukes over the next fifty years and Richard II created six more on the same day in September 1397. Henry VIII introduced a new rank which fell between the dukes and the earls when he created his Lord Treasurer, William Paulet, Marquess of Winchester, in 1551.

We have to remember that the monarch was ruler in name but rarely in presence. At its height, the Angevin Empire (that of the House of Anjou, which ruled England in the twelfth and thirteenth centuries) stretched hundreds of miles from end to end, from as far north as the Scottish border to as far south as the Pyrenees. It took time to send messages across the kingdom when the only means of travel was the horse on land, and at the mercy of the weather on the sea.

A king was kept busy dealing with business in his royal court and would rarely visit the outlying parts of the kingdom, if at all, unless there was a problem. He would only go to the northern border if he intended to attack Scotland and usually only visited areas on the continent if there was a problem. The huge distances and slow communications meant that many nobles were left to self-govern their areas. They had to maintain justice and security as well as keeping the peace. They also had to manage their estates, build castles and fortifications and raise taxes, all in the name of the king.

The story begins in 1066, when William the Bastard of Normandy invaded Anglo-Saxon England to take what he thought was rightfully his. He immediately replaced the earls who ran the country with his own Norman men and then the ruling started in earnest. It culminated with an audit of his territories, the Domesday Book in 1085.

England has changed its borders several times over the centuries covered in these pages. It made a rapid conquest of Ireland in 1170s, which would result in a succession of uprisings and rebellions over the centuries. Then there was the difficult campaign to subdue the Welsh princes a century later. England's nobles were at the forefront of expanding the kingdom, sometimes supporting their king and occasionally allying with the rebels.

On England's northern border, there were continual wars and alliances with Scotland, which resulted in victories and defeats on both sides. They also resulted in a complicated connection between the English and Scottish royal families. The family connection would end with the union of the crowns, when James VI of Scotland was invited to become James I of England following the death of the childless Elizabeth I in 1603. The book ends with the Acts of the Union of the English and Scottish Parliaments in May 1707.

There were many problems with the kingdom's continental possessions in what is now France. The Angevin Empire, as England became known in the 1100s, expanded due to a combination of effective diplomacy, successful campaigns and lucrative marriages. There was Normandy and Brittany in the north-west, Maine, Anjou and Touraine south-west of Paris, Guyenne and Aquitaine in the south-west. By the 1170s the Angevin kings of England controlled more territory south of the English Channel than north of it and the monarch had to rely on his barons to rule these areas on his behalf. But there were many problems holding these vast areas and they fell into French hands one by one, either through battles, diplomacy or treachery, over the next 200 years.

England has been involved in many alliances and wars with France and Spain over the centuries as their empires jostled for power in Western Europe. The nobles were often at the forefront of the diplomacy and when that failed they raised armies and led them into battle. They would then be rewarded or disgraced according to their fortunes in war.

England's nobles were a real mixed bunch of characters. There are a few well-known cases who dramatically changed, or tried to change, the kingdom's history. We have Simon de Montfort, 6th Earl of Leicester, who led the barons' rebellion against Henry III, in the hope of introducing democracy into the kingdom in 1285. Then there was Thomas Stanley, 1st Earl of Derby, who decided the Battle of Bosworth, ending the Wars of the

Roses with Richard III's death and the crowning of Henry VII in 1485. We also have Thomas Boleyn, 1st Earl of Wiltshire, who pushed his daughters, Mary and Anne, in front of Henry VIII for personal gain, with tragic results for the family. They are just three of many who contributed to the kingdom's story in one way or another.

This is a story of powerful people who lived in deadly times. On the one hand the nobles were upstanding men of honour who were prepared to fight for what they believed in (with the lives of their peasants of course). On the other hand they could be treacherous or debauched; men who abused the privileges of their rank. Here are the stories of their strengths, their frailties and their excesses.

Some nobles were chivalrous, loyal and brave while others were cowardly, violent and brutal. There were those who were self-serving, treacherous and masters at back-stabbing. Some were clever and calculating while others were reckless and foolhardy. Some were driven insane by the responsibilities they faced while others were born insane in the incestuous world of England's nobility. Some would eat or drink excessively, while others gambled, quarrelled and overspent. Many were passionate men, becoming involved in secret marriages for love, while others were lustful, leaving a trail of illegitimate children, mistresses and divorces in their wake.

We also have their long-suffering wives to consider in a time when women's rights were ignored in favour of the family name and financial rewards. Girls were often betrothed at a young age and sometimes spent their childhood living with a ward or guardian. They were married young for money or to form an alliance rather than for love. Many also had to suffer their husband's infidelity in silence.

The nobles' wives were then expected to produce children as soon as they could, all in the name of keeping the bloodline strong and at a time when pregnancy and childbirth was dangerous for women. Medical understanding was limited; people believed more in God's judgement than a doctor's skills. A sudden death was often incorrectly blamed on malicious poisoning, and the miracle of giving birth to a healthy child was attributed to divine intervention.

The monarch had the right to approve a marriage license and he also had the right to block marriages. He had to consider the power balances across his kingdom when it came to marrying his nobles to each other. He knew that the right marriage could create loyal supporters, but he did not want powerful families forming unions in case they opposed his rule. It was a complex power game in which rich brides were offered as rewards to create the right power balances across the kingdom. Love did not come in to it and woe betide any noblewomen who married in secret or who had children out of wedlock; unless it was with the king's consent of course.

Chapter 1

William I
1066–87

Planning the Invasion, 1066

The childless King of England, Edward the Confessor, originally promised his throne to the illegitimate Duke William of Normandy. But he changed his mind on his deathbed in January 1066 and named Harold Godwinson as his successor. Duke William declared his intention to take what he believed was his at his first council and then organised the invasion details at a second meeting. William's legitimate half-brother Robert, Count of Mortain, promised over one hundred ships, the largest contingent, and Hugh d'Avranches provided another sixty. Roger de Montgomerie and William FitzOsbern, William de Warenne and Bishop Odo of Bayeux vowed to send more.

The Invasion, 1066

Tostig Godwinson and Harald Hardrada invaded Northumbria in September 1066, and Harold Godwinson marched north and defeated and killed them at the battle of Stamford Bridge on 25 September. William's Norman fleet landed in Pevensey Bay three days later and his army raided the Hastings area until Harold returned.

Many of the men who would soon rule England fought alongside William at the battle of Hastings on 14 October: Brian of Brittany, Alan the Black, Robert de Beaumont, Alan Rufus, William de Warenne, Gerbod the Fleming, Robert of Mortain, Roger de Montgomerie, William FitzOsbern and Ralph de Gaël. They defeated the Anglo-Saxon army and Harold died in the battle.

Delegating Norman Rule, 1067

A few Anglo-Saxon landowners declared Edgar the Ætheling their new king but he had little support and William seized London and was crowned at Westminster Abbey on Christmas Day. He told his supporters to conquer areas of England, promising earldoms and estates as rewards. William the Conqueror's half-brother Odo was created Earl of Kent in 1067 and he ruled England when William visited Normandy. Another large estate owner was Robert of Mortain, Earl of Cornwall, and he conquered land across the kingdom.

Northumbria Rebels, 1067
Morcar resisted the Norman invasion of Northumbria until he was imprisoned. Copsi was rewarded with the Earldom of Northumbria after paying homage to William but he was instructed to bring Yorkshire under control. Osulf ambushed Copsi in Newburn-upon-Tyne and then beheaded him as he escaped from a burning church. Osulf was killed by outlaws soon afterwards and William accepted Gospatric's offer of money for the Earldom of Northumbria.

Conquering England, 1068
Following a brief visit to Normandy, William brought south-west England under control. Gerbod the Fleming had been created Earl of Chester but he was harassed by both the Anglo-Saxons and the Welsh as he fought to control the north part of the Welsh border. William FitzOsbern was created Earl of Hereford, Gloucester, Worcester and Oxfordshire and he too struggled to conquer the south part of the Welsh border.

Henry de Beaumont, 1st Earl of Warwick, joined William in 1068, at the start of a campaign across the Midlands. FitzOsbern agreed peace terms with the Anglo-Saxons in York, securing the north. His next task was to invade the Welsh kingdom of Gwent. Meanwhile, William's new earls secured their new lands by building castles and fortifying the towns across the kingdom.

The Harrying of the North, 1068-72
Gospatric, Earl of Northumbria, Edwin, Earl of Mercia, and Edgar the Ætheling rose up in Northumbria in 1068, so William confiscated their titles. Northumbria was given to Robert Comine and he marched north to Durham where he ignored Bishop Ethelwin's warnings. Gospatric's rebels attacked in January 1069 and Comine was killed when they burnt the bishop's house down. Ethelwin then gathered an army and marched on York forcing William to send troops north to raid villages across Northumbria. Gospatric and Edgar the Ætheling tried in vain to stop what became known as the Harrying of the North. William forgave Gospatric but he rebelled and was defeated again in 1072; this time he was exiled to Scotland.

The Godwinsons and Eadric the Wild, 1069

Harold Godwinson's sons, Godwin and Edmund, had escaped to south-east Ireland where Diarmait of Leinster lent them a fleet of ships. Their attacks on the Normans began in 1069 and Brian of Brittany, 1st Earl of Cornwall, defeated a raid on Devon. Around the same time, Ralph de Gaël defeated Norsemen who invaded Norfolk and he was rewarded with the Earldom of the East Angles.

Brian and William FitzOsbern, Earl of Hereford, failed to relieve the siege of Shrewsbury but they defeated the army besieging Exeter and then 'punished their audacity with great slaughter'. Brian of Brittany then marched north to help William defeat Eadric the Wild at the battle of Stafford and he was rewarded with estates in Suffolk and Cornwall. After Brian left England, Robert, Count of Mortain, was given his title and estates as a reward for defeating the Danes at the battle of Lindsay.

Odo the Fraud, 1076

Odo, Earl of Kent, was arrested and tried for defrauding the crown in 1076 and his Diocese of Canterbury was forced to return the properties it had stolen. He was imprisoned six years later for planning an unauthorised military expedition to Italy and his estates and earldom were confiscated. Robert, Count of Mortain, persuaded his half-brother, King William, to release Odo on his deathbed.

Northumbria Rebels Again, 1079-85

William entrusted the Earldom of Northumbria to Waltheof, 1st Earl of Huntingdon and Northampton, after Gospatric had been exiled to Scotland in 1072. But Waltheof rebelled in 1079 and the earldom was sold to William Walcher, the Bishop of Durham. He was unable to deal with Scottish raiders or the locals' complaints and he eventually murdered the critical Ligulf of Lumley. Eadulf Rus trapped Walcher in a church in Gateshead, set it on fire, and killed him as he escaped. The Northumbrian rebels then besieged Durham castle.

William sent his half-brother Odo of Bayeux north and he broke the power of the Anglo-Saxon rebels in Northumbria. The earldom was given to Aubrey de Coucy but he resigned around 1085 when the Danes threatened to invade Northumbria.

Robert Curthose Rebels, 1077

William's son Robert rebelled against his father at the end of 1077 and was supported by Robert of Bellême, William de Breteuil, and Roger FitzGilbert. King Philip I of France gave the rebels Gerberoy Castle as a base so they could raid Normandy. Robert nearly killed King William during the siege of the castle and Henry de Beaumont, 1st Earl of Warwick, organised a reconciliation between father and son. William later confirmed Robert would inherit Normandy, to appease him.

The Domesday Book, 1085

At the end of 1085 William called for a survey of his lands during the Great Gemot held at Old Sarum, Salisbury. The audit would be a list of landowners, what they owned and what tax they were due to pay. Osmund, Earl of Dorset, was the chief commissioner for drawing up the Domesday Book and it took over six months to complete. The landowners had to swear their allegiance to William once the records had been accepted.

Inheriting Flanders, 1070-1

King William's brother-in-law Count Baldwin VI of Flanders died in 1070 and his young sons were left in the care of his widow Richilde. She asked William FitzOsbern to marry her when their uncle Robert the Frisian challenged their inheritance. He hurried to Flanders to claim his bride only to be killed in the battle of Cassel in February 1071.

An Unpleasant Marriage Proposal

Ascelin Gouel de Perceval wanted to marry Isabella, daughter of Roger de Breteuil, 2nd Earl of Hereford. Perceval captured Breteuil when he refused and then tortured him until he gave consent to the union.

Marriage Rebellion, 1075

King William refused to permit Ralph de Gaël, Earl of the East Angles, to marry Emma, sister of Roger de Breteuil, 2nd Earl of Hereford, in 1075 because it would unite two powerful families. So Gaël and Breteuil rebelled and were joined by Waltheof, Earl of Northumberland and Huntingdon. But the Worcestershire militia stopped Breteuil along the River Severn while Odo of Bayeux and Geoffrey de Montbray pursued Gaël to Norwich.

Gaël's wife held on in Norwich Castle while Ralph sailed across the North Sea looking for help from Scandinavia. Danish and Swedish fleets failed to lift the siege but the countess eventually negotiated her freedom. Roger and his wife were exiled to Brittany and Roger was imprisoned until William I died. Every rebel peasant captured by Geoffrey de Montbray had their right foot cut off as a punishment. Waltheof was beheaded a few months later and his daughter Maud gave the Earldom of Huntingdon to her husband Simon de Senlis and then to the King David of Scotland.

The Earldom Shrewsbury, 1079

Robert de Bellême inherited vast estates in France when his mother was murdered in 1079 and William exercised his right to garrison his castles. But Robert still gained a reputation as being 'grasping and cruel, an implacable persecutor of the Church of God and the poor'. His brother, Hugh, had to wait until his father, Roger de Montgomerie, died in 1094 before he could inherit The Earldom of Shrewsbury.

North-East Wales, 1081

Gerbod the Fleming, 1st Earl of Chester, had been captured at the battle of Cassel in 1071 but he escaped and fled to Rome where Pope Gregory VII advised him to become a monk. His important Earldom of Chester was given to Hugh d'Avranches. Hugh captured part of north-east Wales and gave it to his cousin Robert of Rhuddlan to rule on his behalf. Hugh met Gruffudd ap Cynan, King of Gwynedd, at Corwen in 1081, only to arrest and imprison him in Chester Castle. Robert was then allowed to rule Gwynedd on behalf of the king.

Chapter 2

William II
1087–1100

Rebellions, 1088

There was a conspiracy to replace William Rufus with his brother, Robert Curthose, Duke of Normandy, soon after he was crowned. The main conspirators were his uncles Odo of Bayeux, Robert of Mortain and Geoffrey de Mowbray, his cousin, Robert de Mowbray as well as Eustace of Boulogne, and the brothers Roger, Hugh and Robert de Montgomery.

The rebels burned properties belonging to the king and his supporters over Easter 1088 and William called for them to be hanged 'or by some other form of execution utterly removed from the face of the earth'. He did however, try to parley with some, and Roger of Montgomerie was rewarded with the Earldom of Shrewsbury for pledging his support. Montgomery would negotiate Robert de Bellême's surrender after he was cornered in Rochester Castle.

William handed out rewards for those who had supported him, including the Earldom of Warwick for Henry de Beaumont and the Earldom of Surrey for William de Warenne. But Warenne did not have long to enjoy his new title because he was mortally wounded besieging Pevensey Castle in Sussex.

The king also punished the rebels, imposing fines and confiscating estates and titles. Only a few were pardoned, like Roger de Mowbray. Robert of Mortain was snubbed when he asked for his father's Earldoms of Mortain and Cornwall in 1090. Seven years later he demanded with 'shameless arrogance' the Earldom of Kent when his uncle Odo of Bayeux died, leaving him a rich man, even if most of the wealth had been acquired through extortion and theft.

Alan Rufus, Odo of Champagne, Roger of Poitou and Walter d'Aincourt tracked William de St-Calais down to Durham castle where he surrendered after a promise of safe conduct. But there was an outcry and Alan threatened to withdraw his support because the king had tried to bully him into committing perjury in court. St-Calais' life was saved and he was exiled to

Normandy. But Alan stuck by William and he persuaded him to assemble England's very first 'High Court of Parliament' at York in 1089 to restore order across the kingdom.

Securing Loyalty
William Rufus had to hand out titles and appointments to many barons to get their loyalty. For example, Walter Giffard of Longueville was created Earl of Buckingham and was appointed the Justiciar of England. William also had to buy the support of the Norman barons, who backed Robert, Duke of Normandy. He paid to fortify their castles and garrisoned them with his own men, so he could secure his hold on the Duchy.

Founding the English Church, 1092
Osmund, Earl of Dorset, worked to found the constitution of a cathedral body on the Norman model. He also supervised the building of the cathedral at Old Sarum, Salisbury, only to see the roof destroyed in a thunderstorm five days after it was consecrated in 1092. Despite the bad omen, the cathedral was repaired and Osmund regulated the Divine Office, the Mass, and the Church Calendar under the collective title, 'Sarum Use'. Saint Osmund's canonisation took almost 350 years to complete.

Scotland's Problems, 1093-4
Malcolm III of Scotland had made peace with William I in 1072, handing over his son Duncan as security in exchange for lands. William Rufus confiscated the lost lands in 1091 so Malcolm invaded two years later, looking to retake them. Robert de Mowbray, 9th Earl of Northumbria, ambushed the Scottish army at Alnwick on 13 November. Both Malcolm and his son Edward were killed; Queen Margaret died of grief a few days later.

Donald banished Malcolm's sons and seized the Scottish throne but Duncan returned with an army provided by William in May 1094. While Duncan was victorious, he was seen as an outsider. He eventually had to send William's army back to England, only to be ambushed and killed by Donald in November 1094. Malcolm's son Edgar eventually returned with another Anglo-Norman army led by his uncle Edgar, and Donald was either assassinated, exiled or imprisoned in 1099.

Mowbray's Rebellion, 1095
While Scotland had been subdued, the Norman earls were unhappy with William II's rule. Robert de Mowbray, Earl of Northumbria, William of Eu and William of Aldrie were offended when Stephen of Aumale, son of William's daughter Adela and the Count of Blois, was made heir to the throne.

Mowbray ignored William's summons after he illegally seized four Norwegian vessels in the Tyne. But his supporters abandoned him when the king led his army north. Mowbray escaped a besieged Bamburgh Castle but he was captured at Tynemouth and his wife surrendered when the king threatened to blind her husband. Mowbray was imprisoned for life and eventually became a monk. But he was the lucky one because William of Aldrie was executed while William of Eu was castrated and blinded.

A Murdered Wife
The marriage of Roger de Montgomerie, 1st Earl of Shrewsbury, and Mabel de Bellême, brought together two powerful families. But the Bunel brothers believed she had taken their inheritance so they broke into their castle and murdered her in her bed. As was the Norman tradition, her eldest son, Robert, received the Normandy estates while her second son, Hugh, received the English estates and the Earldom of Shrewsbury.

Crusaders, 1096
The king's brother Robert, and Ralph de Gaël, Earl of the East Angles, joined the First Crusade in 1096. They took part in the siege of Nicaea and then joined Bohemund I in Antioch. Ralph died on Crusade in 1101.

North-West Wales, 1093-8
Robert of Rhuddlan held north-west Wales until he was killed by Gruffudd ap Cynan in 1093. Hugh d'Avranches, 1st Earl of Chester, inherited Robert's lands but he lost most of Gwynedd and Anglesey when the Welsh revolted in 1094.

Hugh de Montgomerie, 2nd Earl of Shrewsbury, supported Hugh d'Avranches' invasion of Gwynedd in 1098. D'Avranches became known as the Wolf because of his savagery and Gruffudd had to withdraw to Ireland when his mercenary fleet abandoned him. Gruffudd was joined by King Magnus Barefoot of Norway and they counter-attacked and killed Montgomerie, forcing D'Avranches to withdraw from Anglesey. It allowed Gruffudd to return to Wales and agree a truce over the ownership of Gwynedd. D'Avranches soon become so fat he could barely walk and he became a monk just before he died in 1101.

Chapter 3

Henry I
1100–35

Seizing the Crown, 1100

King William II was accidentally shot and killed while hunting in the New Forest in Hampshire on 2 August 1100. The earls gathered to choose a successor and while most barons favoured Duke Robert, who was on crusade, Henry de Beaumont, 1st Earl of Warwick, advised them to select his younger brother, Henry. De Beaumont became the king's companion, one of the few barons faithful to the king.

Duke Robert Rebels, 1101

Henry I quickly upset many barons. He accused William of Mortain, 3rd Earl of Cornwall, of taking lands without permission and confiscated them. William de Warenne, 2nd Earl of Surrey, had wanted to marry Matilda, daughter of Malcolm III of Scotland but Henry took her for his wife instead. Ranulf Flambard also escaped from the Tower of London and fled to Normandy. They all wanted to see Henry's brother, Duke Robert Curthose, on the throne.

Mortain started by attacking Henry's Normandy estates along with his exiled uncle Robert de Bellême, 3rd Earl of Shrewsbury. They all rallied to Duke Robert as soon as he returned from the First Crusade and then persuaded him to invade England and depose his brother.

Robert landed at Portsmouth in July 1102 but he immediately sued for peace and agreed the Treaty of Alton with Henry I. The treaty included an amnesty for the rebels but Henry intended to 'soothe them with promises' so they could be 'driven into exile'. He compiled evidence and then accused them of unlicensed castle building.

Robert de Bellême, 3rd Earl of Shrewsbury, refused to answer the charges and he captured Duke Robert's English castles to try to appease the king. But he and his brothers had to forfeit their English titles and estates before they were exiled. William de Warenne, 2nd Earl of Surrey, suffered the same penalties, but Robert Curthose convinced his brother to restore William's earldom. Henry had also wanted Warenne to marry one of his illegitimate daughters to assure his loyalty but Archbishop Anselm of Canterbury refused permission because they were related. For the time being Henry's position was safe, but for how long?

A Power Struggle with the Church, 1105

Pope Gregory VII had declared that only he could appoint or depose bishops in 1075. The announcement resulted in the Investiture Controversy which saw the Holy Roman Emperor Henry IV appoint a series of antipopes. When Henry had problems with the English Church in 1105, Robert de Beaumont advised him to select his bishops, so he could control them. Pope Paschal II excommunicated the king but the exiled Archbishop Anselm of Canterbury cancelled it. De Beaumont was rewarded with the Earldom of Leicester after pledging allegiance to the king.

Normandy, 1106-12

King Henry defeated William of Mortain, 3rd Earl of Cornwall, at the battle of Tinchebrai in 1106. It meant that all of Normandy was under Henry's rule and he placed his supporters in key positions across the Duchy to secure it. William spent the rest of his life in the Tower, becoming a monk in 1140.

The barons along Normandy's frontier opposed Henry's policies in 1110 and they rebelled when he tried to capture Robert Curthose's son William Clito. The French King Louis VI sent Robert de Bellême, 3rd Earl of Shrewsbury, to negotiate Robert's release in 1112, but Henry arrested de Bellême and he died in custody. The Normandy rebellion ended soon afterwards.

The Welsh Rebel, 1114

Henry I, Alexander of Scotland and Richard d'Avranches, 2nd Earl of Chester, joined forces to attack Gruffudd ap Cynan in Gwynedd in 1114. Alexander married Henry's illegitimate daughter Sibylla in the hope of bringing the two crowns closer together, but they had no children to continue the union.

Richard d'Avranches, 2nd Earl of Chester, drowned in the *White Ship* disaster in 1120 and Gruffudd ap Cynan took the opportunity to raid his estates along the Welsh border. King Henry created Ranulf le Meschin the 3rd Earl of Chester and instructed him to drive Welsh rebels back and secure the north-west.

The *White Ship* Sinks, 1120

Henry's only legitimate son, William Adelin, drowned when the *White Ship* sank near Barfleur on 25 November 1120. Henry immediately made his illegitimate son, Robert Fitzroy, the Earl of Gloucester, his heir. It was an unpopular decision which would create future problems between Henry's daughter Matilda and her cousin Stephen.

William Clito Rebels, 1124

The twins Robert and Waleran de Beaumont had been taken into the royal household when their father died in 1118. They inherited their lands when they came of age two years later and while Robert received the English estates and became the 2nd Earl of Leicester, his brother took the French lands and became the 1st Earl of Worcester. Robert also acquired Breteuil through his marriage.

While Robert was busy dealing with a rebellion in the Breteuil area, Waleran was drawn into a conspiracy with Amaury de Montfort, Count of Évreux, who supported Robert Curthose's son and King Henry's nephew William Clito. King Henry soon learnt of the conspiracy and he sent his bastard son Robert Fitzroy, 1st Earl of Gloucester, and Ranulf le Meschin, 3rd Earl of Chester, to deal with Clito. They captured Waleran at Vatteville castle in March 1124. Many of the rebels were blinded while Henry paid Pope Callixtus to annul the marriage of William Clito and Sibylla to stop them having children who would be potential heirs to the throne.

King David of Scotland, 1124

David, the heir to the Scottish throne, had been exiled to the English court when his father, King Malcolm III, was killed attacking Northumbria in 1093. In 1113 he was married to Maud (or Matilda), daughter of Waltheof, Earl of Huntingdon, the last Anglo-Saxon earl to have any power under Norman rule.

Henry helped David take his throne when Alexander I died in 1124 but he could only exercise power in the south of Scotland and was 'king of Scots in little more than name'. The Scots rose behind his nephew Malcolm when David visited Henry in 1130 but the two kings allied to imprison the rebel. David would introduce a Norman style administration into the Scottish government and he spread feudalism across his kingdom with the help of his Anglo-French and French supporters.

Chapter 4

Stephen and Matilda
1135–54

The Anarchy Begins, 1135

Henry had declared his daughter Matilda his heir and then married her to Geoffrey of Anjou when it was clear his marriage to Adeliza was going to be childless. The king's nephew Stephen of Blois, and the barons, had sworn to accept the king's decision, but Hugh Bigod, 1st Earl of Norfolk, announced that Henry had named Stephen his successor when he died in 1135 after he ate too many lamprey fish. Stephen crossed the English Channel and seized the throne, arguing he would be better at keeping order across the kingdom. He was wrong because many barons supported Empress Matilda. Stephen initially had the support of the English barons but his powers waned when he fell sick and rumours of his death spread in 1136. Hugh took the opportunity to seize Norwich castle, but he surrendered the city when the king recovered.

The Beaumonts and Normandy, 1135-54

Stephen betrothed his infant daughter Matilda to Waleran de Beaumont before sending him to secure Normandy. But Matilda died in 1137 and de Beaumont joined Geoffrey of Anjou, Empress Matilda's husband, when he invaded England. Empress Matilda created Waleran the Earl of Worcester and his brother Hugh the Earl of Bedford after they defeated an attack on Normandy in 1138. Waleran then went to Paris to agree a peace treaty between England and France. Robert de Beaumont and Waleran had to fight off more attacks on Normandy, starting in 1140.

Robert de Montfort would capture Waleran de Beaumont when he was fighting for King Louis VII in 1153. Duke Henry's friends took the opportunity to seize his Norman estates, ending his power.

Scotland Attacks, 1136-49

David I of Scotland switched his support to Empress Matilda after hearing that his son Henry had been insulted at Stephen's court. He captured several towns, including Carlisle, Alnwick and Newcastle, before he met Stephen, Richard Fitz Gilbert de Clare and Robert de Ferrers at Durham in February 1136. The Scots were given Cumberland in return for the lost Northumbrian castles but they included the estates of Ranulf, 4th Earl of Chester, and he vowed to win them back.

King David again harried the north of England in 1138, in support of Matilda, until was defeated at the Battle of the Standard near Northallerton on 22 August. Robert de Ferrers was created Earl of Derby for defeating the Scots. Stephen granted the Earldom of Northumbria to David's son and heir Henry at the Second Treaty of Durham in 1139.

The young Henry FitzEmpress joined King David and the outraged Ranulf II, 4th Earl of Chester, during an attack on York in May 1149 and Stephen marched north to meet them. Henry was attacked by Stephen's son Eustace, so Ranulf attacked Lincoln, encouraging Stephen to attack him while Henry escaped. Stephen eventually granted Ranulf the southern half of Lancashire and he gave up his claim on his Cumberland estates.

The Welsh Rebel, 1136

Stephen negotiated the support of the two Marcher Lords, Walter FitzWalter and his son Miles, when he met them at Reading in 1136. But he refused to help when there was an uprising on the Welsh border and Richard Fitz Gilbert de Clare was killed in Gwent by Iorwerth ab Owain. Owain ap Cynan of Gwynedd and Gruffydd ap Rhys of Deheubarth joined the rebellion and they defeated the Normans at the battle of Crug Mawr. Miles FitzWalter had to rescue de Clare's widow from Cardigan Castle.

Matilda Seizes Power, 1139-41

Miles FitzWalter and Robert Fitzroy, Matilda's illegitimate half-brother, recognised Matilda as their sovereign and they invited her to England in the summer of 1139. Miles would later be created Earl of Hereford and Robert Fitzroy Earl of Gloucester for giving their support. Ranulf, 4th Earl of Chester, also joined Matilda because Stephen had given his lands to King David of Scotland and he wanted to capture King David's son Henry as he returned to Scotland.

Stephen's queen, also Matilda, heard about the plan and she persuaded her husband to escort Henry to Scotland. Ranulf made a plan to intercept the royal party at Lincoln Castle. He and his half-brother, William de Roumare, sent their wives to visit the constable's wife and then entered the castle in disguise, pretending they were to collect them. Once inside, they seized weapons, let their men in, threw out the royal garrison and took the king prisoner. All Stephen could do was to give Ranulf control of Lincolnshire and Derbyshire and make William the Earl of Lincoln.

Dubious Supporters, 1140-1

Although Stephen had plenty of supporters, their allegiance was dubious and self-serving. Reginald de Dunstanville was another of Henry's illegitimate sons and Stephen created him Earl of Cornwall in 1141 hoping to get his support. But Reginald stood by his half-sister and the title was confiscated. Simon II de Senlis, 4th Earl of Northumberland, only supported his cause because he believed Matilda would give his Earldom of Northampton to David of Scotland; he was rewarded with the Earldom of Huntingdon.

The worst case of dubious support was Geoffrey de Mandeville. Henry I had confiscated William de Mandeville's title and estates after an important prisoner escaped while he was in charge of the Tower. Geoffrey de Mandeville wanted them back and was created Earl of Essex when he declared for Stephen in 1140. But he switched to support Matilda when Stephen was captured at Lincoln the following year. She made him custodian of the Tower, cancelled his father's debts and returned his grandfather's lands. But the gifts meant nothing because he switched his allegiance back as soon as Stephen was released.

Stephen later arrested Geoffrey and threatened to execute him until he surrendered his castles. Geoffrey resigned as custodian of the Tower of London when he was freed and became an outlaw who had to be tracked down and killed by the king's men in September 1144.

The Battle of Lincoln, 1141

Ranulf, 4th Earl of Chester, proved to be a corrupt landlord and the citizens of Lincoln complained about his treatment of them. So the king returned to Lincoln, pretending that Ranulf and William had failed to return the castle to him. The townspeople let his army into the town in January 1141 and he laid siege to the castle. Ranulf escaped, leaving his wife Maud behind to make sure his father-in-law Robert Fitzroy, Earl of Gloucester, would help him rescue her.

Advisors told Stephen to escape from Lincoln but he chose to stay and there was a battle on 2 February 1141. William de Warenne, 3rd Earl of Surrey and Waleran de Beaumont, 1st Earl of Worcester, fled from the first charge and Stephen's attempts to rally them failed. Warenne and Beaumont escaped to join Matilda but Stephen was captured and imprisoned at Bristol.

Gilbert Fitz Gilbert de Clare, 1st Earl of Pembroke, joined Matilda. So did Aubrey de Vere and Hugh Bigod and they were created the Earls of Oxford and Norfolk, respectively. Ranulf de Gernon, 4th Earl of Chester, captured Alan of Penthièvre, 1st Earl of Richmond, and tortured him until he surrendered the Earldom of Cornwall.

The Battle of Winchester, 1141
It seemed all was going well for Matilda but no one would crown her queen in London and she was given the title 'Lady of the English' instead. Empress Matilda and her half-brother, Robert Fitzroy, Earl of Gloucester, besieged Winchester in September 1141. Stephen's queen, Matilda, and William of Ypres marched to relieve the city and while Ranulf, Earl of Chester, and Miles FitzWalter, Earl of Hereford, escaped, Robert Fitzroy was captured. Empress Matilda would hand over Stephen in exchange for him later in the year, giving up her best chance of becoming queen.

Ranulf Rebels, 1144-6
Stephen abandoned his attempt to take Lincoln Castle from Ranulf, 4th Earl of Chester, in 1144 when a siege tower collapsed killing dozens of men. Ranulf changed his allegiance after Empress Matilda allied with David of Scotland because he was still trying to reclaim his northern estates. So he visited Stephen at Stamford in 1145 and was restored to favour after repenting his crimes. The king allowed him to keep Lincoln Castle until he could recover his old estates.

Ranulf de Gernon, 4th Earl of Chester, encouraged Stephen to support his invasion of Wales but his advisors warned that Ranulf might be planning to ambush him. So the king started an argument with Ranulf at Northampton and then had him imprisoned for treason. Ranulf was forced to surrender all the royal lands and castles he held, hand over all his hostages and take an oath not to resist the king. He was freed after Gilbert Fitz Richard de Clare, 1st Earl of Hertford, handed over his nephew Geoffrey to guarantee Ranulf's good conduct.

Ranulf immediately rebelled and 'burst into a blind fury of rebellion, scarcely discriminating between friend or foe.' He failed to capture Lincoln and Stephen tried to seize him at Coventry but captured Gilbert instead and confiscated his castles. Gilbert joined his uncle as soon as he was freed and they were joined by Gilbert de Clare, Earl of Pembroke. While Stephen reconciled with the two Gilberts, Ranulf joined Henry of Anjou instead.

Crusaders, 1146-8
The Second Crusade was announced at Vézelay in 1146 and both Waleran de Beaumont, 1st Earl of Worcester, and William de Warenne, 3rd Earl of Surrey vowed to take part. They were with the French-Norman crusaders when they were defeated before Damascus and William was killed by the Turks at Mount Cadmus in January 1148. Waleran returned to build an abbey, to thank God for allowing him to survive a shipwreck on the coast of Provence.

The Siege of Newbury, 1152-3

Stephen considered exceptional steps when he tried to force John Marshal to capture Newbury Castle in 1152. He announced his 5-year-old son William would be hanged if he did not surrender. John told him to carry out his threat, saying, 'I still have the hammer and the anvil with which to forge more and better sons!' Stephen talked about catapulting William into the castle but could not bring himself to harm the boy. So John made the most of Stephen's indecision to alert Matilda's forces and young William was released unharmed.

The Treaty of Wallingford, 1153-4

Matilda's son Henry FitzEmpress, Duke of Normandy, landed in England in 1153 to assert his claim. Henry began by laying siege to Stamford while Hugh Bigod, Earl of Norfolk, held Ipswich. Stephen withdrew to London for the winter, Henry was joined by Robert de Beaumont, Earl of Leicester, leaving him in control of a large part of England.

The barons sued for peace as Stephen and Henry faced each other at Wallingford in the summer of 1153. King Stephen recognised Prince Henry as his successor under the Treaty of Wallingford, leaving Stephen's son Eustace furious about being disinherited; he conveniently died a month later.

Peace terms were agreed under the Treaty of Winchester in November 1153. Henry would do homage to Stephen as his adopted son and successor while Stephen's surviving son William had to renounce his claim to the throne. But it was a perilous peace and there were rumours that William planned to assassinate Henry. Stephen set about reasserting his authority over his kingdom, only to die in October 1154. One of Henry's first acts was to create William the Earl of Surrey.

Chapter 5

Henry II
1154–89

Early Problems, 1154-7

Henry II had inherited a vast empire stretching from Scotland in the north to the Pyrenees in the south. Recent acquisitions by his family, the House of Anjou, had left England in control of around one third of modern France. Henry's father, George of Anjou, had become Duke of Normandy in 1144, while Henry had married Eleanor of Aquitaine. He was also Matilda's son and he had inherited her claim to the English throne.

Henry II had granted Staffordshire to Ranulf II, 4th Earl of Chester, while he was young and some barons were jealous of the gift. Ranulf was served poisoned wine at the house of William Peverel and three of his men died; Ranulf died in agonising pain soon afterwards. Henry exiled Peverel as soon as he was crowned.

Henry II also introduced 'cutage', a tax paid in lieu of military service. In 1157 Hugh Bigod, Earl of Norfolk, refused to pay, so the king marched his army into Hugh's area and forced him to submit.

The Welsh Border, 1157-65

Roger de Clare, 2nd Earl of Hertford, and William Fitz Robert, 2nd Earl of Gloucester, promised to aid each other against all others except the king along the Welsh border in 1154. Three years later Henry II instructed Roger to invade South Wales, telling him he could keep all the lands he could conquer. But Rhys ap Gruffydd harassed Roger's advance towards Carmarthen until he was forced to agree a truce. But an angry Gruffydd raided Clare's new lands after his nephew Einion was assassinated. Clare refused to hand over Einion's murderer so Gruffydd recaptured Cardigan, forcing Henry II to invade the area in 1165.

The Pope Interferes, 1163

Aubrey de Vere, 1st Earl of Oxford, was betrothed to Agnes, the daughter of Henry of Essex in 1163. But the marriage ran into problems when his father-in-law was accused of treason and then lost the judicial duel that followed. So de Vere tried to have the marriage to his child-bride annulled only to learn that Pope Alexander III refused permission. Aubrey refused to take Agnes back until he was threatened with excommunication if he did not restore her conjugal rights. They would eventually have four sons, securing the de Vere line.

Brittany Rebels, 1166-72
Henry II had claimed he was Brittany's overlord when Conan de Penthièvre died in 1148. His son, also Conan, inherited the Earldom of Richmond when he came of age in 1156 but his stepfather, Odo, seized his inheritance when his mother died. Conan turned to England, hoping for support, but Henry II annexed Nantes while his brother, Geoffrey, banished Conan's uncle Hoël. Conan fought to reunite Brittany, only to have Henry II cancel his earldom.

Peace in Brittany was achieved in 1160 when Conan married Henry's cousin Margaret. Six years later Conan asked Henry II for help against the rebellious Breton barons but he had to betroth his 5-year-old daughter to the king's teenage son Geoffrey to secure it. Henry then invaded Brittany and forced Conan to abdicate, so he could claim it on behalf of his son. Henry II eventually claimed Brittany for himself when Conan died in 1171.

Meanwhile, an argument over how the money destined for the Crusader States should be collected had caused a war between England and France. King Louis VII had joined with the Welsh, the Scots and Bretons in an attack on English-owned Normandy. The French would be forced to retire and desert their allies after their military arsenal was destroyed. Henry counter-attacked the rebels in Brittany but Geoffrey wanted it for himself and he joined the revolt against his father in 1172; they would reconcile two years later.

The Invasion of Ireland, 1169-71
Henry II had confiscated Richard de Clare's Earldom of Pembroke because he had sided with Stephen against Empress Matilda. Richard, also known as Strongbow, soon became involved in an Irish feud. Diarmait Mac Murchada had abducted Derbforgaill, wife of King Tighearnán Ua Ruairc of Breifne, back in 1152. The High King, Ruaidrí Ua Conchobair, retaliated by seizing Leinster from Diarmait in 1167, so he went to Aquitaine to ask Henry II for help to recover his province. Although the king was unable to send troops, he did offer his moral support to Diarmait.

Diarmait then visited Richard de Clare and he agreed to send an army to Leinster in return for marrying Diarmait's daughter Aoife and becoming heir to his province. Clare sent Raymond FitzGerald across the Irish Sea, when Henry gave his consent two years later, and he captured Leinster; Clare joined him soon afterwards. Diarmait died in May 1171 and his son Domhnall rebelled, so Clare captured more territory. King Henry was concerned about this developing rival kingdom so he forced Clare to surrender his towns and castles and return to Wales. He left behind a mixture of Irish and English lords ruling south-east Ireland on behalf of the English crown.

An Archbishop's Murder, 1170

Thomas Becket was appointed Archbishop of Canterbury in 1162 and immediately tried to recover the rights associated with his new post. Henry put forward the Constitutions of Clarendon in 1164, demanding a weakening of Rome's influence and less powers for the Church, but Beckett stormed out of a meeting in Northampton Castle in October and went into exile in France.

Becket returned to his post in 1170 after prolonged negotiations with King Louis VII and Pope Alexander III. But he immediately upset Henry by handing out excommunications to those who had crowned Henry the Young king a few months earlier. Henry uttered a curse along the lines of 'who will rid me of this troublesome priest?' (versions vary) and four knights decided to murder the archbishop.

Reginald FitzUrse, Hugh de Morville, William de Tracy and Richard le Breton, entered Canterbury Cathedral and tried to arrest Becket. He refused, so they murdered him. Becket was made a saint and Henry paid penance at his tomb while the murderers were excommunicated and sent on crusade.

Young Henry's Revolt, 1173

Young Henry was unhappy. He was not allowed to make any decisions and he was kept short of money. Matters came to a head when King Henry gave three of his castles to his youngest son John. Young Henry and his brothers Geoffrey and Richard fled to Paris where they were welcomed by King Louis. Queen Eleanor tried to reach them but she was captured en route.

Young Henry promised lands to William of Scotland and the Counts of Boulogne, Flanders and Blois to get their support. Several barons also gave him their support because they had personal grievances against the king. William de Ferrers had had the title of the Earl of Derby and Peveril Castle taken from him because his father had supported Stephen while Hugh Bigod, 1st Earl of Norfolk, was eager to revive feudal power and had been promised Norwich Castle by Young Henry.

Henry secretly travelled back to England in the spring of 1173 to organise an attack on the rebels and he then returned to the Continent to face Louis and the Young King. Robert de Beaumont, 3rd Earl of Leicester, landed at Walton, Suffolk, in September where he was joined by Hugh Bigod, 1st Earl of Norfolk, at Framlingham. But Henry's chief minister, Justiciar Richard de Luci, captured them both at the battle of Fornham in Suffolk on 17 October.

Henry crushed the opposition in south-west France early in 1174 while Henry's illegitimate son Geoffrey stopped William the Lion's raids across the Scottish border. Philip, Count of Flanders, then invaded southern England but Henry's visit to Becket's tomb in Canterbury Cathedral restored everyone's confidence in his royal authority. The rebellion in England ended following the capture of William the Lion at Alnwick and Henry then returned to Normandy to defeat Louis at Rouen. King Henry would release the rebellious barons and let them keep their titles but he confiscated a number of strategic castles. He also charged them for the cost of stopping the rebellion with a new tax called the 'Forest Fine'.

Scotland Invades, 1174-5
William the Lion had succeeded Malcolm the Maiden as king of Scotland in 1165. He wanted to retake Northumbria because Henry had confiscated it from him in 1157 and he seized the opportunity during Henry the Young King's revolt in 1173. He was captured as he led a charge at the battle of Alnwick in 1174 shouting, 'now we shall see which of us are good knights.'

William was forced to swear allegiance to Henry II at York Castle in 1175 and had to pay for the English army which occupied Scotland. Henry II also chose William's bride, Ermengarde, under the Treaty of Falaise, taking Edinburgh Castle as the dowry. Only then was William allowed to return to Scotland where he faced prolonged revolts in Galloway. It was many years before Ermengarde bore William an heir but they eventually had four children. Meanwhile, William was busy fathering six illegitimate children, and their descendants would lay claim to the Scottish crown in years to come.

The King's Wayward Brother, 1181-6
Geoffrey had angered his brother, King Henry, by joining Henry the Young King's rebellion. He also annoyed King Philip II with his treacherous deals at the French court and then upset Rome by robbing churches. Geoffrey eventually married Constance, Duchess of Brittany, in 1181 but not many mourned him when he was trampled to death by a horse during a tournament in Paris in 1186. Henry II married the widowed Constance to the loyal Ranulf de Blondeville, 6th Earl of Chester, one of England's most powerful earls.

The Earldom of Gloucester, 1186-9
William, 2nd Earl of Gloucester, made Henry II's youngest son John his

heir, when his own son Robert Fitz Robert died in 1166. John was also betrothed to William's daughter Isabella in 1176 even though they were cousins and the marriage contract included a promise to find an alternative husband if Pope Alexander III banned the wedding. William died in 1186 and John assumed Isabella's Earldom of Gloucester but Pope Clement III banned them from having sexual relations when the couple married three years later. The Archbishop of Canterbury then voided the marriage and placed their lands under interdict.

One of Robert's sisters, Amice, had been married to Richard de Clare, 3rd Earl of Hertford. They too were cousins and the Pope instructed them to separate even though they had been married for twenty-five years. In doing so he was stopping Clare's claim on the Gloucester estates.

Securing Aquitaine, 1188

King Phillip II of France tried to seize the province of Berry south of Paris in 1188 so Henry offered it to the loyal William Marshal. He included the hand of Dionisia of Châteauroux in the deal and Marshal accepted. Henry had argued with Richard, Count of Poitou, over Aquitaine for some time but their feud escalated when the king refused to let his heir go on a crusade. It resulted in war when Richard attacked France, undermining Henry's attempts to make a truce with King Philip. The French King exploited the situation by allying with Richard in 1189. Philip and Richard ambushed the ailing King Henry at Le Mans but William Marshal skilfully covered the English retreat to Chinon. He unhorsed Richard during a skirmish but only killed his horse, as a warning to the treacherous prince.

Chapter 6

Richard I
1189–99

Fulfilling a Father's Promises
Teenage Isabel de Clare became the Countess of Pembroke when her brother Gilbert died in 1185. Henry II had placed the rich heiress in the Tower of London and promised her to the 43-year-old Earl Marshal, William Marshal. Richard stuck by his father's promise and they were married, but while Isabel was 'the good, the fair, the wise, the courteous lady of high degree', Marshal treacherously supported the king's brother, John. He soon discovered John's interests were at odds with his own, so switched his support back to Richard in 1193 and was eventually created Earl of Pembroke in 1199, making him one of the most powerful barons in the kingdom.

The Crusade Begins, 1190
Richard had taken the cross, a promise to go on a crusade, in 1187 and King Philip did the same when he heard that Saladin had captured Jerusalem. They agreed to go together so that neither could attack the other's territories in their absence. But Richard needed money to pay his troops and he ended the Treaty of Falaise with Scotland in return for a payment of 10,000 silver marks, returning William the Lion's independence. Richard also sold appointments and estates and even said 'I would have sold London if I could have found a buyer.' Richard and Philip set off together on the Third Crusade in 1190.

A King's Ransom, 1193-4
Baldwin of Bethune, Earl of Aumale, served with Richard I on the crusade and together they defeated Saladin at the siege of Acre and the battles of Arsuf and Jaffa in 1191. The crusade ended with the Treaty of Jaffa but Richard was disgusted to hear that Conrad had been elected the King of Jerusalem. Four days later Conrad was murdered by assassins and one

admitted under torture that Richard had organised the killing. The fact that Conrad's pregnant wife Isabella was married to Richard's nephew Henry of Champagne only a week later increased the mystery.

Richard and Baldwin were sailing home across the Mediterranean Sea when their ship was blown ashore, so they continued their journey overland. A disguised Richard was captured near Vienna early in 1193 and was handed over to Emperor Henry VI. Baldwin was sent on his journey so he could organise the huge ransom but Leopold V, Duke of Austria, also wanted two brides for his sons, including Richard's niece Eleanor. Baldwin was returning to Vienna with the two princesses when Leopold died and Richard was released.

Meanwhile, Richard's unpopular brother, John, had seized Windsor Castle and was about to invade England when his mother, Queen Eleanor, took action to stop him. Richard returned home in May 1194, only to find that John had joined forces with King Philip II of France. On hearing the news, Philip warned John to 'look to yourself, the devil is loosed,' so John fled to the French court. Richard was recrowned at Winchester and soon restored order across his kingdom.

William of Scotland thought Richard would be short of money after paying his ransom, so he offered another 15,000 marks for Northumbria. But the deal fell through because Richard refused to include the castles; Anglo-Scottish relations remained tense.

The Fair Maid of Brittany

Geoffrey, Duke of Brittany and Earl of Richmond, had been trampled to death at a jousting competition in 1186, leaving the infant Eleanor to be raised by her grandmother Eleanor of Aquitaine. Saladin's brother, Al-Adil, refused to marry both King Richard's sister Joan and Eleanor in 1190 because he wanted a Muslim bride. Three years later Eleanor was betrothed to Frederick, son of Leopold V, Duke of Austria, as part of the conditions to release Richard, a prisoner of Emperor Henry VI. But Frederick died while she was travelling to meet him and the marriage contact was cancelled.

Unsuccessful discussions about a match between Eleanor and Louis, son of King Philip II, in 1195 led to a weakening in the relations between England and France. Meanwhile, the unfortunate Eleanor had become known as the Fair Maid of Brittany and the Beauty of Brittany as she was touted around the royal marriage market.

Arthur the Heir

Geoffrey, Duke of Brittany, had died before Eleanor's brother Arthur was born. He became second in line to the throne when his uncle Richard was crowned in 1189 and he was adopted and declared heir to the throne in a treaty with Philip II of France. It placed 3-year-old Arthur ahead of Richard's treacherous brother, John. Richard also betrothed Arthur to King Tancred's daughter but his interest in Sicily waned when Emperor Henry VI conquered the Mediterranean kingdom in 1194.

Arthur's mother Constance had increased Brittany's independence while Richard I was on the Third Crusade, and boldly proclaimed young Arthur the Duke of Brittany in 1196. When he returned from the crusades Richard was far from impressed with her declaration. He summoned her to Bayeux in Normandy but secretly gave Constance's husband Ranulf de Blondeville, Earl of Chester and Lincoln, instructions to seize her en route. Her abduction was then blamed on their marital problems. Brittany's barons rebelled against her imprisonment and they took Arthur to Brest for safe keeping. Constance would annul her marriage when she was released in 1198.

Richard also intended to take Arthur into custody, but the boy was smuggled to Paris leaving the heir to the English throne in King Philip II's hands. Richard was worried young Arthur would be influenced by the French court, so he made his brother John his heir just before he died in April 1199.

Chapter 7

John
1199–1216

A Rival Heir, 1200

Richard had declared his brother John heir to the English throne on his deathbed but the French nobility wanted 12-year-old Duke Arthur of Brittany to be king because he had pledged his support to King Philip II. Philip gave Arthur's supporters an army and they led it into Anjou and Maine until the Treaty of Le Goulet settled the matter in 1200. Under the terms of the treaty, John recognised Philip as ruler of the Angevin Empire's continental possessions while Philip recognised John as King of England. Philip was also paid for recognising John's sovereignty of Brittany and Arthur was handed over to John. He soon returned to Paris, suspicious of John's motives.

Arthur's supporters sought their revenge by invading Normandy in 1202 but he and his sister Eleanor were captured at Château de Mirebeau; King John's mother, Eleanor of Aquitaine, was also taken hostage. John wanted the young duke mutilated (probably by blinding), to stop him inheriting the throne, but Hubert de Burgh refused to maim the teenager. Duke Arthur vanished in April 1203 never to be seen again and King John was suspected of arranging his disappearance.

The French Attack Normandy, 1200-4

The French attacked Normandy in 1200 and Robert de Beaumont, 4th Earl of Leicester, was captured trying to retake Pacy Castle. William Marshal, 1st Earl of Pembroke, was also forced to negotiate a truce, pay homage to King Philip II, and hand over his son as a hostage, so he could keep his Normandy estates.

Beaumont died in custody in 1204 and his possessions were divided between his two nieces. Amicia was then married to Simon de Montfort, 5th Earl of Leicester, and Margaret was married to Saer de Quincy, Earl of Winchester. But the French renewed their attacks until John ordered Saer de Quincy to surrender Vaudreuil Castle to King Philip II rather than send reinforcements. Saer and his cousin Robert FitzWalter were also forced to pay huge amounts of money so they could keep their estates.

A Crusade to the Holy Land, 1202

Simon de Montfort was a French noble who joined in the Fourth Crusade in 1202. Pope Innocent III warned the Crusaders not to attack Zara on the Adriatic Sea, but the Venetians wanted the port. Simon urged Zara not to surrender, promising he would convince the Frankish troops not to attack, but they were forced to join the siege because they were in debt to the Venetians. After sacking Zara the crusaders headed for Constantinople rather than the Holy Land, so de Montfort returned home.

Wales, 1204-9

Ranulf de Blondeville, Earl of Chester and Lincoln, was suspected of being involved in a Welsh revolt in 1204, so King John confiscated his estates. Ranulf had to promise his loyalty to get his Marcher lands back and he would fight alongside the king during an invasion of Welsh territory in 1209.

Brittany, 1203-15

Arthur's disappearance in 1203 left his sister, Eleanor the Fair Maid, heiress to Brittany but the Breton barons were unhappy because they wanted a male duke. King John took Eleanor when he left Normandy in December 1203 and she was imprisoned in Corfe Castle on the Dorset coast. Twenty-five of her squires escaped but most were recaptured and starved to death as a warning.

King Philip II wanted Eleanor to marry his son so he could become Duke of Brittany, but John refused and forced her to entrust the duchy to him in 1208. The Bretons made Eleanor's young half-sister Alix their duchess to counter the claim, but Philip wanted a strong and loyal ruler for Brittany. He cancelled Alix's betrothal to Henry of Penthièvre in 1213 and married her to his cousin Peter instead.

King John countered by offering Eleanor's Earldom of Richmond to Peter, but he refused to take the bribe even after his brother Robert was taken hostage. John took Eleanor with him when he invaded Brittany in 1214, hoping to invest her as the Duchess of Brittany, but his campaign ended at the battle of Roche-au-Moine.

John gave up his claim on Brittany because he had to deal with the First Barons' War back in England. King Philip's son Louis of France was then invited to invade England to make a claim on the English throne on behalf of his wife Blanche. It did not help that Pope Innocent III believed Eleanor had a better claim to the throne than John.

The Magna Carta was signed in 1215 and part of the conditions was that John had to release all his hostages. That is all but one, because Eleanor was kept under house arrest and forbidden from marrying. Across in Brittany her rival Alix would die in childbirth in 1221, aged only 20, leaving her baby son John, the new Duke of Brittany.

The Church, 1209-14
John refused to accept Stephen Langton as Archbishop of Canterbury, so Pope Innocent III placed England under an interdict in March 1208 and excommunicated the king in November 1209. Ranulf de Blondeville, Earl of Chester and Lincoln, eventually secured a peace with the Pope in 1214.

The Albigensian Crusade, 1209-18
King John had confiscated Simon de Montfort's Earldom of Leicester so he joined the Albigensian Crusade against the heretic Cathars in southern France in 1209. He became notorious because of his cruelty but he was also a successful commander and was rewarded with territories north of the Pyrenees. Montfort then headed north and seized Normandy from King John. Pope Innocent III wanted Montfort to lead the next crusade but he was too busy defending his new territories. He defeated Peter II of Aragon at the battle of Muret in 1213, but he was killed trying to capture Toulouse in 1218.

Scotland, 1209-16
King John marched his army north to Berwick in August 1209 but William the Lion bribed him to withdraw, promising his daughters would marry English nobles. The controversial Treaty of Falaise was renewed in 1212 and William's only son and heir Alexander was married to John's eldest daughter Joan, uniting the English and Scottish royal families.

The Battle of Bouvines, 1214
John wanted to retake Normandy so he allied with King Otto of Germany in 1214. Otto invaded the north of France but John's Poitou mercenaries refused to fight King Philip's son Louis. John then offered Peter, Duke of Brittany, the Earldom of Richmond, but he too refused to help. While John struggled to capture Nantes, the invasion ended when Otto and John's armies were routed at Bouvines on 27 July 1214.

The Magna Carta, 1215
King John returned from Normandy to learn the northern barons were organising a rebellion. John negotiated with them and promised to go on crusade but he was secretly recruiting mercenaries while he waited for a letter of support from Pope Innocent III. It arrived in April but it was too

late to stop the barons meeting at Northampton in May to renounce their feudal ties to John.

Ranulf de Blondeville, Earl of Chester and Lincoln, and William Marshal, Earl of Pembroke, were just two of the few barons who remained loyal to the king. The rest joined Robert FitzWalter, who was still angry about losing his Normandy estates, when he led his Army of God south to seize London. John was forced to sue for peace and he met the barons at Runnymede near Windsor Castle on 15 June 1215. They agreed on a proposal for the rights of free men, the protection of church rights, fair justice and the baron's consent to taxation.

But neither John nor the rebels appointed to a ruling council tried to implement the Great Charter, later renamed the Magna Carta. John again asked Rome for help and the Pope declared the charter 'not only shameful and demeaning, but illegal and unjust'. He excommunicated the rebel barons and they would soon be rising up against John again.

A Feudal Adventurer, 1215-6
Loyalties were always suspect under King John. William de Forz, 3rd Earl of Albemarle, was loyal to him until London's leaders opposed the king. He joined the executors of the Magna Carta but he was the only one who supported the king when he fought with the barons. That was until Louis captured Winchester in 1216 and he again joined the barons. He would switch sides two more times. He was 'a feudal adventurer of the worst type' who always made sure he was on the winning side.

Louis of France, 1216
Saer de Quincy, Earl of Winchester, and his cousin Robert FitzWalter, had been humiliated by King John's order to surrender Normandy to King Philip II. So they invited the French Dauphin, Louis, to claim the English throne on behalf of his wife Blanche of Castile. A storm scattered John's fleet when it sailed out to intercept Louis' fleet in May 1216 and the French landed in Kent.

Several barons, including William de Forz, 3rd Earl of Albemarle, and Robert de Vere, Earl of Oxford, joined Louis when he captured Winchester. Then King Alexander II of Scotland crossed the border, captured Carlisle, and headed to Dover in 1216 to meet Louis. Even William Longespée, Earl of Salisbury and Wiltshire, turned his back on his half-brother the king.

John went on the counter-attack in September, retaking key rebel areas, but he died of dysentery in October and there were rumours he had been poisoned. William Marshal, Earl of Pembroke, made sure John's 9-year-old son Henry became king and he proved to be a popular choice. The English barons united behind their new sovereign, so the Scottish and French armies returned home.

Chapter 8

Henry III
1216–72

The First Barons War, 1217

King John had appointed thirteen ministers to reclaim the kingdom on behalf of his young son Henry. Many had expected Ranulf de Blondeville, Earl of Chester and Lincoln, to be regent but he rejected the post so the king's council appointed William Marshal, Earl of Pembroke, to be the kingdom's regent and the king's protector.

Prince Louis returned from France with extra troops only to find that Cardinal Guala had declared that the war against the rebels was a crusade. Ranulf de Blondeville, 6th Earl of Chester, was ordered to stop the northern barons marching south to meet Louis. But first he seized Mountsorrel Castle in Leicestershire, because the Quincy family had taken it from his grandfather. Roger de Quincy asked for help to secure the north, so Louis sent half his troops to Lincoln while the rest went to Dover.

Marshal and Blondeville were joined by William de Forz, 3rd Earl of Albemarle, and William de Ferrers, 4th Earl of Derby, and they were let into Lincoln through a side gate. They surprised Louis' supporters and took many prisoners, including the Earls of Lincoln, Winchester and Hereford. Gilbert de Clare, Earl of Hertford and Gloucester, was also captured and he had to hand over his daughter. William Marshal was around 75 years old when he married Isabel on her seventeenth birthday.

Marshal was preparing to besiege London when Hubert de Burgh attacked and scattered the fleet carrying reinforcements for Louis off the coast at Sandwich on 24 August 1217. He captured the flagship, the *Great Ship of Bayonne*, and executed the captain, Eustace the Monk. Hubert was later rewarded with the Earldom of Kent and named the king's chief minister for life. Louis was forced to negotiate a truce and Marshal was criticised for the generosity of the terms afforded to the rebels, but the Magna Carta could be reissued and England was at peace once more.

De Forz Rebels, 1219

William Marshal, Earl of Pembroke, did not trust the other barons to be regent, so he offered the post to the papal legate Pandulf Masca as he lay dying in 1219. Pandulf, Peter des Roches and Hubert de Burgh were appointed to run the regency council. William de Forz, 3rd Earl of Albemarle, was eager to revive the barons' independence so Burgh had him excommunicated and declared a rebel. He then confiscated some of his castles after he attended a forbidden tournament. Burgh tried to retaliate by accusing Roches of treason in 1221 but no one believed him so he was sacked from the regency council. Pandulf was recalled by Rome soon afterwards, leaving Hubert running the government.

Forz was excommunicated a second time when he rebelled again. He was pardoned after promising to go on a crusade but he just rebelled a third time in 1224. He died at sea when he finally headed to the Holy Land.

Trouble in Wales, 1223-32

Hubert de Burgh, 1st Earl of Kent, invaded Wales in 1223 to suppress Llywelyn the Great. William Marshal, 2nd Earl of Pembroke, and Gilbert de Clare, Earl of Hertford and Gloucester, would defeat the Welsh but Burgh forced them to surrender Cardigan and Carmarthen castles rather than being allowed to keep them, as was the custom. Burgh then made himself more unpopular by trying to resurrect sheriffdoms on behalf of the crown. Peter des Roches led the opposition when he returned from the crusades and Burgh was imprisoned in the Tower in 1232, accused of squandering royal money and lands.

Roches took control of the king's government and the Poitevin barons took the opportunity to seize lands from Burgh's followers. Burgh was moved to Devizes Castle but he soon escaped and rebelled with Richard Marshal, 3rd Earl of Pembroke. Roches would invade Marshal's lands in South Wales but Marshal and Llywelyn drove him back.

An Irish Rebellion, 1224-34

Hugh de Lacy started raiding royal estates in Ireland in 1224. William Marshal, 2nd Earl of Pembroke, was appointed Ireland's chief minister only to be sacked after two years of campaigning because of his unacceptable treatment of Aodh O'Connor's supporters in Connacht. The Bishop of Ferns cursed Marshal, prophesying his sons would have no children and his estates would be scattered. The prediction came true when Marshal died in 1231. His five sons died in quick succession and the family estates were divided between his sons-in-law. William de Valence, husband of one of Marshal's granddaughters, inherited the earldom.

The king's supporters retaliated by attacking Marshal's Irish manors so

William's brother, Richard, allied with Llywelyn the Great and sailed across to Ireland. They would defeat Ireland's new justiciar, Maurice FitzGerald, at the battle of the Curragh in 1234.

An Unlicensed Marriage, 1232

Hubert de Burgh, 1st Earl of Kent, was guardian (known as a ward) to the orphaned Richard de Clare, the heir to the Earldoms of Hereford and Gloucester. He married his daughter to Clare without a royal license in 1232 and then protested he had nothing to do with the union. The king then found out the newly-weds were only 12 years old at the time, so Burgh was fined. Margaret died three years later and John de Lacy, 1st Earl of Lincoln, bought the marriage rights to the soon-to-be-wealthy Clare on behalf of his daughter Maud.

The Kingdom of Sicily, 1236–43

Henry III's brother, Richard of Cornwall, was one of the wealthiest men in Europe. Pope Innocent IV offered to sell the kingdom of Sicily to him in 1236 as he returned from the Holy Land. Richard replied, 'You might as well say, I make you a present of the moon; step up to the sky and take it down.' But Henry III was interested and he promised to pay a huge sum and drive Manfred from the kingdom. The king's 10-year-old son Edmund was invested as the ruler and Pope Alexander IV confirmed the grant of Sicily. But England's barons refused to contribute to what they scornfully called the 'Sicilian business', leaving Henry unable to pay. Simon de Montfort, 6th Earl of Leicester, eventually had to step in to negotiate a retraction on behalf of the king.

Inheritance Problems, 1238

Margaret de Quincy inherited the Earldom of Lincoln from her mother Hawise of Chester, and her husband John de Lacy was created the 2nd Earl of Lincoln in 1232. They also paid Henry III for permission to marry their daughter Maud to Richard de Clare, Earl of Gloucester, in 1238. Margaret retained the vast estates when John died and their young son was raised at court. Edmund succeeded the earldom but he died before his mother, leaving her controlling a large part of the Earldom of Pembroke. Margaret made her grandson Henry de Lacy her heir after quarrelling with her daughter.

The King and de Montfort Argue, 1238

Simon de Montfort's father and brother had been killed in the Albigensian Crusade in southern France so he had gone to England to claim his inheritance in exchange for his France estates. He convinced his cousin Ranulf de Blondeville, Earl of Chester, to hand over the Earldom of

Leicester but it was nine years before he was formally invested by Henry III.

Henry III's young sister, 16-year-old Eleanor, had sworn a vow of chastity when her husband William Marshal, 2nd Earl of Pembroke, died in 1231, but Simon de Montfort pursued her. They were married in 1238 and the senior barons complained she had been married to a French man of modest rank without their knowledge. Eleanor's brother, Richard the Earl of Cornwall, was particularly against the marriage, so Henry had to bribe him with gifts. Even the Archbishop of Canterbury, Edmund Rich, condemned the marriage so Montfort went to Rome and was given Pope Gregory IX's approval, so he could return home and finally receive the long sought-after Earldom of Leicester.

But Montfort took his family connection too far when he named the king as security for a debt he owed to Queen Eleanor's uncle Thomas of Savoy. A furious Henry threatened to imprison Montfort in the Tower when he found out in August 1239. Henry also revealed how Montfort had secured such a lucrative marriage with the words 'you seduced my sister and I gave her to you, against my will, to avoid a scandal.' So Eleanor went into exile in France and Simon went on crusade until the rumours died down.

De Montfort returned from crusade in 1241 and joined Henry's invasion of Poitou. But he courted trouble again by stating that the king deserved to be thrown in prison when the campaign failed. His next appointment was viceroy of the Duchy of Gascony but there was criticism over his maltreatment of the rebel prisoners so he remained in France for the next twenty years to avoid a controversy.

The Palatine of Chester, 1239
William de Forz, 4th Earl of Albemarle, claimed the Palatine of Chester could not be divided when he married Christina, co-heiress to the Earldom of Chester. But the royal court disagreed and he had to renounce the earldom in exchange for other lands when Christina died in 1239. Forz secured a second lucrative marriage to 11-year-old Isabella de Redvers, heiress to the Earldom of Devonshire, in 1241. He died in 1260 having seen all of his six children die before him, so Isabella inherited his lands and called herself the Countess of Devon and Albemarle.

A Banned Tournament, 1241
Tournaments were exciting sporting events where the nobility could show off their jousting skills and settle arguments. But they were also dangerous events and Henry III had banned them because he did not want his subjects killing one another for sport. But the barons kept jousting in secret and Gilbert Marshal, 4th Earl of Pembroke, was mortally injured at a forbidden

tournament in 1241. The king stopped his son Walter claiming his inheritance for some time because he had also attended the tournament.

Attempts to Recapture Poitou, 1241-43

Henry III had made his brother Richard, Earl of Cornwall, Count of Poitou in 1225, but it was a token appointment because he did not own the area. Ranulf de Blondeville, Earl of Chester and Lincoln, led a failed attempt to secure Poitou (in what is now western France) in 1230 which ended with a three-year truce with the French king.

The teenage Louis IX gave Poitou to his brother Alphonse in 1241 but Henry was determined to recover it. The excuse came when his mother Isabella claimed she had been insulted by Louis' queen Margaret. Isabella's husband, Hugh of Lusignan, encouraged his stepsons to attack Poitou and then betrayed Richard's plans to the French. The invasion was a disaster and Richard had to give up his claim to Poitou in 1243.

Peace was achieved with the Treaty of Paris and Richard's marriage to Margaret's sister Sanchia (whom the English called Cynthia); a third sister, Beatrice, married Charles I of Naples. A strong union between England and France had been formed by the marriages of the two kings and their two brothers to the four sisters from Provence. The closeness of the marriages was bound to end in trouble.

Acquiring the Welsh Marches, 1246

John the Scot, Earl of Huntingdon and Chester, died childless in 1237 and his title was given to his brother-in-law Christian. But the estates were divided between his four sisters, leaving Henry III unhappy that 'so fair a dominion should be divided among women'.

Llywelyn the Great died in 1240 and his son Dafydd died in 1246. Llywelyn's grandsons, Owain and Llywelyn, agreed to give Henry some of their Welsh lands under the Treaty of Woodstock in 1246. The same year, Henry bought the Marcher estates and gave them to his loyal supporters. The Welsh border was then quiet until Llywelyn ap Gruffudd rebelled in 1256.

King Alexander of Scotland, 1251-5

Ten-year-old King Alexander III of Scotland married Henry III's daughter Margaret in 1251. There were rumours the children were being mistreated by their guardians, Robert de Roos and John Balliol, so Richard de Clare, Earl of Hertford and Gloucester, was sent to Edinburgh in 1255 to investigate. He dressed in Roos' colours, tricked his way into the castle, and discovered that the young king and queen were being held separately under house arrest conditions. So he sneaked his men into the castle and seized it.

The Scottish barons were furious that their sovereigns had been taken hostage but they were powerless to attack the castle, because their king and queen were inside. Clare later escorted Alexander across the border so he could meet Henry III at Newminster in Northumberland.

A New King of Germany, 1256

Henry III's brother, Richard, Earl of Cornwall, had great ambitions for himself. He stood against Alfonso X of Castile for the throne of Germany in 1256 and he was crowned 'King of the Romans' after bribing Pope Alexander IV and the French King, Louis IX. But after all the trouble Richard went to get the crown, he only made four brief visits to Germany before he died in 1272.

The Oxford Provisions, 1258-64

The king had given the French baron William de Valence the important Earldom of Pembroke, and rich estates, making other barons jealous. Rivalry in Wales also led to a quarrel between Valence and Simon de Montfort, 6th Earl of Leicester, who had just returned from self-imposed exile in France.

Montfort and Richard de Clare, Earl of Hertford and Gloucester, led the revolt against Henry III's government during the Mad Parliament in 1258. They drew up the Oxford Provisions, a series of proposals designed to reform Henry III's administration. Some, like John de Warenne, 6th Earl of Surrey, initially opposed the reform plan but they eventually took the oath. Others, like William de Valence, refused to comply so he was imprisoned and forced into exile. But Henry successfully divided the barons over the Oxford Provisions and Montfort left the country in disgust when the king revoked his agreement.

Someone was angry about Richard de Clare's involvement because he and his brother William were poisoned soon after the Provisions were declared. But they survived and their steward Walter de Scotenay was hanged for the crime. A second poisoning attempt at the table of Peter of Savoy, Earl of Richmond, succeeded in killing Clare in 1262.

The Second Barons War, 1263-5

The barons invited Simon de Montfort back to England in 1263 but they objected to him taking control of the Council of Fifteen. He disrupted parliament so they held him prisoner until Prince Louis of France agreed to arbitrate. Montfort was unable to meet Louis because of a broken leg but he was as surprised as everyone else when the Prince declared the Oxford Provisions to be unlawful and invalid at the beginning of 1264. It gave Henry III control of his kingdom back.

Prince Louis' plan to cause unrest in England had worked because the royalists and reformists went to war. Robert de Ferrers, 6th Earl of Derby, attacked Worcester and then joined Simon de Montfort at Gloucester, but Prince Edward escaped after making a truce with de Montfort's son Henry. Edward got his revenge in March 1264 when he captured Ferrers' brother William and attacked Ferrers at Chartley Castle. Simon de Montfort then massacred the Jewish community in Leicester while Gilbert de Clare, Earl of Hertford and Gloucester, did the same in Canterbury; both men were denounced as traitors on 12 May.

Simon immediately marched out of London and confronted the royal army at Lewes on 14 May. Prince Edward was winning the battle when the king was driven back and was forced to take refuge in St Pancras Priory. Henry III and Prince Edward were captured and Richard, Earl of Cornwall, was found hiding in a nearby windmill.

Simon de Montfort was now able to rule England and he established a government based on the Oxford Provisions. While Henry retained the title and authority of King, Montfort's council discussed how to run the country; their decisions were to be approved by parliament. Pope Clement IV was not impressed; he excommunicated the rebels and placed England under an interdict.

The Great Parliament of 1265 formally introduced the Oxford Provisions and they allowed each county and select boroughs to put forward two representatives. They also granted a vote to everyone who owned the freehold of land to an annual rent of forty shillings. It was an early form of democracy but some barons felt the Provisions had gone too far and support for them soon declined.

De Montfort's plans to release Prince Edward included confiscating Ferrers' estates and then imprisoning him in the Tower for trespassing on them. But Montfort's support was waning until even Clare defected to the king's side. The barons were so enraged by Montfort's behaviour that Clare even helped Edward escape from Kenilworth Castle in May 1265. The Welsh Marcher Lords rallied around the freed prince and Edward and de Clare captured more of Montfort's allies at Kenilworth.

At the beginning of August Simon de Montfort thought he saw his son's army approaching as he marched towards Evesham, but it was Edward's army carrying captured de Montfort banners. The two armies clashed in the 'murder of Evesham, for battle it was none' on 4 August 1265. When Simon heard his son Henry had been killed, he lamented 'then it is time to die' and he was slain alongside Peter de Montfort and Hugh Despenser. Simon's corpse was decapitated, his testicles were cut off and hung across his nose. They were then sent to his wife while his hands and feet were sent to his enemies. The Dictum of Kenilworth ended the Second Baron's War.

Stealing Lands, 1266-9

The rebels had been defeated but Henry III needed extra support in the Midlands, so he pardoned Robert de Ferrers, 6th Earl of Derby, and allowed him to return home. The treacherous Ferrers immediately rebelled and Henry III's nephew Henry had to defeat him at Chesterfield in May 1266. Ferrers then lived as an outlaw for two years before he was captured and imprisoned in Windsor Castle.

The Derby estates were given to Henry's second son Edmund, and while the Kenilworth Dictum nominally returned them to their owner in 1269, the king had a cunning plan to keep them. Ferrers was kept in Wallingford Castle, leaving him insufficient time to pay his fines, so the administrators transferred them to Edmund of Almain, 2nd Earl of Cornwall. Ferrers would later present his case to Edward I, arguing that the agreement was made under duress, but the transfer was declared legal because it had been signed by the chancellor. The rebellious Robert de Ferrers eventually died in 1279, ending the power of one of England's most powerful families.

A Reluctant Wife, 1268

Isabella de Fortibus became one of the richest heiresses in England when she inherited the Earldom of Devonshire from her brother Baldwin de Redvers, and the Earldom of Albemarle from her husband William de Forz. Simon de Montfort, 6th Earl of Leicester, wanted to marry her after defeating the king's army at the battle of Lewes but she went into hiding. The king then gave his son Edmund Crouchback, 1st Earl of Lancaster, permission to marry 31-year-old Isabella in 1268 but again she refused. Instead she offered her 11-year-old daughter to Edmund instead; young Aveline would die four years later.

The Crusades, 1274

The Holy Land was in its final death throes when Henry III's sons Edward and Edmund left for the Ninth Crusade. Edmund gained a reputation for being a ruthless warrior and was called 'Crouchback', meaning the crossed back, because he was a crusader. The brothers headed home when they heard their father had died in 1272 but they did not return until 1274.

Chapter 9

Edward I
1272–1307

Securing the Kingdom, 1272
Edward had joined Louis on the Eighth Crusade in 1270 but the French king died in Tunis. A sick Henry wanted his son to return home but Edward joined the Ninth Crusade to Acre instead in 1271. But there was little to do after Hugh III of Cyprus, the nominal King of Jerusalem, made a truce with the Muslim states, so Edward decided to return home. Although the new king heard of his father's death in November 1272, he took his time travelling home across Europe. Gilbert de Clare, Earl of Hertford and Gloucester, secured Edward's right to succeed to the throne in his absence and he served as the Guardian of England until Edward I returned in August 1274.

Claiming Back Lancaster, 1269-74
Henry III's queen, Eleanor, had betrothed their second son Edmund, 1st Earl of Lancaster, to young Aveline de Forz in 1269. But the Earldoms of Devon and Albemarle were confiscated on behalf of the king when 15-year-old Aveline died in 1274, stopping Edmund from inheriting them when he returned from the crusades.

Reclaiming Royal Rights, 1278
Edward I, who was known as 'Longshanks' because he was tall, wanted to reclaim his royal judgement rights and called a parliament at Gloucester in 1278. Many of the barons answered his writ with the words 'by what warrant', but John de Warenne, 6th Earl of Surrey, went a step further. With sword in hand, he stood before the new king and said 'my ancestors came with William the Bastard and conquered their lands with the sword, and I will defend them with the sword against anyone wishing to seize them.'

The Conquest of Wales, 1282
Henry III had given Humphrey de Bohun, Earl of Hereford and Essex, the

Welsh Marcher lands in 1270. Llewelyn ap Gruffudd believed the grant was in violation of the Treaty of Montgomery so he refused to pay homage to the new king of England. So Edward I declared war on Gruffudd in 1277 and Bohun was joined by William de Beauchamp, 9th Earl of Warwick, a 'vigorous and innovative military commander', as they secured the disputed lands.

The Welsh rose up again in 1282 but the earls rejected Edward's call for mercenaries because it meant he could claim the conquered territory himself. Instead they insisted the king issue a feudal summons, so they could claim any captured lands for themselves. Roger Bigod, 5th Earl of Norfolk, and John de Warenne, 6th Earl of Surrey, joined the campaign into South Wales, but it was Edward I's brother, Edmund Crouchback, and William de Valence, Earl of Pembroke, who defeated and captured Gruffudd. Valence negotiated the surrender of the Dolwyddelan Castle, completing the conquest of Wales; it had taken over 200 years.

Marrying the King's Daughter
Gilbert de Clare, Earl of Gloucester and Hertford, had inherited his father's considerable estates at the age of four. He was soon betrothed to Alice, daughter of Hugh of Lusignan, but the contract was annulled in 1267 because she loved her cousin Prince Edward. King Edward then betrothed the young Clare to his daughter Joan of Acre and promised him estates on the proviso they would be inherited by the king's grandchildren. But the widowed Joan fell in love with Ralph de Monthermer, one of de Clare's squires, before Clare came of age. She convinced her father to knight the squire and then she married him in secret.

Edward I imprisoned Monthermer when he found out about the marriage, ignoring Joan's complaint that 'no one sees anything wrong if a great earl marries a poor and lowly woman. Why should there be anything wrong if a countess marries a young and promising man?' Anthony Beck, Bishop of Durham, eventually convinced Edward to release Ralph and sanction the marriage. Monthermer was then created Earl of Gloucester and Hertford but only for as long as Joan was alive. She died in 1307 and Gilbert de Clare finally inherited his Earldoms of Gloucester and Hertford when he came of age in 1308.

A Claimant to the French Throne, 1285
Edward I's brother, Edmund Crouchback, had been married to Blanche, widow of Henry I of Navarre in 1276. He governed the Champagne and Brie regions (now in northern France) on behalf of her daughter Joan until 1284. Edmund agreed Edward could relinquish his continental lands to the French so they would restore his possessions, but the new King Philip IV

refused to give them back. Prince Edward's marriage to Philip's daughter Isabella brought about a temporary peace but it would also produce an English claimant to the French throne. That claim would cause problems for many years in the future.

A Dispute between the Marcher Barons, 1287-95

The successful Welsh campaign had increased resentment between Humphrey de Bohun, Earl of Hereford and Essex, and Gilbert de Clare, Earl of Gloucester. Clare had been Bohun's guardian and he claimed he had not paid him enough for his marriage rights, as was the tradition. Bohun was in turn annoyed that Clare had been given command of the campaign which had ended in their defeat at the battle of Llandeilo Fawr in 1282.

Tension mounted during another campaign against Rhys ap Maredudd in 1287. Edward I was away in Gascony so the kingdom's regent, Edmund of Almain, 2nd Earl of Cornwall, tried to mediate between Clare and Bohun. Edward was far from pleased to learn that Almain had been accused of mismanaging the kingdom in his absence and he was also annoyed that his Marcher lords had been arguing with each other rather than fighting the Welsh.

Clare reignited the feud when he ignored the king's order to stop building Morlais Castle on land claimed by Bohun. Bohun asked the king to intervene because he faced the rebellious Welsh to the west and his rival de Clare to the east. But Edward I refused because it would set a precedent which would undermine one of the Marcher barons' greatest privileges; the right to settle feuds privately.

Clare carried on building his castle and even raided Bohun's lands in a show of defiance, so Edward used the January 1292 parliament to stamp his authority on the situation. He took Glamorgan from Clare and fined him 10,000 marks. He also confiscated Brecon from Hereford and fined him 1,000 marks. The fines would be cancelled and the lands were restored but the king had proved his point; he had the power to punish any disobedient earl.

Edward I headed to North Wales when Madog ap Llywelyn rebelled in 1294, only to find himself trapped inside Conwy Castle. William de Beauchamp, 9th Earl of Warwick, raised the siege and defeated Madog at the battle of Maes Moydog in March 1295. This ended the Welsh rebellions, reducing the role the Marcher lords played in the defence of England. So Edward took the opportunity to restrict their liberties, reducing the chance of them fighting each other in the future.

A Dubious Transaction, 1293

Isabella de Fortibus, 8th Countess of Devonshire, owned the Isle of Wight and Edward I wanted it. She had outlived her six children and there was no chance of having any more, so the king offered to buy her southern estates in 1276. Unfortunately, an inquiry discovered that John de Eston was her distant heir, blocking Edward's offer, but he still claimed her northern lands. One of his servants, Walter Langton, rushed to see Isabella when she was taken ill in 1293 and she sold the Isle of Wight to the king on her deathbed, in what can only be described as a dubious transaction.

Marrying the King's Nephew, 1294

Henry de Lacy had endured a double tragedy when his son Edmund drowned in a well at Denbigh Castle and his son John fell to his death from the walls of Pontefract Castle. Their sister Alice became Countess of Lincoln, Salisbury and Wiltshire, and the king married the 13-year-old heiress to his nephew Thomas, heir to the Earldoms of Lancaster, Leicester and Derby, in 1294. While Thomas and Alice produced no legitimate heirs to their combined estates, he fathered several illegitimate children and the couple eventually separated.

The Loss of Aquitaine and Brittany, 1294-7

John of Savoy inherited the Dukedom of Brittany and the Earldom of Richmond in 1286 and he was expected to support the English cause. But he did not retake Bordeaux after King Philip IV seized Guyenne and declared Aquitaine forfeit in 1294. Edmund Crouchback and Henry de Lacy, 3rd Earl of Lincoln, tried to capture territory but their army dispersed during the siege of Bayonne when they were not paid. A broken-hearted Edmund died in 1296.

Edward I wanted to retake his lost lands so he asked his earls to support him at the Salisbury Parliament in March 1297. His plan was for his Earl Marshal, Roger Bigod, 5th Earl of Norfolk, to attack Gascony while he invaded Flanders. But Bigod argued he was only obliged to serve abroad in the company of the king and when the king angrily stated 'by God, you shall either go or hang,' Bigod replied, 'by the same oath, I will neither go nor hang.' Others also protested against feudal service in yet another expensive foreign war.

Humphrey de Bohun, 3rd Earl of Hereford, demanded the restoration of the ancient liberties detailed in a list of complaints called the Remonstrances because he was busy fighting the Welsh in the Marches. Although he eventually pledged support, he interfered with the raising of reinforcements for Edward's invasion, forcing him to abandon the campaign and issue the 'Confirmation of Charters', confirming the Magna Carta's terms as part of statute law.

John the Red, Duke of Brittany, abandoned the English cause after the failure to recover Aquitaine and he was deprived of the Earldom of Richmond. Instead he allied with the French and married his grandson John to King Philip's cousin Isabella of Valois. He would spend the next decade supporting King Philip against Count Guy of Flanders. John was leading Pope Clement V's horse at his coronation in Lyon when a wall collapsed under the weight of spectators, crushing him to death.

Scotland Attacks, 1306

Scotland and France had agreed a treaty of mutual support which became known as the Auld Alliance in 1295. Each promised to help the other if they were attacked by England. But events went badly for Scotland when Robert Bruce rebelled and seized the crown in February 1306. When he attempted to invade England most of his family were killed or captured and his estates were confiscated. Edward would later become known as the 'Hammer of the Scots' for inflicting the crushing defeat on the Scottish rebel. Robert fled to the Isle of Rathlin off the Irish cost to consider his next move while Humphrey de Bohun, 4th Earl of Hereford, became Queen Elizabeth's custodian.

Gilbert de Clare, Earl of Gloucester and Hertford, was appointed Warden of Scotland, Captain of Scotland and Warden of the Northern Marches. But Bruce did not give up and he returned to Scotland where he soon gained the initiative as Clare struggled to contain his raids.

Prince Edward's Friend, 1306

The teenage Piers Gaveston had arrived in England in 1300 and he joined Prince Edward's household where the two became firm friends. But they became too close and were both banned from court when Gaveston became involved in the prince's argument with the Treasurer, Walter Langton.

The two young men soon returned to court but Gaveston was again in trouble in 1306 when he convinced twenty-one knights to abandon Edward's campaign into Scotland and attend a tournament instead. They were arrested and then pardoned but Gaveston was exiled. King Edward hit Prince Edward and threw him out of the royal chambers when he tried to give his county of Ponthieu (now in northern France) to Gaveston.

Edward I fell ill while campaigning along the Scottish border at the beginning of July 1307. He worried that Gaveston would be a bad influence on his son and his dying wish was to stop Gaveston returning. He was right to be concerned.

Chapter 10

Edward II
1307–27

The King's Legitimacy, 1307
Edward I had many children with his first wife Eleanor of Castile but only Edward II had survived into adulthood. The elderly king then married Margaret of France and they had two children, Thomas and Edmund. But Edmund was born when the king was 62 years old, starting rumours over his legitimacy. He was only 5 when his father died.

Piers Gaveston's Rise, 1307-9
Edward II immediately recalled his friend Piers Gaveston and gave him the estates and the Earldom of Cornwall which had been promised to his brother. He then arranged Gaveston's marriage to Margaret, sister of the powerful Gilbert de Clare, Earl of Gloucester and Hertford, making him one of the country's richest nobles. It also made him many enemies.

The king organised a tournament in his friend's honour at Wallingford Castle in December 1307 but Gaveston and his supporters cheated, humiliating the Earls of Warenne, Hereford, and Arundel. Even so, Edward appointed Gaveston his regent when he went to France in 1308 to marry King Philip IV's daughter Isabella. But he went a step too far when he ignored his new wife and spent all his time with his friend at the coronation feast. The French king was insulted when he heard about his daughter's mistreatment.

Henry de Lacy, Earl of Lincoln, led the calls to exile Gaveston. Edward had to agree because Philip IV supported the demands. Gaveston was appointed the Lieutenant of Ireland instead, even though Richard de Burgh, Earl of Ulster, had just been given the same position. At first he alienated many by replacing long-standing officers but became popular when his new men put an end to the Irish rebellion.

Edward II convinced the earls to let Gaveston back, with Gilbert de Clare's help, and Pope Clement V lifted the ban on him after John of

Brittany, 4th Earl of Richmond, made a plea on his behalf. He was reinstated with the Earldom of Cornwall. In July 1309 Edward II agreed to the Statute of Stamford, a document based on the Magna Carta, to appease the barons. But the compromise did not last long because Gaveston was handing out favours and appointments to his friends. He also enjoyed inventing offensive nicknames for anyone who opposed him. Henry de Lacy, 3rd Earl of Lincoln, became 'Burst Belly'; Aymer de Valence, 2nd Earl of Pembroke, was 'Joseph the Jew'; Thomas Plantagenet, Earl of 3rd Lancaster was 'the Fiddler'; and Guy de Beauchamp, 10th Earl of Warwick, was 'the Black Dog of Arden'. It was only a matter of time before they secured their revenge.

The Lords Ordainers, 1310-11
Several earls refused to attend parliament in February 1310 in protest against Gaveston's actions. A few weeks later several barons, including John of Brittany, 4th Earl of Richmond, and Guy de Beauchamp, 10th Earl of Warwick, broke parliamentary rules wearing their armour and carrying their weapons in parliament. But they were allowed to explain their grievances and Edward was then forced to appoint a committee called the Lords Ordainers to rule the kingdom. The committee consisted of eight earls, seven bishops and six barons, and they were led by Robert Winchelsey, Archbishop of Canterbury and the Earls of Warwick, Lincoln and Lancaster.

Henry de Lacy, 3rd Earl of Lincoln, was the most experienced member, Thomas Plantagenet, Earl of Lancaster and Leicester, was the richest and Guy de Beauchamp, 10th Earl of Warwick, was the most aggressive. Between them they drafted the directives, or Ordinances, which would control the king's spending and stop him from appointing his own ministers. They also sent the troublesome Gaveston into exile once more. Gilbert de Clare, Earl of Gloucester and Hertford, would join the Ordainers following the death of Henry de Lacy in March 1311.

Piers Gaveston's Fall, 1311-13
Although Edward II had raised taxes for an invasion of Scotland, Robert Bruce continued to raid the north of England. Edward eventually called upon his barons to support a military campaign in June 1311 but most ignored him because they hated the new Lieutenant of Scotland, the corrupt Piers Gaveston. Calls to exile him again were ignored and only Gilbert de Clare, 8th Earl of Gloucester, John de Warenne, 7th Earl of Surrey, and Gaveston accompanied Edward when he invaded Scotland in September. Bruce refused to negotiate with Edward and the Scots skilfully withdrew as the English army blundered forward. Edward's troops withdrew when he ran out of money and Bruce went on the offensive, raiding northern

England as Gaveston watched, powerless to intervene, from Bamburgh Castle in Northumberland.

Gaveston briefly went into exile but Archbishop Winchelsey excommunicated him and he was declared an outlaw on his return. Edward and Gaveston were nearly captured at Newcastle in May 1312 and while the king was taken to York for his own safety, Gaveston was trapped in Scarborough Castle. Aymer de Valence, Earl of Pembroke, and John de Warenne, 7th Earl of Surrey, guaranteed his safety and Valence then took him to Deddington in Oxfordshire. But not everyone was feeling so gallant.

Guy de Beauchamp, 10th Earl of Warwick, took Gaveston to Warwick castle while Pembroke was away visiting his wife on 10 June. Thomas Crouchback, Guy de Beauchamp, Humphrey de Bohun, 4th Earl of Hereford, and Edmund FitzAlan, 9th Earl of Arundel, then condemned Gaveston to death in a mock trial and he was beheaded at Blacklow Hill on the Kenilworth road on 19 June. Many barons disliked the fact that his guarantee of safekeeping had been ignored and Valence and Warenne were just a few who switched their support to the king. The king was also annoyed that Gaveston's captors had not returned the jewels he had given his friend.

The Bannockburn Campaign, 1314

John of Brittany, 4th Earl of Richmond, and Gilbert de Clare, Earl of Gloucester and Hertford, reconciled the king with the barons who had executed Gaveston. They were pardoned but they were then ignored. Meanwhile, Edward turned his attentions to Scotland only to find that Thomas Plantagenet, Earl of Lancaster and Guy de Beauchamp, Earl of Warwick, refused to give him assistance because they had been marginalised. Edward even had to cancel the debt Edmund FitzAlan, 9th Earl of Arundel, owed to the crown to get him to participate.

The experienced Humphrey de Bohun, 4th Earl of Hereford, had been sacked as Constable because he had taken part in Gaveston's execution. He had been replaced by the loyal, but inexperienced, Gilbert de Clare, Earl of Gloucester and Hertford. So Edward was marching north with a new commander and a depleted army.

The English army encountered the Scots at Bannockburn on 23 June and there were arguments as they approached their enemy. Bohun wanted to lead the cavalry attack but Clare was thrown off his horse after charging ahead without orders. Both Clare and Bohun survived the melee and the rout that followed but Bohun's cousin Henry was killed in hand-to-hand combat with Robert Bruce.

De Clare was called a coward when he suggested avoiding battle the following day and Edward went as far as to accuse him of treason. So de

Clare led a new attack, against his better judgement, to prove his loyalty. Bohun's archers were overrun by the Scottish cavalry, Clare was killed and the English army withdrew in disarray.

Aymer de Valence, 2nd Earl of Pembroke, escorted Edward away from the field of battle while Bohun Humphrey led the rest of the barons to Bothwell Castle. The castle commander declared for Bruce as soon as he heard of the Scottish victory and he took the English nobles prisoners. Bohun was eventually exchanged for Bruce's queen, Elizabeth, and his daughter, Princess Marjorie.

Edward escaped to England where he was forced to submit to the barons and reconfirm the Ordinances. But many of the barons were still hostile to him. A sick Guy de Beauchamp, 10th Earl of Warwick, withdrew to his estates and died; there were rumours he had been poisoned on the king's orders. It was a bad decision if he had: Guy was sorely missed because he was 'the wisest of the peers' and the 'other earls did many things only after taking his opinion'. The country descended into turmoil as Thomas Plantagenet tried to govern, with little success. The Scots even captured Carlisle, taking Andrew Harclay, Sheriff of Cumberland and Warden of the West Marches, prisoner.

Retaliation in Ireland, 1314

Roger de Mortimer, 1st Earl of March, acquired lands in the Welsh Marches and Ireland through his marriage to Joan de Geneville. But he had to fight Henry de Lacy, 3rd Earl of Lincoln, for his estates in Ireland in 1308 so he asked Edward Bruce, brother of Robert Bruce, King of the Scots, for help. Edward invaded Ireland following the victory at the battle of Bannockburn in 1314 so Edward II appointed Mortimer his new Lord Lieutenant of Ireland and defeated both Bruce and the Lacys.

The Rise of the Despensers, 1314-8

Hugh le Despenser had been only 4 years old when his father was killed fighting alongside the rebel Simon de Montfort at the battle of Evesham in 1265. But he kept the Earldom of Winchester because his grandfather had been loyal to Edward. It also helped that his son, also Hugh, was a favourite of Edward II, encouraging the Despensers' enemies to start rumours about a royal homosexual relationship.

Hugh the Elder was one of the few who remained loyal to Edward during the arguments over Piers Gaveston. He was appointed the king's chief administrator when Gaveston was executed in 1312 and both father and son filled their pockets as they took control of the government, increasing the jealousy against them.

Gilbert de Clare, Earl of Gloucester and Hertford, died in 1314, and the king married his three sisters, Eleanor, Margaret and Elizabeth, to his favourites, Hugh Despenser the Younger, Hugh de Audley and Roger d'Amory. The frustrated Marcher barons were outraged to see the valuable estates they coveted given to the king's favourites.

The tension increased after Humphrey de Bohun, 4th Earl of Hereford, suppressed a revolt in Glamorgan in 1316. Hugh the Younger had executed Llywelyn Bren without a trial and Bohun, Mortimer and Clare used it as an example of the Despensers' oppressive rule. They were even more annoyed when some of their lands were confiscated and given to the Despensers.

The Treaty of Leake in August 1318 reconciled the king with the Welsh Marcher lords. But the Despensers conspired to depose their leader, Thomas Plantagenet, Earl of Leicester and Lancaster, so his supporters ignored a king's summons in 1321. Even the steward of the royal household, Bartholomew Badlesmere, rebelled against his master. The Lords Ordainers took steps to restore order in the kingdom by forcing Edward to banish the Despensers in July.

Aymer de Valence, 2nd Earl of Pembroke, failed to appease the Marcher Lords so Roger de Mortimer, 1st Earl of March, marched on London. He was refused entry to the capital so he put it under siege until Edmund of Woodstock, 1st Earl of Kent, forced him to withdraw. Mortimer surrendered to the king at Shrewsbury in January 1322 and was imprisoned in the Tower. He escaped in August 1323, after arranging for someone to drug the constable, and went into exile in France, vowing to reclaim his lost lands from the Despensers.

The King's Half-Brother, 1316
Edward II's younger half-brother was named Thomas, after Thomas Becket. He was heir presumptive until his nephew Edward was born in 1312 and was then created Earl of Norfolk, although the Norfolk estates were split between Thomas and his brother Edmund. 16-year-old Thomas was appointed Earl Marshal in 1316; not the wisest of appointments because he had a violent temper. He was also made the Keeper of England while the king campaigned in Scotland.

Unlucky in Marriage, 1322
Thomas Plantagenet, Earl of Lancaster and Leicester, had become one of the kingdom's richest nobles when he married Alice de Lacy, Countess of Salisbury and Lincoln. In 1316 Lancaster stopped John de Warenne, Earl of Surrey, from getting a divorce and he then persuaded the Bishop of Chichester to excommunicate him for adultery.

Thomas took control of the kingdom following the reissuing of the Ordinances; he struggled to run it. There was intrigue at court when

Warenne kidnapped and imprisoned Thomas's wife in Reigate Castle. Some believed Alice had arranged the abduction to escape her miserable marriage but Thomas thought Edward II had exploited Warenne's frustration over his failed divorce to humiliate him.

Whatever the motive, an outraged Thomas seized two of Warenne's castles, but he did not ask for his wife back. The king eventually forced the two earls to make a truce and while Alice got her divorce, Thomas kept her Earldoms of Lincoln and Salisbury, as stipulated in their marriage contract. Alice's failed marriage continued to haunt her when she was imprisoned in York when her ex-husband rebelled in 1322.

The Battle of Boroughbridge, 1322

Many nobles were disappointed by Edward's lack of effort against Scotland and Thomas Plantagenet, Earl of Lancaster, tried to incite a rebellion in March 1322. He marched north only to find the Sheriff of Cumberland, Andrew Harclay, holding Boroughbridge with 4,000 men. Lancaster only had 700 troops and Harclay refused his promises of estates so he was forced to attack the following day.

Lancaster's men failed to cross the River Ure by a ford and Humphrey de Bohun, 4th Earl of Hereford, was crossing the bridge when disaster struck. A pike thrust between the bridge planks skewered his anus and his dying screams created panic. Many rebels defected during the night while reinforcements joined Harclay, leaving Lancaster no option but to surrender next day. He was taken to Pontefract, condemned to death and beheaded on 22 March. Harclay was rewarded with the Earldom of Carlisle.

A Truce with Scotland, 1322-3

The English army invaded Scotland in 1322 but Robert Bruce withdrew north, using a scorched earth policy to starve Edward's troops. The king and queen were at Rievaulx Abbey in Yorkshire when the Scots counter-attacked and the new Warden of the Marches, Andrew Harclay, 1st Earl of Carlisle, was unable to march south in time to help them. John of Brittany, 4th Earl of Richmond, was captured at Old Byland on 14 October 1322 while Edward II and his half-brother Edmund of Woodstock, 1st Earl of Kent, were lucky to escape to York.

The defeat convinced Harclay that he could not defend the Marches, so he met Robert the Bruce at Lochmaben in January 1323. They agreed a peace treaty which recognised Scotland as an independent kingdom in return for a hefty payment. Edward would also be allowed to marry one of his relatives to Bruce's son, allying the two countries. The deal was a favourable one but it had been agreed without the king's permission.

Harclay was accused of treason because he only had the authority 'to make a truce, to give safe-conducts or make any agreement without proper grant of powers' with the king's enemies. He had gone beyond his powers and a furious Edward ordered Sir Anthony Lucy to arrest him. On 3 March Harclay was proclaimed to be 'no knight, but a knave', his spurs were cut off, his sword was broken over his head and he was stripped of his robes. He was then hung, drawn and quartered and his head was taken to the king at Knaresborough before it was displayed on London Bridge. The four parts of his body were displayed in the four corners of the kingdom; at Carlisle, Newcastle, Bristol, and Dover.

Edmund of Woodstock, 1st Earl of Kent, was appointed Warden of the Marches and given responsibility for the Scottish border. It only took him two months to come to the same conclusion as Harclay: it was impossible to hold the Scots back. Edmund referred the problem to his half-brother and he was on the council which agreed a thirteen-year truce with Scotland.

The Loss of Aquitaine, 1324
Having made his peace with Scotland, Edward turned his attentions to his possessions in France. He had avoided paying homage to Charles IV so the French king was threatening to confiscate the Duchy of Aquitaine under the pretext of a local dispute. The king again used his half-brother Edmund of Woodstock, 1st Earl of Kent, as his troubleshooter and sent him to hold it in July 1324. But promised reinforcements never arrived and the French overran the duchy. Edmund was captured at La Réole in September and he was forced to agree to a six-month truce.

The Fall of the Despensers, 1326
Edward had found it difficult to manage without the Despensers so he recalled them in October, claiming he had been forced to exile them under duress. They helped the king 'legally' obtain the Lacy lands and were given some while Alice de Lacy was forced to buy the rest back. She kept the Earldom of Lincoln but her Earldom of Salisbury reverted to the crown.

Alice was kept under house arrest 'for her own protection' until she was married to Eubulus le Strange, who was hoping to make money by claiming the land given to the Despensers. But she stopped him taking the estates and the king showed his approval by cancelling the debts left to her by Thomas, her ex-husband who had been executed after the battle of Boroughbridge.

But Queen Isabella was enraged that the Despensers had returned; even more so when Hugh the Elder was created Earl of Winchester. The Queen's supporter (and possibly her lover) Roger de Mortimer rebelled and took Hugh the Elder and Hugh the Younger prisoner. Although Mortimer wanted the Despensers put on trial for treason, Hugh the Elder was immediately hanged in his armour, at Bristol in October 1326. His head was cut off and sent to Winchester while his body was chopped up and fed to dogs.

The Overthrow of Edward II, 1327

Edward II had refused to go to France to pay homage to King Charles IV, so he instructed Queen Isabella to negotiate with her brother on his behalf. She was anxious to escape from the king and happily left for Paris in March 1325. Both parties agreed Prince Edward could act on the king's behalf so he was sent over to France to meet his uncle.

Although the two kings were satisfied with the arrangement, Isabella refused to return to England. Instead she met up with the exiled Roger de Mortimer, 1st Earl of March, and the two became lovers, maybe reviving a romance they had started in England. They plotted how to remove King Edward from the throne and they were soon joined by the king's enemies. Both John of Brittany, 4th Earl of Richmond, and Thomas of Brotherton, 1st Earl of Norfolk, had lost estates to the crown and Isabella promised to return them in return for their support. Even the king's half-brother Edmund of Woodstock, 1st Earl of Kent, joined the growing rebellion because he hated the Despensers more than Mortimer.

But the scandal of Isabella's and Mortimer's affair forced them to leave the French court and head to Flanders. While she raised a mercenary army, he organised the fleet which carried them to the River Orwell in Suffolk on 24 September 1326. The people of London came out in support of the queen so Edward fled the capital, pursued by Mortimer and Isabella.

Few nobles were prepared to help the king because they hated the Despensers. Edmund FitzAlan, 9th Earl of Arundel, was the last loyal earl and he was captured in Shrewsbury and taken to Isabella at Hereford to be executed. It took the executioner twenty-two strokes with a blunt sword to sever his head.

Henry Crouchback captured Edward II at Neath in South Wales on 16 November and took him to Kenilworth Castle. He would be rewarded by having the Earldoms of Lancaster, Derby, Salisbury and Lincoln returned. Isabella and Mortimer faced a problem because the king could not be legally deposed or executed, but the barons gave their support when they asked how to deal with the situation.

Edward was taken Berkeley Castle and in January 1327 was told he had been found guilty of incompetence; he was forced to abdicate. Mortimer then arranged his murder in September 1327 and the popular story is that he was killed by having a red-hot poker thrust into his anus. It left his teenage son Edward III under the control of Isabella and Mortimer.

Chapter 11

Edward III
1327–77

Roger de Mortimer's Fall, 1327-30

Fourteen-year-old Edward III was crowned on 25 January 1327 but the kingdom was ruled by his mother Isabella and her lover Roger de Mortimer. Mortimer was created Earl of March, received estates and appointments, and was granted the Montgomery Marches. He was even allowed to choose spouses for his three sons and eight daughters, giving him a powerful position in the west.

As Mortimer's dominance at court increased, so did the hatred against him. In the autumn of 1328 the king's uncles, Thomas and Edmund of Woodstock, joined forces with Henry, 3rd Earl of Lancaster and Leicester, but their plot to overthrow Mortimer failed. The teenage king did nothing.

In 1329 William Montagu accompanied young Edward III to France to negotiate a marriage alliance with King Philip VI. Montagu took the opportunity to secretly contact Pope John XXII in Avignon to tell him that England was being ruled by Isabella and de Mortimer. They agreed that genuine letters from the king would contain the words *Pater Sancta* (Holy Father) in Edward's own handwriting; everything else was a forgery.

To begin with, only Edward, Montagu and Richard Bury, Keeper of the Privy Seal, were party to the scheme. Mortimer soon discovered the conspiracy but neither Edward nor Montagu gave anything away when they were questioned. Montagu suggested it was time for Edward to remove Mortimer, telling him, 'it was better they should eat the dog than the dog should eat them.'

In March 1330 Mortimer laid a trap for Edmund by making him think that his brother Thomas was still alive. Edmund was caught plotting again and while he offered to walk from Winchester to London with a rope around his neck as atonement, Edward III ignored his appeal. He sanctioned the death sentence but did not set a date. Meanwhile, Mortimer struggled to find anyone willing to execute a member of the royal family and he eventually had to pardon a convicted murderer so he would do the deed. Edward III was furious when he heard about the execution. Henry, 3rd Earl of Leicester and Lancaster, convinced the teenage Edward to assert his independence and he declared Mortimer a traitor in Nottingham in October.

Edward gave instructions to the constable of Nottingham Castle to let his men in through a secret tunnel. They arrested Mortimer, took him to the Tower, condemned him without trial, and hanged him like a common criminal at Tyburn. His estates were forfeited to the crown and Edmund's name was cleared. Queen Isabella was left in control of the estates of Alice de Lacy, 4th Countess of Lincoln. Meanwhile, the king gave Montagu her Earldom of Salisbury as a reward for bringing down Mortimer.

The King's Brother, 1327-30
John of Eltham was Edward III's brother and he became heir to the throne when he was 11 years old. John was created Earl of Cornwall and he remained heir until 18-year-old Edward had a son in June 1330. John was then betrothed to Maria, illegitimate daughter of King Afonso IV, to strengthen England's alliance with Portugal; he would die of fever before they married.

Campaigning against the Scots, 1332-3
Edmund of Woodstock, 1st Earl of Kent, had joint command of the Scottish Border with Henry Crouchback, 3rd Earl of Lancaster and Leicester. But the two fell out and Henry was made Captain General of all the Scottish Marches. David of Scotland had been betrothed to Edward III's sister Joan under the Treaty of Northampton. He came to the throne in 1329, when he was only 5, but the pretender Edward Balliol was crowned after Ralph de Stafford, 1st Earl of Stafford, defeated the Scots at the battle of Dupplin Moor on 11 August 1332.

David was forced to flee across the border and he returned with English troops the following year, only to be defeated at the battle of Halidon Hill on 19 July 1333. John of Eltham, 1st Earl of Cornwall, then defeated Edward Balliol in south-west Scotland.

Edward Balliol told William Montagu, 1st Earl of Salisbury, that he refused to pay homage to Edward III in 1334. So English troops crossed the border and the Scots were forced to cede the Lowlands. Henry of Grosmont was appointed the king's lieutenant in Scotland in 1336 and was created Earl of Derby soon afterwards for his loyal service. Montagu's second invasion in 1337 failed to capture Dunbar, so Edward III decided to turn his attention back to France.

A Violent Marriage, 1335
Fifty-three-year-old Alice de Lacy, 4th Countess of Lincoln, took a vow of chastity when her husband Eubulus died in 1335. The king had already granted her estates and the Earldom of Salisbury to William Montagu because he had helped dispose of Roger de Mortimer, Earl of March. But Alice was kidnapped from Bolingbroke castle by Hugh de Freyne, then raped and forced to marry her assailant. But Freyne died soon afterwards and Alice renewed her vow of chastity as her relatives argued over her inheritance. Eubulus's nephew Roger le Strange was the first to imprison her in Bolingbroke castle. Then her illegitimate half-brother Sir John de Lacy detained her. The unfortunate Alice died childless in 1348 and her Earldom of Lincoln became extinct.

Kidnapping a Wife for Money, 1336
After his first wife died, Ralph de Stafford, 1st Earl of Stafford, abducted Margaret de Audley because her estates were worth ten times his own. Although her parents filed a complaint, the king supported Stafford's marriage in 1336 and he compensated Margaret's father with the Earldom of Gloucester.

The Hundred Years War Begins, 1337
In 1331 the 19-year-old King Edward III and William Montagu, 1st Earl of Salisbury, travelled to France disguised as merchants to spy on the new King Philip VI's regime. Six years later, Philip declared that Edward had forfeited Aquitaine due to his rebellious and disobedient behaviour. The announcement started the Hundred Years' War. Edward III immediately created six new earls to increase the number of loyal nobles he could take on campaign. They included William Montagu, Earl of Salisbury, Henry of Grosmont, Earl of Derby, Robert de Ufford, Earl of Suffolk, and William de Bohun, Earl of Northampton. Some were even given annuities or estates to supplement their income.

Hugh de Courtenay, 9th Earl of Devon, stopped a French invasion of Cornwall in 1339, while Montagu and Ufford joined the expedition to besiege Cambrai, only to be captured the following year. John of Bohemia persuaded King Philip VI not to execute them, so they were freed in a prisoner exchange after agreeing they would never fight in France again.

In June 1340 the English fleet destroyed the French at the battle of Sluys but Philip then played a waiting game on the land. He knew Edward was short of money to pay his troops so he avoided challenges to hold single combats or staged fights between small groups of knights to decide the outcome of the war.

The Low Countries, 1338-45

William Montagu, 1st Earl of Salisbury, was sent to Valenciennes on a diplomatic mission to meet the princes of Flanders and Germany. He voiced concerns about the king's plans for costly alliances but he remained loyal and was appointed Marshal of England and Earl of Norfolk. Edward III's treaty with the Low Countries would result in a huge debt, so Montagu and Henry of Grosmont, 1st Duke of Lancaster, had to stay behind with the king's family as security, until it was paid off. Expeditions into Flanders in 1340 and 1345 achieved little.

A Bigamous Marriage, 1340-1

Joan was the daughter of Edmund of Woodstock, 1st Earl of Kent, and the king's cousin. Her father had been executed by Queen Isabella's lover, Roger de Mortimer, when she was only 2 years old and she, her mother and siblings had been imprisoned in Arundel Castle ever since.

Thomas Holland secretly married 12-year-old Joan in 1340 but he was overseas when her family married her to William Montague, son and heir of the 1st Earl of Salisbury. Joan did not disclose her secret marriage, fearing Thomas would be executed, but he announced their union when he returned from the crusades a rich man.

Montagu kept Joan a prisoner until the second, bigamous, marriage had been annulled in 1349 and she was allowed to join her husband in the Low Countries after Pope Clement VI approved of their marriage. After all their difficulties, all five of Thomas and Joan's children died young.

The Breton War of Succession Begins, 1341-3

John the Good, Duke of Brittany and 5th Earl of Richmond, hated his stepmother Yolande. He did not want to leave Brittany to his half-brother John de Montfort, so he left it to the French King when he died in 1341. Philip VI in turn gave it to Charles of Blois, husband of his niece Jeanne of Penthièvre, and the Breton barons rebelled.

It was the start of the prolonged War of the Breton Succession which was also known as the War of two Jeannes after Jeanne de Penthièvre and John de Montfort's wife Jeanne de Flanders. Philip summoned Montfort to court and arrested him, leaving his wife Joanna (or Jeanne) to fight for his inheritance. Pope Clement VI organised a truce in 1343 and while John de Montfort was freed he fought in vain to retake Brittany until he died, using English troops provided by Edward III.

Jeanne of Flanders wanted to continue the fight on behalf of their 6-year-old son, also John, but they were forced to flee to England. Jeanne la Flamme, or Fiery Joanna as she was known, was then declared insane and imprisoned while her son was raised in the king's household.

John of Flanders would return to Brittany when he came of age in 1364, and he defeated and killed Charles de Blois at the battle of Auray. Charles's widow Joanna gave up her rights to Brittany under the Treaty Guérande. Unfortunately, for Edward III, John declared he was a vassal to Charles V of France until the Breton barons forced him to flee to England in 1373. Charles V tried to capture the duchy so the Bretons invited John back and he was reinforced by an English army led by Edward's son Thomas of Woodstock, 1st Duke of Gloucester. The new French king, Charles VI, decided to pay off Thomas to avoid a confrontation, and John ruled for over a decade until Brest was taken from English control using a mixture of diplomacy and bribes in 1397.

The Battle of Crécy, 1346

Edward III planned a three-pronged attack on France in 1345. The Earl of Northampton would advance west from Brittany, Henry of Grosmont, 1st Duke of Lancaster, 4th Earl of Leicester and Lancaster, would move north from Aquitaine, while the king attacked from Flanders. Many of England's principal earls were present when they met the French army at Crécy on 26 August 1346. John de Vere, 7th Earl of Oxford, was fighting alongside Prince Edward, 1st Duke of Cornwall, when he asked reinforcements; Edward III replied, 'let the boy win his spurs,' and he did so, defeating the French army. The following morning Robert de Ufford, 1st Earl of Suffolk, and William de Bohun, 1st Earl of Northampton, located and defeated the rest of the French.

The Battle of Neville's Cross, 1346

King David and his Queen spent eight years in France before they returned to Scotland. David got his revenge when Edward III was campaigning in France by invading England in 1346 in support of the Auld Alliance, but he was defeated and captured at the battle of Neville's Cross and was then imprisoned for eleven years.

William de Bohun, 1st Earl of Northampton, negotiated his release in 1357 for an enormous ransom which had to be paid over ten years. David's plans to bequeath Scotland to England or hand over a son to Edward III were rejected, leaving him unable to pay the ransom. So David had no choice but to make peace with England.

The Lady with the Garter, 1348

William Montagu, 1st Earl of Salisbury, had married Catherine Grandison in 1327. She is remembered as the countess who dropped her garter in front of the king, giving Edward III the idea for the name of the new Order of the Garter, a new honour he could give his barons. There was also a rumour that Edward III lusted after Catherine and that he arranged to be alone with her so he could rape her. The story did the rounds but it was probably just French propaganda.

Married against her Will, 1350

Margaret Brotherton had been married to John Segrave in 1335 when she was 15 years old and she became the Countess of Norfolk and Earl Marshal (the only woman to hold the appointment) as soon as she came of age. But she wanted a divorce by the time she was 30 and argued she had never consented to be married so young. Her plan was to visit Rome to ask for a divorce but Edward III banned her from leaving England. She was caught trying to escape in disguise but her problem was resolved when her husband died. Margaret had not learnt her lesson because she remarried without the king's permission in 1354.

Prince Edward in France, 1355-60

The fighting rumbled on in France until the Black Death struck in 1348, killing one-third of Europe's population. The English kept the upper hand in the war against the French when Henry of Grosmont, Earl of Leicester, Lancaster, Derby and Lincoln, and Robert de Ufford, 1st Earl of Suffolk, won the naval battle of Winchelsea on 29 August 1350.

Edward of Woodstock, 1st Duke of Cornwall, made a daring raid into Aquitaine and Languedoc in 1355, crippling the economy of southern France. Then came the battle of Poitiers on 19 September 1356. An attack by John de Vere, 7th Earl of Oxford, against the French cavalry, helped secure an English victory. Hugh de Courtenay, 10th Earl of Devon, was in charge of the English baggage train which blocked the bridge on the French escape route, allowing Thomas de Beauchamp, 11th Earl of Warwick, William Montagu, 2nd Earl of Salisbury, and Robert de Ufford, 1st Earl of Suffolk, to complete the victory. King John II of France and his son Louis were amongst the prisoners.

Edmund of Langley, 1st Duke of York, and Roger de Mortimer, 2nd Earl of March, invaded French territory again in 1359 but they failed to capture Reims and the campaign was indecisive. King Edward decided to renounce his claims to the French throne so King John granted him full sovereignty of his Continental possessions (about a third of modern France). Henry of Grosmont, Duke of Lancaster, and William Montague, 2nd Earl of Salisbury, had helped negotiate the Treaty of Brétigny.

Love Blossoms from a King's Ransom, 1356-64

King John II of France was taken to England and ransomed for three million crowns while his son Louis was held in Calais as a guarantee. Enguerrand de Coucy was one of the forty French noble hostages handed over as a guarantee of the king's release in 1359. He soon became a favourite at the English court and Edward III's headstrong daughter Isabella fell in love with him after her official betrothals had failed.

Louis escaped in 1363 but John voluntarily returned to captivity in England to agree the Treaty of Brétigny which established territorial adjustments between England and France and set the payments for John's release. King John died in 1364 and Coucy married Isabella a few months later. He was released without having to pay a ransom, created Earl of Bedford and given estates in England.

Married to the Princes

Edward of Woodstock, Duke of Cornwall, was the eldest son of Edward III and Philippa (he would be given the name the Black Prince 200 years after his death). Edward was raised with his cousin Joan, and while she was married off at a young age, Edward never forgot his cousin, the Fair Maid of Kent. They married in secret in 1360 and while Pope Innocent VI blessed the union, many opposed it because they thought the Prince of Wales should have been married to a foreign princess.

Edward's brother Prince Lionel of Antwerp, 1st Duke of Clarence, was betrothed to Elizabeth, 4th Countess of Ulster, when he was aged 8. Lionel became the Earl of Ulster and was appointed governor of Ireland in 1361, but he failed to secure his Irish estates and returned to England five years later. Lionel was then betrothed to Violante, daughter of Galeazzo Visconti, lord of Pavia, with the promise of a huge dowry. They married in 1368 but Lionel died of illness during the festivities and some believed he had been poisoned by his unimpressed father-in-law.

Prince Edward in Castile, 1367-77

Edward was invested as Prince of Aquitaine in 1362. After France had been defeated, he saw an opportunity in Castile, where King Peter had been exiled by his illegitimate brother Henry of Trastámara. Edward was promised huge estates in 1367 in return for offering help; he helped defeat the French and Castilian forces at the battle of Nájera. But Peter was murdered in 1369 and Edward did not receive anything. King Charles V took advantage of the resentment caused by the new taxes being raised in Aquitaine and besieged Limoges in 1370.

Edward was eventually forced to retire due to illness and his brother John of Gaunt preferred to fight in Castile rather than in France. Edward III and his eldest son would sail for France with 400 ships and thousands of troops, only for bad weather to drive them back to England. After years of campaigning against the French and Spanish, Prince Edward died one year before his father, aged 46. His 10-year-old son, Richard II, would be crowned when Edward III died in 1377.

John of Gaunt in Aquitaine, 1369-73

John of Gaunt was the third surviving son of Edward III and Philippa. He was so called because he was born in Ghent (then called Gaunt) and rumours of him being the son of a butcher angered him every time he heard them. He married Blanche of Lancaster in 1361, becoming the Earl of Lancaster with huge estates in the north-west. He inherited the rest of the Lancaster estates and was elevated to the Duke of Lancaster when Blanche's sister Maud, the Countess of Leicester, died the year later.

King Charles V wanted Edward of Woodstock to answer charges in 1369 in Paris but the sick king's son refused to go. So the French renewed their war on England and John of Gaunt was sent to raid northern France with Thomas de Beauchamp, 11th Earl of Warwick, and Humphrey de Bohun, Earl of Hereford, Essex and Northampton. They had a stand-off with Philip, Duke of Burgundy, and then failed to capture Harfleur, so they fell back to Calais, where Beauchamp died of plague.

Gaunt's incursion forced Charles V to abandon his plans to invade England and John reinforced his brothers Edward and Edmund of Langley, Earl of Cambridge, in Aquitaine the following summer. He captured Limoges and then took charge of the area after Edward returned home. He then married Princess Constance to form an alliance with Castile but he was unhappy about his lack of troops and resigned his command in 1371, joining his father in a failed invasion of France.

John of Gaunt and William de Ufford, 2nd Earl of Suffolk, invaded southern France in 1373 and while they travelled huge distances during the raid, they achieved nothing. Their exhausted troops deserted when they reached a plague-ridden Bordeaux and John had no money to raise another one, so he sailed home to England.

Seizing Estates to Gain Loyalty, 1373

The powerful Humphrey de Bohun, Earl of Hereford, Essex and Northampton, died in 1373. His vast estates should have gone to his cousin Gilbert but the king split them between Humphrey's daughters and then married them to his close relatives. Eleanor was married to Edward III's son Thomas of Woodstock, 1st Duke of Gloucester, and Mary married Edward III's grandson Henry Bolingbroke.

John of Gaunt's Rule, 1376

John of Gaunt became the effective head of the English government in 1374, running the kingdom on behalf of his ill father and elder brother. But his wealth, his arrogance and failed policies made him unpopular and Earl Marshal Edmund de Mortimer, 3rd Earl of March, supported Edward, Prince of Wales, as he opposed his rule.

The Good Parliament of 1376 stopped the crippling war taxes, prosecuted corrupt officials and exiled the king's mistress Alice Perrers. But Gaunt took control of the country when Prince Edward died in 1376 and reversed the council's decisions, impeached the reformers and recalled the king's mistress. Mortimer was ordered to inspect the remotest of royal castles, to remove him from court, so he resigned. The Bad Parliament of 1377 annulled everything introduced by the Good Parliament and it started an unpopular poll tax to finance the war.

Chapter 12

Richard II
1377–99

The King's Minority, 1377-80

Ten-year-old Richard succeeded to the throne when his grandfather died in 1377. Attempts by Thomas de Beauchamp, 12th Earl of Warwick, to reform the government failed so he was made the king's Governor instead. The barons were worried that Richard's uncle, John of Gaunt, would usurp the throne and they did not want his other uncles to form a Regency Council. Richard's government was in the hands of a series of councils but Gaunt and another royal uncle, Thomas of Woodstock, Duke of Buckingham, remained influential. The councils would increase taxes to fund unsuccessful military expeditions abroad, raising dissatisfaction across the kingdom. Richard eventually took control when he reached his majority in 1380.

Many Problems, 1378-81

John of Gaunt's first target was Brittany in 1378 but he was unable to capture St Malo. It left him believing England would never be able to defeat France because it had superior wealth and manpower. He also faced rebellion at home and a war with Scotland, so he headed home. Then there was the Peasants' Revolt, as Gaunt marched north in 1381. He was called a traitor and forced to flee to Scotland where King Robert II looked after him until the uprising had been put down.

The Heir Presumptive, 1379

Edmund de Mortimer, Earl of March and Ulster, joined the government council when Richard took the throne. He wisely abstained from taking office because he was married to Richard's heir, 16-year-old Philippa Plantagenet. The marriage of Edmund and Philippa would eventually give rise to the House of York's claim to the throne.

Edmund knew John of Gaunt was jealous of his wealth, so he accepted the office of Lord Lieutenant of Ireland so he could escape court politics in 1379. He was unable to subdue the O'Neills in Ulster so he headed south to suppress the Munster chieftains where he caught a winter chill and died in Cork in December 1381.

Edmund's son Roger inherited his father's title and he took on his mother's claim to the throne, making his wardship a big political issue. Richard FitzAlan, Earl of Arundel and Surrey, looked after him until 6-year-old Edmund was appointed Lord Lieutenant of Ireland to remove him from court, like his father. The youngster was then handed over to Richard II's half-brother Thomas Holland, 2nd Earl of Kent, and Roger married to his daughter Eleanor.

Roger was kept in Ireland until he died in 1398 aged 24, and his 7-year-old son Edmund then became the heir presumptive to the throne. Young Edmund and his brother Roger would be imprisoned when Henry Bolingbroke deposed Richard in September 1399.

The Fight for Brittany, 1380-1
Richard II's uncle Thomas of Woodstock, Earl of Essex and Buckingham, and Ralph Neville, 1st Earl of Westmorland, took an army to the continent in July 1380 to support Duke John's claim for Brittany. France supported the rival claimant Charles of Blois, but their troops were plunged into confusion when King Charles V died in September. The English army was forced to end the siege of Nantes after John reconciled with the new French King, Charles VI.

The First Royal Marriage, 1380
Richard II's trusted friend William de Ufford, 2nd Earl of Suffolk, and Michael de la Pole, negotiated the king's marriage to Anne of Bohemia, daughter of the Holy Roman Emperor, Charles IV, in 1380. The union gave England a strong ally against France in the Hundred Years War. John Holland, 1st Duke of Exeter, escorted Anne to England and Edward Courtenay, 11th Earl of Devon, accompanied her to London. De la Pole was awarded the Earldom of Suffolk when Ufford died.

Problem Marriages
Eight-year-old John Hastings, 3rd Earl of Pembroke, was married to 17-year-old Elizabeth, daughter of John of Gaunt, in 1380. But the king's hot-headed half-brother John Holland, 1st Duke of Exeter, made her pregnant. The unconsummated marriage was annulled and while Hastings was later married to Philippa, daughter of Edmund de Mortimer, 3rd Earl of March, he was mortally injured jousting soon afterwards.

Robert de Vere, 9th Earl of Oxford, was also married at a young age to the king's cousin Philippa de Coucy. He was created Duke of Ireland and Marquess of Dublin, but he divorced her in 1387 so he could marry his mistress Agnes de Launcekrona, Queen Anne of Bohemia's Czech lady-in-waiting.

The Peasants' Rebellion, 1381
A poll tax was introduced in 1381 and the Lollards, religious reformers determined to have the Bible distributed in English, rebelled in Suffolk. William de Ufford, 2nd Earl of Suffolk, was ordered to supress John Wycliffe's uprising but he was taken prisoner by Geoffrey Litster while eating his dinner in Bury St Edmunds. Litster failed to convince Ufford to join the rebellion and he was able to escape in disguise. Henry Despenser, Bishop of Norwich, soon stopped the rebellion.

There was also an uprising on the outskirts of London and Richard II rode out to meet the rebels. Wat Tyler refused to believe the teenage king's promises and he was killed in the scuffle which followed. Richard led the crowds away from the scene and allowed the rebels to go home. He then went to Essex to calm the situation down and silenced the last group of rebels at Billericay. Richard's personal intervention in stopping the rebellion had improved his reputation.

Support for Portugal, 1381
Edmund of Langley, 1st Duke of York, went to Portugal in 1381 on an abortive expedition to help the Portuguese attack Castile. He betrothed his 8-year-old son Edward to Princess Beatrice, the daughter of King Ferdinand I of Portugal. But the proposed marriage was annulled when Portugal and Castile made their peace.

Holland and Stafford Argue, 1385
Richard II's half-brother John Holland, 1st Duke of Exeter, had a violent temper and he murdered Ralph Stafford, son of the 2nd Earl of Stafford, during an argument while they were campaigning in Scotland. Holland was arrested in Beverley and sentenced to death but their mother Joan, Countess of Kent, pleaded with Richard to spare his half-brother. She died from the worry at Wallingford Castle so a repentant Richard pardoned Holland and he was ordered to go to the Holy Land.

Invading Scotland, 1385
Richard appointed Thomas de Beauchamp, 12th Earl of Warwick, Warden of the West March, and Henry Percy, 1st Earl of Northumberland, Warden of the East March, and he instructed them to survey the border fortifications. Richard II decided to attack Scotland in 1385 after the impatient Robert III

seized the throne from his elderly father King Robert II. Earl Marshal Thomas de Mowbray, 1st Duke of Norfolk, led the invasion and Henry Percy, 1st Earl of Northumberland, acquired the nickname *Haatspore*, or Harry Hotspur, because of his rapid marches and aggressive attacks. But the English army failed to defeat the Scots and it was forced to withdraw. The counter-attack came in 1388 and Percy was captured at the battle of Otterburn on 10 August.

The king's half-brother John Holland, 1st Duke of Exeter, was appointed Warden of the West March while Earl Marshal Thomas de Mowbray, 1st Duke of Norfolk, was appointed Warden of the East March. Thomas de Beauchamp, 12th Earl of Warwick, was kept busy in peace negotiations with Scotland while the border fortifications were strengthened.

The Fight for Castile and Aquitaine, 1386-96

John of Gaunt decided to pursue his claim on Castile through his marriage to Princess Constance in 1386. He concluded an alliance with Portugal by marrying his daughter Philippa to the new Portuguese king, John the Good. But John of Trastámara refused to fight the English, leaving Gaunt unable to pay his troops, and he renounced his claim in return for money after his soldiers were struck down by disease. His daughter Catherine married Trastámara's son Henry to seal the deal.

John returned to England in 1390 where he was made Duke of Aquitaine. The Gascons rebelled against his appointment in 1394 and he was forced to negotiate the Truce of Leulinghem with them two years later.

The Lords Appellant Take Over, 1387

Thomas de Beauchamp, 12th Earl of Warwick, and Thomas le Despenser turned Richard against his most trusted advisor, Lord Chancellor Michael de la Pole, Earl of Suffolk. So Pole was accused of embezzlement and negligence during the Wonderful Parliament of 1386. Those jealous of the king's close relationship with Robert de Vere, 9th Earl of Oxford, spread rumours about a homosexual friendship. They increased when he was created Marquess of Dublin in 1385 (the first ever Marquess) and the Duke of Ireland the following year.

The king wanted to maintain peace with France but his uncle Thomas le Despenser, Earl of Gloucester, was calling for a war. Despenser and Richard FitzAlan, Earl of Arundel and Surrey, pressured Richard into including them onto the Regency Council in 1386 but he limited their appointments to only one year.

FitzAlan may have defeated a combined Franco-Spanish-Flemish fleet off Margate in March 1387 but the king wanted his favourites on the council and he dismissed Despenser and FitzAlan a few months later. Thomas of

Woodstock, 1st Duke of Gloucester, led the rebellious Lords Appellant who seized control of the king and government in November. He was joined by Thomas de Beauchamp, 12th Earl of Warwick, Richard FitzAlan, 11th Earl of Arundel, Thomas de Mowbray, Earl of Nottingham, and Henry Bolingbroke, Earl of Derby.

The Lords Appellant engaged the Council's army at the battle of Radcot Bridge near Oxford on 20 December 1387, but Robert de Vere and Michael de la Pole fled the field and the rest of the army surrendered. The Lords Appellant condemned the king's favourites during the Merciless Parliament and an absent Vere was sentenced to death. Meanwhile, Despenser and FitzAlan continued their warlike stance with France and they refused to honour a peace with the French King.

Pole and Vere went into exile where they both died. Richard II had Vere's embalmed body brought back to England in 1392 and had the coffin opened so he could kiss his friend's hand one last time.

The Crusades, 1390-4

John Beaufort, illegitimate son of John of Gaunt, 1st Duke of Lancaster, served with Louis II, Duke of Bourbon, during his crusade to North Africa in 1390. He then served with the Teutonic Knights in Lithuania. John Montacute, 3rd Earl of Salisbury, also crusaded through Lithuania with John of Gaunt's son Henry Bolingbroke and they returned with 300 captured princes. Bolingbroke then made a second pilgrimage to the same region and then went to the Holy Land. John of Gaunt joined the Crusade against the Ottomans which ended in the disastrous battle of Nicopolis in 1396 and he returned home suffering from ill-health.

Legitimate Bastards, 1396

John of Gaunt, 1st Duke of Lancaster, always exerted considerable influence over his nephew Richard II. His legitimate male heirs would include Kings Henry IV, Henry V, and Henry VI; his daughters included Queen Philippa of Portugal and Queen Catherine of Castile. He also had five illegitimate children and the four he had with Katherine Swynford were surnamed Beaufort. He eventually married Katherine in 1396 and Pope Boniface IX agreed that their children could be legitimised. But John Beaufort, 1st Marquess of Somerset and Dorset, and his siblings were barred from the line of succession as part of the deal. John of Gaunt died in 1398, having seen his son Henry Bolingbroke exiled by Richard.

A Second Royal Marriage, 1396

Queen Anne died of the plague in 1394 and Richard FitzAlan, Earl of Arundel and Surrey, arrived late for her funeral. A furious king hit him and then pretended to forgive him, but he had not forgotten the insult. Twenty-nine-year-old King Richard was soon betrothed to 6-year-old Isabella of Valois as part of a peace deal with France in 1396. Edmund of Langley, 1st Duke of York, collected the young princess from the court of the insane King Charles VI.

The End of the Lords Appellant, 1397
Richard II dismissed the Lords Appellant and resumed power in 1397. He rewarded those who had supported him, creating Despenser the Earl of Gloucester, John Beaufort the Marquess of Somerset and Dorset, and Ralph Neville, Earl of Westmorland. He also arrested those who had opposed him, accusing Thomas de Mowbray, 1st Duke of Norfolk, and Thomas de Beauchamp, 12th Earl of Warwick, of plotting to imprison him. King Richard and his half-brother John Holland also arrested the king's uncle Thomas of Woodstock, 1st Duke of Gloucester, and Richard FitzAlan, 11th Earl of Arundel. Holland seized Arundel Castle at the king's request and was rewarded with the Dukedom of Exeter.

Richard FitzAlan was executed while Thomas of Woodstock was imprisoned in Calais. Thomas was soon murdered and Henry Bolingbroke and Edward of Norwich, Earl of Rutland, were suspected of organising his murder with the Captain of Calais, Thomas de Mowbray, 2nd Earl of Nottingham. There were also suspicions that Richard II had ordered his death.

Whoever carried out the deed, Thomas de Mowbray was elevated to Duke of Norfolk and Henry Bolingbroke was created Duke of Hereford. Rutland was given Gloucester's title, the Duke of Aumale, and his office of Constable of England.

Thomas de Beauchamp, 12th Earl of Warwick, was also imprisoned in the Tower but his life was spared because he pleaded guilty and pleaded for mercy. He still had to forfeit his estates and titles and was sentenced to life imprisonment.

The End of the Mortimers, 1398
Roger de Mortimer, 4th Earl of March, had been sent to Ireland because he had a claim to the throne. He was summoned to attend Parliament at Shrewsbury in January 1398 but Richard was concerned how he was 'rapturously received' by supporters wearing his colours. So he sent his brother-in-law Thomas Holland, 1st Duke of Surrey, across to Ireland to arrest Mortimer. Only he arrived too late because Mortimer had been ambushed and killed while scouting in front of his army near Kells. So Richard threw his son Edmund into prison to stop Mortimer's supporters rallying around the 7-year-old.

Henry Bolingbroke's Exile, 1399

Thomas de Mowbray and Henry Bolingbroke blamed each other as the rumours over Gloucester's murder in Calais Castle circulated. In September 1398 Mowbray accused Henry of making treasonable remarks so Edward of Norwich, Duke of Aumale, planned a duel to settle the argument. But Richard intervened and he exiled Thomas and Henry, taking their titles and their estates. Edward was made to marry the elderly and childless Philippa Mohun. Richard also made Edward ward of the Mortimer estates, knowing he would never have any children to claim them.

Bolingbroke planned to marry the Duke of Berry's daughter in 1399 but Richard sent John Montacute, 3rd Earl of Salisbury, to France to stop the match. Richard II then called Henry a traitor and condemned him to a life in exile. This was the final straw for Bolingbroke and he started planning to seize the throne. He was joined by Thomas Arundel, the exiled Archbishop of Canterbury, and his nephew Thomas FitzAlan who had been treated cruelly as a child by Richard's half-brother John Holland.

Henry Bolingbroke Seizes the Crown, 1399

Richard travelled to Ireland to avenge the death of Roger de Mortimer and Henry Bolingbroke seized the opportunity to return to England. He landed at Ravenspurn in East Yorkshire at the end of June and was soon joined by loyal Lancastrians. Richard and Edward of Norwich immediately headed back across the Irish Sea, landing at Milford Haven in South Wales on 19 July. They marched north to join the part of the army which had landed in North Wales, but false rumours of Richard's death caused the troops under John Montacute, 3rd Earl of Salisbury, to desert.

Custodian of the Realm, Edmund of Langley, 1st Duke of York, was raising an army to stop Henry when his son Montacute sent him news that his army had dispersed. Langley also dismissed his troops and he surrendered to Bolingbroke at Berkeley on 27 July; others did the same including Michael de la Pole, 1st Earl of Suffolk.

Richard II sent his half-brother John Holland, Duke of Exeter, to meet Henry Bolingbroke but blood ties were deciding loyalties across the kingdom. Earl Marshal Ralph Neville, 1st Earl of Westmorland, was married to Henry Bolingbroke's sister Joan Beaufort, and he supported his brother-in-law. Henry Percy, 1st Earl of Northumberland, was married to Neville's daughter Margaret, so he and his sons Henry and Thomas, 1st Earl of Worcester, joined Bolingbroke at Doncaster.

Richard and his councillors were imprisoned in the Tower while his enemies were released. Titles were cancelled and estates forfeited so they could be given to Henry's supporters. Neville and Percy accepted Richard's abdication and some, including the recently released Thomas de

Beauchamp, 12th Earl of Warwick, urged Henry to execute Richard. While Henry took his time over deciding what to do, Richard's closest supporters were executed, including Queen Isabella's guardian William le Scrope, 1st Earl of Wiltshire.

Henry was crowned in October 1399, the first king from the Lancaster side of the Plantagenets. Richard died in Pontefract Castle in February 1400; he may have been starved to death. His body was displayed in St Paul's Cathedral to prove he was dead.

Chapter 13

Henry IV
1399–1413

The Epiphany Rising, 1400

Henry IV settled many scores with Richard's supporters when he took the throne. Thomas le Despenser, 1st Earl of Gloucester, was attainted for murdering his uncle Thomas of Woodstock, 1st Duke of Gloucester, in Calais (even though Henry had been a chief suspect). Edward of Norwich was sacked as the Constable of the Tower, deprived of the Dukedom of Aumale and imprisoned at Windsor Castle. Richard II's half-brother John Holland, 1st Duke of Exeter, was also reduced to Earl of Huntingdon.

Those who had been demoted planned to assassinate King Henry and his sons so they could restore Richard to the throne. They were joined by John Montacute, 3rd Earl of Salisbury, and Exeter's nephew Thomas Holland, 1st Duke of Surrey. The attack was due to be made during the Epiphany celebrations in January 1400 but Edward of Norwich betrayed the plot and the conspirators scattered. Montacute was caught and executed by a mob in Cirencester and Despenser met the same fate in Bristol. Thomas FitzAlan, Earl of Arundel and Surrey, tortured Richard's half-brother John Holland, because he had treated him cruelly as a child, before the two Hollands were executed.

The Welsh and the Percy's Rebel, 1402-4

Owain Glyndŵr rebelled along the Welsh border in March 1402. The two Henry Percys, 1st Earl of Northumberland and Hotspur, defended the North March while Richard of Conisburgh, 3rd Earl of Cambridge, protected Herefordshire. But Owain captured Edmund de Mortimer at the battle of Bryn Glas on 22 June 1402 and Henry accused him of desertion, refused to ransom him, and confiscated his properties. So Edmund married Owain's daughter and declared his imprisoned nephew Edmund de Mortimer, 5th Earl of March, rightful heir to the throne.

Henry Percy was also Warden of the Scottish East March and he and his son Henry Hotspur defeated the Scots at the battle of Homildon Hill on 14 September 1402, with Edmund de Mortimer's help. Although Henry appreciated the victory, he failed to pay the Percys and made them hand over their prisoners rather than let them claim their ransom money. A furious Henry Percy denounced Henry's 'tyrannical government'.

The following summer, Henry Percy the younger and his uncle Thomas Percy, Earl of Worcester, joined forces with Glyndŵr and Mortimer. The king's army engaged the Percys at Shrewsbury on 21 July 1403 and Percy's army fled after Henry was killed. Thomas was captured and beheaded in Shrewsbury; his head was displayed on London Bridge. Even Henry Percy's corpse was exhumed and displayed in Shrewsbury's market place to prove he was dead. His head was then impaled on Micklegate, a gateway into York, while his body was quartered and the pieces sent to the four corners of the kingdom.

Henry IV ordered Percy's old enemy Earl Marshal Ralph Neville, 1st Earl of Westmorland, to engage the rebels and he drove them back to Warkworth Castle. As a temporary measure, the king secured the Scottish border by appointing Neville Warden of the West March while his teenage son John of Lancaster, 1st Duke of Bedford, was made Warden of the East March. Richard Neville, 5th Earl of Salisbury, arrested Henry Percy, 1st Earl of Northumberland, for treason and he then took command of both the Scottish Marches. Hotspur's son, another Henry Percy, was imprisoned for supporting the rebellion.

Meanwhile, Thomas FitzAlan, Earl of Arundel and Surrey, had been appointed to coordinate operations in all the Welsh Marches. He allied with the king's half-brothers the Beauforts before defeating Glyndŵr in North Wales while Edward of Norwich, 2nd Duke of York, campaigned in South Wales. The Welsh were finally defeated by Richard de Beauchamp, 13th Earl of Warwick, at the battle of Mynydd Cwmdu in the summer of 1404.

The Mortimers Rebel, 1404

Henry pardoned Henry Percy, 2nd Earl of Northumberland, in June 1404 but only after he had handed over his grandson. The hostage situation made no difference because Percy contacted Edmund de Mortimer and Owain Glyndŵr and they decided they would divide the conquered kingdom into three in February 1405. Glyndŵr would take the west, Percy the north and Mortimer the south.

At the same time the heirs to the throne, Edmund and Roger de Mortimer, were abducted from Windsor Castle and were being taken to their uncle when they were recaptured near Cheltenham. Constance of York was arrested and accused of helping them to escape but she blamed her brother Edward of Norwich, 2nd Duke of York, and he was imprisoned in Pevensey

Castle. Edmund and Roger would be kept in prison for the rest of Henry IV's reign.

The Percys Rebel, 1405
Henry Percy, 2nd Earl of Northumberland, was furious that a Neville now held both the West and East Warden of the Scottish Marches. So he rebelled again with the Archbishop of York, Richard le Scrope, and Thomas de Mowbray, Earl of Norfolk and Nottingham. Percy attacked Witton Castle, near Durham, in May 1405 only to discover that Ralph Neville, 1st Earl of Westmorland, had already fled. Neville defeated Percy's allies at Topcliffe in Yorkshire before marching towards York with Henry IV's son John of Lancaster.

They encountered the rebels on Shipton Moor near York, where an outnumbered Neville convinced the rebels that their demands would be accepted and their safety guaranteed. So they disbanded on 29 May and Neville took them to the king at Pontefract Castle. Henry disregarded Neville's promise and the rebel leaders were condemned to death. Archbishop Thomas Arundel objected to the execution of a fellow archbishop, but Richard le Scrope, Thomas de Mowbray and William Plumpton were beheaded in York on 8 June 1405.

Meanwhile, Henry Percy had fled to Scotland and the king instructed Neville to seize his castles. Percy continued plotting and he returned to England in 1408 only to be killed at the battle of Bramham Moor in Yorkshire on 19 February. His head was later displayed on London Bridge.

A Portuguese Alliance, 1405
Richard II had supported John the Good, illegitimate son of Peter the Cruel of Portugal, in his struggle with Castile in 1385. Henry wanted to do the same and he secured the alliance with a double marriage in November 1405. His sister Philippa of Lancaster was married to King John I, and Thomas FitzAlan, Earl of Arundel and Surrey, was married to John's illegitimate daughter Beatrice.

Chapter 14

Henry V
1413–22

The Lollards Rebel, 1414

Henry V faced civil unrest at the start of his reign when the religious movement known as the Lollards called for the introduction of an English language Bible in January 1414. Richard de Beauchamp, 13th Earl of Warwick, helped put down the uprising and John Grey, 1st Earl of Tankerville, escorted the Lollard leader, Sir John Oldcastle, from Powys to London. Oldcastle would be burned at the stake in 1417.

The Southampton Plot, July 1415

Henry V felt confident enough to release the claimants to the throne Edmund and Roger de Mortimer when he came to the throne. Roger died soon afterwards but Edmund married Anne, daughter of Edmund Stafford, 5th Earl of Stafford, without a license in 1415. Both were descendants of Edward III and their children could have made a claim to the throne so Henry fined them. Although Edmund remained loyal to the king, others decided to use him in their scheming.

Edmund's brother-in-law Richard of Conisburgh was the chief conspirator. Henry V had created him the Earl of Cambridge but he received no estates, leaving him 'the poorest of the earls'. The king's instructions to raise troops for an invasion of France drove him deeper into debt. Conisburgh's co-conspirator was Henry Scrope, 3rd Baron Scrope of Masham.

Conisburgh and Scrope planned to take Mortimer to Wales and proclaim him king. But when he heard of the plot, Mortimer went immediately to Portchester, where the English army was preparing to sail, and told the king on 31 July. Conisburgh and Scrope were arrested and beheaded on 5 August 1415 but Mortimer was pardoned for being loyal. Henry's fleet set sail for France a few days later.

The Agincourt Campaign, 1415-17

Henry's army captured Harfleur in September 1415. William de la Pole, 1st Duke of Suffolk, was seriously wounded while Thomas FitzAlan, Earl of Arundel and Surrey, fell ill during the siege, returned to England and died.

Henry then ignored his council's warning and ordered Edward of Norwich, 2nd Duke of York, to lead the army towards Calais. His tired and hungry troops were intercepted by a much larger French army at Agincourt on 25 October 1415. Despite the disadvantages, Henry's archers defeated the French men-at-arms on a muddy battlefield. The only criticism that could be levelled at Henry was his decision to execute his prisoners when he thought they might overwhelm their guards.

Richard de Vere, 11th Earl of Oxford, and Henry Percy, 2nd Earl of Northumberland, sailed across the English Channel to relieve Harfleur in 1416, taking part in the naval battle at the mouth of the Seine. Henry V would have to launch a second invasion of Normandy in 1417.

Defending the Northern Border, 1415-7

The Scots crossed the border in 1415 hoping to take advantage of Henry V's absence in France, but Earl Marshal Ralph Neville, 1st Earl of Westmorland and Warden of the West March, defeated them at Yeavering in Northumberland. Henry V reconciled with the Percys by creating Henry Percy the 2nd Earl of Northumberland and making him Warden of the East March. He defeated another Scottish invasion in August 1417 and was joined by Richard Neville, 5th Earl of Salisbury, as the Warden of the West March in 1420.

A Royal Marriage, 1421

Edward of Norwich, 2nd Duke of York, had visited Paris to negotiate a marriage between the new king and Catherine of Valois at the start of Henry's reign. The match was postponed because of Henry V's successful campaign in France and then delayed by prolonged negotiations on behalf of the insane Charles VI of France. The 1420 Treaty of Troyes recognised Henry V as regent and heir-apparent to the French throne. He married Charles's daughter Catherine of Valois and Edmund de Mortimer, 5th Earl of March, accompanied the couple back to England in February 1421.

Raiding Anjou and Maine, 1421

Henry V left his brother Thomas of Lancaster, 1st Duke of Clarence, in command of the English forces in France. But Charles's son, the Dauphin, refused to accept the situation and he was joined by a Scottish army led by John Stewart, Earl of Buchan. So King Henry instructed Lancaster to raid Anjou and Maine. Foraging English archers captured a Scottish man-at-arms as the army camped near Baugé on 21 March 1421. Lancaster decided to attack immediately because the following day was Easter Sunday, a holy day. But the English cavalry were ambushed and many including Lancaster and his uncle Thomas Beaufort, 1st Duke of Exeter, were killed.

The Conquest of Normandy, 1417-22

Thomas Beaufort had been rewarded with the Dukedom of Exeter and appointed Lieutenant of Normandy following the victory at Agincourt. Edmund de Mortimer, 5th Earl of March, was with the army which invaded Normandy in 1417 and he was joined by Thomas Beaufort for the sieges of Evreux, Ivry, and Rouen. Thomas Montacute was appointed lieutenant general of the conquered area and created Count of Perche, part of Henry V's policy of creating Norman titles; he was later rewarded with the Earldom of Salisbury. Edmund de Mortimer, 5th Earl of March, was still campaigning when the king died of dysentery during the siege of Meaux on 31 August 1422.

Chapter 15

Henry VI – Peacetime
1421–55

The Regency, 1422-5
Henry was only nine months old when he succeeded to the English throne
in August 1422. He also became the titular King of France in accordance
with the Treaty of Troyes when his grandfather Charles VI died in October
1422. Henry V's brother John, Duke of Bedford, was appointed regent in
September 1423 but his French mother Catherine of Valois was not allowed
to take part in the young king's upbringing. John took over the running of
the war in France while his brother Humphrey of Lancaster, Duke of
Gloucester, ruled the kingdom in his absence. Humphrey claimed the
regency when John died but the rest of the Council protested, particularly
when he lost control of the kingdom's justice and finances resulting in unrest
across the kingdom.

The Lieutenant of Ireland, 1423
Edmund de Mortimer, 5th Earl of March and Ulster, was appointed the
king's lieutenant in Ireland in 1423. He sent a deputy to carry out his duties,
but was 'sent out of the way to Ireland' after arguing with the king's
protector, Humphrey of Lancaster, Duke of Gloucester, only to die soon
afterwards. Richard of York, 3rd Duke of York, inherited Mortimer's title
and his claim to the throne. His inheritance also made the 12-year-old one
of the wealthiest men in England.

York was sent to Ireland to deal with the feud between the Lord
Chancellor of Ireland, John Talbot, Earl of Shrewsbury and Waterford, and
James Butler, 4th Earl of Ormonde. The hostility dominated Irish politics
for years and it weakened the crown's authority in Ireland, until Butler
married Talbot's daughter Elizabeth.

York eventually allied with the Norman barons who were opposing
Edmund Beaufort, 2nd Duke of Somerset, the leader of Henry VI's council.
He returned to England after the council surrendered Maine and Anjou as
part of the marriage deal between Henry and Margaret of Anjou. York was

again appointed Lieutenant of Ireland, to keep him out of the way, but he soon returned because the crown owed him a huge amount of money.

The Nevilles, 1424-5

Ralph Neville was ward to Richard of York, 3rd Duke of York. Richard was betrothed to Neville's 9-year-old daughter Cecily when he turned 13 in 1424. Richard inherited the valuable Earldom of March from his uncle Edmund de Mortimer the following year. Neville inherited the Earldom of Westmorland the same year but he struggled to get his inheritance from his grandfather's widow Joan Beaufort, daughter of John of Gaunt, Duke of Lancaster.

Joan died in 1440 but Neville conceded the rest of the disputed lands to his great-uncle Richard Neville, 5th Earl of Salisbury, in 1443. Ralph eventually 'succumbed to a mental disorder' and was eventually placed under the guardianship of his brother Thomas. Maybe it was because he had been so busy finding husbands and wives for his twenty children.

Succession Worries, 1427

Edmund Beaufort, 2nd Duke of Somerset, was suspected of having an affair with Henry V's widow Catherine of Valois in 1427. The match worried many because any children from the match would be illegitimate half-siblings of the king, which created problems for the succession to the throne. So Parliament had to rush through a new law regulating the remarriage of widowed queens. Beaufort later married Eleanor, daughter of Richard de Beauchamp, 13th Earl of Warwick, in secret but their unlicensed marriage was later pardoned.

The Nevilles and the Percys Quarrel, 1434-49

Henry Percy, 2nd Earl of Northumberland, was married to Eleanor Neville, and his sister Elizabeth was married to Ralph Neville, 2nd Earl of Westmorland. Henry resigned as Warden of the East March in 1434 but he was made warden of both marches when Richard Neville, 5th Earl of Salisbury, resigned as Warden of the West March a year later because the crown owed him money. The appointment merely increased tension between the two families.

Richard Neville would be reappointed Warden of the West March in 1443 but he started recruiting tenants on Percy's estates, increasing tensions between the families. Henry Percy also argued with the Archbishop of York but the king supported the Church when the dispute escalated into violence.

The Loss of Burgundy, 1430-5

John of Lancaster, 1st Duke of Bedford, had continued the fight in France while his younger brother Humphrey, Duke of Gloucester, acted as Lord

Protector of England. Lancaster defeated the French at the battle of Verneuil but Joan of Arc rallied the French until she was captured by the Burgundians at the siege of Compiègne in May 1430. They handed her over to the English and she was burned at the stake.

There was a stand-off as John protected Normandy and Humphrey held Calais. But Philip, Duke of Burgundy, switched to Charles VII when John died during the Congress of Arras in 1435. It sparked a resurgence in French confidence and Charles used the opportunity to strengthen his army. Philip, Duke of Burgundy, attacked Calais in 1436 but Humphrey and the garrison escaped. John de Mowbray, 3rd Duke of Norfolk, and John de Vere, 12th Earl of Oxford, then helped Edmund Beaufort, 2nd Duke of Somerset, lift the siege.

Richard Plantagenet, 3rd Duke of York, was appointed lieutenant general and Governor of France and Normandy in 1439. But he refused to send reinforcements to John Talbot, 3rd Earl of Shrewsbury, because the crown wanted him to pay for them out of his own pocket. Instead he sent a separate army under the new Duke of Somerset and Earl of Kendal, John Beaufort. Talbot reorganised and trained the English army when he was appointed Constable of France.

The King's Half-Brothers, 1437-42

Owen Tudor married Henry V's widow Catherine in secret but the marriage was not recognised by the authorities, making their two children, Edmund and Jasper, illegitimate. Catherine died in childbirth in 1437 and Owen Tudor was imprisoned while their children were sent to Barking Abbey in Essex. They were raised by the abbess Katherine de la Pole, the sister of the king's favourite, William de la Pole, 1st Duke of Suffolk.

Katherine brought the youngsters to the king's attention when he turned 21 in 1442 and he allowed them to be educated in court; he also released their father from prison. Ten years later they were declared legitimate and recognised as the king's brothers. Edmund was created Earl of Richmond and Jasper was created Earl of Pembroke and they were both given large estates.

Arguments in Devon, 1439-47

Thomas Courtenay, 5th Earl of Devon, attacked William Bonville's estates in 1439, even though he was married to his aunt Elizabeth. Two years later Courtenay was appointed Steward of the Duchy of Cornwall, only to see the post cancelled a few days later after the Royal Steward for Cornwall, Bonville, complained. The pair were ordered to appear before the king after Courtenay's men attacked Bonville's friend Sir Philip Chetwynd. But they both ignored his warning and were sent to serve in France.

Henry VI favoured Courtenay because he was married to Margaret, the mother of his favourite, Edmund Beaufort, Duke of Somerset. But William de la Pole, 1st Duke of Suffolk, favoured Bonville when he took control of the court party in 1447. It meant that Courtenay would support Richard Plantagenet, 3rd Duke of York, during the Cade Rebellion in Sussex and Kent in 1450.

The Beauforts, 1440-4

The siege of Harfleur stopped the French invading England in August 1440. Richard, 3rd Duke of York, was reappointed Lieutenant of France with full powers but he was furious to hear that John Beaufort, 1st Duke of Somerset, had advised King Henry to sue for peace. Beaufort would resign before York arrived in Normandy in 1441 but the king would have been wise to accept his advice.

The fall of Pontoise, near Paris, to the Duke of Orléans in September 1441 weakened the English situation while Gascony (now in south-west France) was in danger of being taken. York was ordered to fortify Rouen in 1443 when the French threatened Bordeaux and Aquitaine. Beaufort's promise to reinforce him never materialised, allowing the French to capture Guyenne (now in south-west France).

York was further infuriated to hear that John Beaufort had been elevated to Duke of Somerset and given command of the army in the north of France. Beaufort also declared himself the Lieutenant of Aquitaine and Captain General of Guyenne after the wife of Humphrey of Lancaster, 1st Duke of Gloucester, was charged with treason. It left York only governing Normandy and his position was undermined even further when Beaufort's negotiations failed. The king added insult to injury when he gave money to Beaufort to pay his troops but still gave York nothing, leaving him deep in debt.

Beaufort continued to cause problems in the summer of 1443. First he marched on Cherbourg before heading south to Gascony, accidently breaching a peace treaty when he entered the Breton town of Guerche. His next crime was to set all his prisoners free without permission in return for money from the Duke of Brittany.

Following an aimless march through Maine, Beaufort returned to England and died, possibly taking his own life. His death left William de la Pole, 1st Duke of Suffolk, in charge of Henry VI's government. But Richard of York would not forget John Beaufort's contemptuous behaviour and would always hold a grudge against the Beaufort family.

Accusations of Witchcraft, 1441

Humphrey of Lancaster, 1st Duke of Gloucester, had claimed Henry's regency following the death of his elder brother John, Duke of Bedford, in 1435. But his enemies accused his wife Eleanor of heresy and practising witchcraft against the king in 1441. She was imprisoned and a humiliated Humphrey retired from public life. But it did not end there because Humphrey was arrested for treason in 1447. He died three days later and while some believed he had been poisoned, the shock of imprisonment had caused a stroke.

Securing Powys in Wales, 1447
Henry Grey, 2nd Earl of Tankerville, captured a rebellious Gruffudd Vychan in Powys in 1447. He was then beheaded in Powys Castle despite a promise of safe conduct, maybe as revenge for the death of Christopher Talbot, son of the 1st Earl of Shrewsbury. His execution ended the revolt in central Wales and order was restored in Powys.

The Loss of Maine and Anjou, 1444-48
William de la Pole, 1st Earl of Suffolk, had been forced to surrender to Jean, Count de Dunois, when Joan of Arc relieved Orléans in 1429. Jackanapes, as Pole was known, was ransomed after spending three years as a prisoner of Charles VII. He would negotiate the marriage of Henry VI and Margaret of Anjou in 1444 but he had to include a secret clause in the deal which handed Maine and Anjou to France.

Pole soon became the principal power behind Henry VI's throne and was appointed Chamberlain, Admiral of England and Duke of Suffolk in 1448. However, Pole had never paid the ransom he owed to the Count de Dunois, and he was suspected of handing over council papers so the French could plan an invasion of England.

Two years later Pole was blamed for losing Maine and Anjou and was imprisoned in the Tower. The king intervened and made sure he was exiled rather than have him tried and executed. However, Pole was not safe because his ship was intercepted. He was subjected to a mock trial and beheaded on Dover's beach. Either one of his enemies had arranged his death or the king had had him silenced to stop him revealing how Maine and Anjou had been given away.

A Private War between the Percys and Nevilles, 1448-53
The Percys and the Nevilles were often locked in a private feud along the Scottish Marches. But Richard Neville made sure his children were married to wealthy partners. His son, also Richard, was married to Anne, daughter of Richard de Beauchamp, 13th Earl of Warwick, and he inherited the earldom when he turned 21 in 1449, making him a wealthy and powerful noble. His daughter Eleanor married Thomas Stanley, 'a man of considerable acumen' who would become one of 'the most successful power-brokers of his age'.

Henry Percy, 2nd Earl of Northumberland, disrespected Neville when he marched his forces through the West March, en route to attack Scotland in 1448, without asking permission. Percy's army burnt Dunbar and Dumfries but the Scots retaliated against Alnwick and Warkworth castles. Percy was defeated and his eldest son was captured at the battle of Sark on 23 October. Neville lost many troops driving the Scots back. The feud resulted in Neville and Percy being excluded from the peace negotiations with Scotland, increasing the resentment between the families.

Resentment on the Scottish Border, 1449-53
William Neville, 1st Earl of Kent, guarded Roxburgh Castle on the Scottish Borders for King Henry until he was sent to France on a diplomatic mission in 1449. He was captured at Pont de l'Arche and ransomed four years later, only to learn the crown had not paid him for the upkeep of the castle. It left him deep in debt and hating the king.

The Loss of Gascony and Aquitaine, 1449-53
John Talbot was captured at Rouen in 1449 and had to promise never to wear armour against the French king again. He kept his promise but did fight against other French forces. Talbot's replacement, John Beaufort, was defeated at the battle of Formigny in 1450, resulting in the loss of Normandy.

The French were victorious and both Talbot and his son were killed at the battle of Castillon on 17 July 1453, resulting in the French capture of Gascony and Aquitaine. The battle marked the end of the Hundred Years War (which had lasted 116 years). The loss of all of England's continental territories except Calais would leave John Beaufort, Duke of Somerset, open to criticism from Richard, Duke of York, and the animosity between them would spill over at the start of the Wars of the Roses.

The Duke of York Rebels, 1450-2
Resistance to the king's policies was increasing, with Richard Plantagenet, 3rd Duke of York, leading the opposition. Henry VI's poor judgement and nepotism had caused resentment and the established noble families wanted him to take back the land and money he had given to his favourites.

The troubles resulted in violence, starting with the lynching of Adam Moleyns, Lord Privy Seal and Bishop of Chichester, in January 1450. Then the king's chief councillor, William de la Pole, 1st Duke of Suffolk, was murdered in May. Next Jack Cade led a rebellion in Kent and Sussex in June 1450 and his peasant army seized control of London and killed the Lord High Treasurer, John Fiennes.

On 7 September the Duke of York landed at Beaumaris in North Wales and marched south, meeting the king in London on 27 September. He demanded reform, a better government and the prosecution of the traitors who had lost the Continental territories. The violence in London continued and the king's advisor Edmund Beaufort, 2nd Duke of Somerset, had to be put in the Tower for his own safety. Eventually Henry VI promised to curb his spending and make reforms to restore public order, so York retired to his estates in Ludlow. Somerset was released and appointed Captain of Calais, to keep him away from court. But York wanted more; he wanted to destroy Somerset.

The kingdom was suffering and York was coaxed back from Ireland to help run it in 1452. But he also wanted to be recognised as Henry VI's heir apparent because he had had no children with Queen Margaret of Anjou after seven years of marriage. York gathered a small army and marched on London to make his demands, only to find the king had locked the gates. So a compromise was made: York was allowed into the city under guard and was then held under house arrest until he had sworn an oath of allegiance to Henry. Only then was he allowed to speak to the king.

The King's Madness, 1453
Two factions had developed on the Privy Council by 1453. Richard Plantagenet, 3rd Duke of York, and his brother-in-law Richard Neville, 5th Earl of Salisbury, opposed Edmund Beaufort, 2nd Duke of Somerset, and Humphrey Stafford, 1st Duke of Buckingham. Meanwhile, Henry Percy, 2nd Earl of Northumberland, supported the king while his long-standing enemies, the two Richard Nevilles, supported York. But Beaufort and Stafford remained in control of Henry VI and they encouraged him to overtax York's tenants and sack York as the Lieutenant of Ireland.

News of Margaret's pregnancy lifted everyone's spirits but the king had a mental breakdown after hearing about the loss of Boulogne in August 1453. The strong-willed Margaret opposed York until he was appointed Protector of the Realm the following spring and he immediately threw Beaufort in prison. While Stafford was loyal to Henry VI and Beaufort, he was reluctant to oppose York because his son was married to Beaufort's daughter and he feared for his own life.

Henry VI recovered at the end of 1454 and York had to surrender his appointments while Richard Neville, Earl of Salisbury, resigned as Chancellor. Stafford negotiated Beaufort's release from prison and he immediately advised the king to reverse most of York's decisions. A furious York was determined to depose of the meddling Beaufort for good.

The Percys and the Nevilles go to War, 1453-4
In 1453 Thomas, son of Richard Neville, Earl of Salisbury, married Maud

Stanhope, heiress of Lord Cromwell; he was given Wressle Castle as part of the marriage contract. Thomas Percy thought the castle should be his so he intercepted the wedding party at Heworth near York on 24 August, but Thomas and Maud escaped. Henry Holland, 3rd Duke of Exeter, supported the Percys over another territorial dispute with Cromwell and the feud was in danger of turning into a minor civil war.

The king ordered the families to make their peace but Henry Percy and his sons Henry, Egremont and Richard, fought Richard Neville. John Neville, 1st Marquess of Montagu, also joined the feud because he had been forced to hand over his title and lands to the Percys. The feuding barons were summoned to court in May 1454 but they all refused to attend. The Nevilles would capture Thomas Percy and his brother Richard at the battle at Stamford Bridge the following October in a prelude to the coming civil war.

Chapter 16

Henry VI – Wartime 1455–61

The First Battle of St Albans, 1455

Richard Plantagenet, Duke of York, Richard Neville, 5th Earl of Salisbury, and his son Richard Neville, 16th Earl of Warwick, felt threatened when Henry VI summoned a Great Council in Leicester in May 1455. So York recruited along the Welsh border while the Nevilles gathered men near the Scottish border. They then both marched on London. An alarmed Edmund Beaufort, 2nd Duke of Somerset, did not have time to alert his supporters and both John de Vere, 12th Earl of Oxford, and John de Mowbray, 3rd Duke of Norfolk, would arrive too late to help.

York and the Nevilles intercepted the king's retinue at St Albans on 22 May and while few men died in the skirmish, the outcome was very significant. Edmund Beaufort, Henry Percy, 2nd Earl of Northumberland, and Thomas Clifford, 8th Baron de Clifford, were killed. Somerset's son Henry Beaufort was wounded and would survive to become the 'the hope of the [Lancastrian] party'. But he never forgave York and the Nevilles and would have to face the 'enmities entailed upon him by his father's name'. Not everyone conducted themselves so gallantly. James Butler, 1st Earl of Wiltshire, removed his armour, dressed in a monk's habit and hid in a ditch. He would be accused of fighting 'mainly with the heels, for he was frightened of losing his beauty'.

York wanted to keep Henry VI alive and rule in his name, so he took the king to London and personally recrowned him in a symbolic ceremony. Henry was then held prisoner while York appointed himself Constable of England and made Richard Neville, Earl of Warwick, his Captain of Calais.

Conflict in Devon, 1455-6

The arguments in Devon continued and Thomas Courtenay attacked William Bonville's supporters in 1455. They occupied Exeter and Thomas Courtenay junior murdered the city recorder, Nicholas Radford, a Bonville supporter. The struggle escalated when Courtenay defeated Bonville at the battle of Clyst Heath on 15 December.

Lord Protector York imprisoned Courtenay in the Tower to resolve the situation but the king released him as soon as he recovered from his madness early in 1456. He also appointed Courtenay the Commissioner of the Peace for Devonshire. But another of Courtenay's sons, John, renewed the violence by occupying Exeter in April 1456. Thomas Courtenay was ordered to appear before the king but he died en route to London. The Wars of the Roses would lead to the death of three of Courtenay's sons and the end of the family's power in Devon.

A Lancastrian Heir, 1455-7

Edmund and Jasper Tudor were Henry VI's illegitimate half-brothers and they supported their sibling when the Wars of the Roses began. Edmund was captured by William Herbert, 1st Earl of Pembroke, and he died of the plague in Carmarthen Castle in 1457. His 13-year-old widow Margaret Beaufort gave birth to their son two months later in Pembroke Castle. Edmund and Margaret's child spent his first twelve years in the Herbert household and then went into exile after Herbert was executed for fighting for the Yorkists. He briefly returned to England when Henry VI was restored in 1470 but fled with other Lancastrians to Brittany. He would return to challenge Richard III for the crown in 1485.

The Loveday Council, 1458

Richard, Duke of York, had surrendered the office of Lord Protector when the king recovered in February 1456 and he went north to defend the border against a threatened invasion by James II of Scotland. Both Nevilles, the Earls of Salisbury and Warwick, remained as councillors in London but Henry VI was now under the control of his queen, Margaret of Anjou.

The king's supporters regarded Richard of York with suspicion for three reasons. Firstly, he threatened the succession of the young Prince of Wales. Secondly, he was negotiating for the marriage of his eldest son Edward into the Burgundian ruling family. Finally, he was supported by the powerful Nevilles. Henry was desperate to end the conflict between the factions but suspicions and animosities ran deep. He held the Loveday Council on 25 March 1458, hoping to reconcile the feuding barons, but he failed to stamp his authority on the situation and little changed.

The Battle of Blore Heath, 1459

The uneasy truce between the Lancastrians and Yorkists came to an end in 1459. A Great Council was held in Coventry in June 1459 but Richard of York, 3rd Duke of York, the Nevilles and their Yorkist supporters refused to appear. Instead they assembled their troops and prepared to go to war.

Richard Neville, 16th Earl of Warwick, took part of his Calais garrison to England while Richard Neville, 5th Earl of Salisbury, headed north to join Richard Duke of York. Queen Margaret was anxious to stop them meeting and sent her supporters to intercept them. Henry Beaufort, 3rd Duke of Somerset, nearly clashed with Richard Neville, 16th Earl of Warwick, at Coleshill in Warwickshire. Meanwhile, Thomas Stanley tracked down his father-in-law Richard Neville, 5th Earl of Salisbury, to Blore Heath in Staffordshire on 23 September. Stanley kept part of his army away from the battle that followed and he was defeated by Neville. The two Richard Nevilles met York after the battle but John Neville, 1st Marquess of Montagu, had been captured and taken to Chester Castle.

The Parliament of Devils, 1459
Henry VI wanted to reconcile the factions in October 1458 but Henry Percy, 3rd Earl of Northumberland, was taking no chances and he marched his army south only to be denied entry to London. Percy did attend the Parliament of Devils in October 1459 and he condemned all Yorkists as traitors for killing his father at the battle of St Albans four years earlier. His only consolation was that he did not have to pay relief to the crown because his father had died fighting for the king.

The Battle of Ludford Bridge, 1459
Richard and the Nevilles clashed with King Henry and Humphrey Stafford, 1st Duke of Buckingham, at the battle of Ludford Bridge in Shropshire on 12 October 1459. But Warwick's Calais garrison refused to fight the king, the rest of the Yorkists were scattered, and York's wife and two youngest sons were captured. York escaped to Ireland, taking his second son Edmund, Earl of Rutland, with him, while the Nevilles headed to Calais with York's eldest son Edward, Earl of March. Henry Beaufort, Duke of Somerset, was sent to Calais to seize Warwick but the garrison remained loyal to their captain. Beaufort was forced to occupy nearby Guisnes Castle and he would be defeated at the battle of Newnham Bridge on 23 April 1460.

The Battle of Northampton, 1460
Henry VI attainted Richard Plantagenet, Duke of York, and the Nevilles in December 1459, leaving York with three options if he was to avoid arrest and seize power. He could either become Lord Protector again, claim the throne for himself, or disinherit the king so his son could succeed. Richard Neville, 16th Earl of Warwick, visited Richard in Ireland in March 1460 to plan their next move. The Nevilles landed at Sandwich on 26 June where they captured Richard Woodville, 1st Earl Rivers. London then opened its

gates to the Yorkists on 2 July and Richard Neville, 5th Earl of Salisbury, besieged the Tower while Warwick and York's son Edward Plantagenet, Earl of March, marched north in pursuit of the king.

Their armies clashed near Northampton on 10 July and Humphrey Stafford, 1st Duke of Buckingham, defiantly announced, 'the Earl of Warwick shall not come to the king's presence and if he comes he shall die.' But Edmund Grey, 1st Earl of Kent, turned traitor and ordered his men to lay down arms, allowing the Yorkists to enter the king's camp. Buckingham and John Talbot, 2nd Earl of Shrewsbury, were killed but, more importantly, Henry VI was taken prisoner.

Warwick took the king back to London. York returned to England in September and moved into the royal palace. He then entered Parliament and symbolically placed his hand on the throne to signify he was the kingdom's ruler but not its king. Thomas Bourchier, the Archbishop of Canterbury, asked York if he wished to see the king but his reply failed to impress anyone: 'I know of no person in this realm which oweth not to wait on me, rather than I of him.'

An Act of Accord was eventually agreed under which Henry VI would stay on the throne while his son Edward, Prince of Wales, was disinherited. Instead York and his son Edward would succeed Henry. York was appointed Prince of Wales, Duke of Cornwall and Earl of Chester, to recognise his new role. He was also appointed England's Lord Protector and he would rule the kingdom with the help of Richard Neville, Earl of Warwick.

The Battle of Wakefield, 1460
Richard of York now held all the trump cards. He had control of the king, his troops held London and he had Parliament's permission to succeed the king. But the Lancastrians were gathering in the north, so Richard marched north to meet them taking with him his second son Edmund, Earl of Rutland, and Richard Neville, 5th Earl of Salisbury.

The Yorkists reached Sandal Castle, near Wakefield in Yorkshire, on 21 December while the Lancastrians left their bases at York and Pontefract to meet them. Henry Beaufort, 3rd Duke of Somerset, had captured a large party of Yorkist troops at Worksop, leaving Richard of York short of troops so there was a stand-off. For reasons that are unclear, York left his castle on 30 December; he had either been tricked into deploying or had underestimated the size of the Lancastrian army.

Henry Beaufort, Henry Holland, 3rd Duke of Exeter, and Henry Percy, 3rd Earl of Northumberland, then defeated the Yorkists. York was killed on the battlefield while Neville was captured and executed. York's son Edmund was also captured and his expensive armour betrayed his importance. When John Clifford, 9th Baron de Clifford, heard he had been taken prisoner he took his revenge for his father's death at York's hands at the First Battle of St Albans. He told Edmund, 'thy father slew mine and so will I do thee and all thy kin,' and beheaded him. All three of their heads were displayed on York's Micklegate. A paper crown was placed on Richard of York's head, mocking his short time as successor to the throne.

The Battle of Mortimer's Cross, 1461

Prince Edward, now the 4th Duke of York, heard about his father's and brother's death at Shrewsbury over Christmas. He intercepted and defeated a Lancastrian force at Mortimer's Cross near Leominster in Herefordshire on 2 February 1461. Jasper Tudor, 1st Earl of Pembroke, and James Butler, 1st Earl of Wiltshire, escaped but Owen Tudor, Jasper's father and Henry VI's step-father, was taken prisoner and executed.

The Second Battle of St Albans, 1461

Queen Margaret, Henry Beaufort, 3rd Duke of Somerset, and Henry Percy, 3rd Earl of Northumberland, marched their Lancastrian army south and engaged the Yorkists at St Albans on 17 February 1461. They defeated Richard Neville, 16th Earl of Warwick, William FitzAlan, 16th Earl of Arundel, John Neville, 1st Marquess of Montagu, John de Mowbray, 3rd Duke of Norfolk, and Henry Bourchier, 1st Earl of Essex. The Yorkists dispersed and Henry VI was freed but London refused to let the Lancastrians enter the city because they had a reputation for pillaging. Instead the mayor let Richard of York's son Edward Plantagenet and the Yorkists enter the city instead.

The Battle of Towton, 1461

Richard of York's son Edward Plantagenet was proclaimed King Edward IV on 4 March 1461 and he was determined to finish off the Lancastrians. The Yorkists marched north into Lancastrian territory only to suffer a setback when Richard Neville, 16th Earl of Warwick, was injured at the battle of Ferrybridge in Yorkshire on 28 March.

The following day around 80,000 men clashed in a brutal battle at Towton. No one had an advantage until a combination of strong wind and snow blinded the Lancastrian archers led by Henry Percy, 3rd Earl of Northumberland. John Howard then reinforced the Yorkist right flank, turning the tide against the Lancastrians; he was knighted after the battle and would soon be the Duke of Norfolk.

Losses amongst the Lancastrian nobility were high. Henry Holland, 3rd Duke of Exeter, fled to Scotland and eventually joined Queen Margaret in exile in France. He would be attainted and his estates given to his wife; she then separated from him. Holland's three illegitimate half-brothers served the Lancastrian cause but only one of the 'Bastards of Exeter' would survive the conflict.

Thomas Courtenay, 6th Earl of Devon, and James Butler, 1st Earl of Wiltshire, were captured and beheaded. Henry Percy, 3rd Earl of Northumberland, was killed and his son was imprisoned in the Tower. The Percy's Earldom of Northumberland was later given to John Neville while the Yorkists marched south to London for Edward IV's coronation.

Chapter 17

Edward IV
1461–83

Percy Rebels in the North, 1461-3

Richard Neville inherited the Earldom of Warwick from his father in 1461 and the Earldom of Salisbury from his mother in 1462, making him the richest noble in England. He was also powerful, holding offices including Admiral of England, Captain of Calais and Steward of the Duchy of Lancaster. He managed to keep the north under control and even negotiated a truce with King James III of Scotland in the summer of 1462.

But Henry VI's queen, Margaret of Anjou, was determined to get the throne back and she invaded England with French troops in October 1462. King Edward had to pardon the rebel leaders, including Ralph Percy, so he could secure the Scottish border. But Percy rebelled again and besieged Norham Castle in the spring of 1463, forcing Neville to use a mixture of diplomacy and force to reclaim Northumberland from the Lancastrian rebels.

Yorkist Control of Devon, 1463

Thomas Courtenay, Earl of Devon, had been executed at Towton in 1461. Edward IV created Humphrey Stafford the Earl of Devon in 1463 and he was given Courtenay's estates. Stafford saw his position in Devon secured after serving on the commission which convicted and beheaded Thomas's brother Henry for treason. He received more of the Courtenay lands as a reward, giving King Edward a loyal Yorkist supporter in what was a traditional Lancastrian area.

The Battles of Hedgeley Moor and Hexham, 1464

The Lancastrian Henry Beaufort, 3rd Duke of Somerset, had surrendered Bamburgh Castle in Northumberland to Ralph Percy in December 1462. He was pardoned and restored after submitting to Edward IV but his loyalty was short-lived and he was arrested for supporting Henry VI's cause. He escaped at the beginning of 1464 and headed north to join Queen Margaret on the Scottish border.

Beaufort and Percy led raids across the north of England, seizing Norham Castle and several towns in Northumberland. He then surprised John Neville, Earl of Montagu, at Hedgeley Moor on 25 April as he travelled north to meet King James III. But most of the Lancastrians fled, Percy was killed and Beaufort was lucky to escape. Neville's men found him hiding in a barn at Hexham on 15 May, and he was beheaded.

Bamburgh surrendered soon afterwards, ending Lancastrian resistance in the north of England. Edward IV rewarded John Neville by giving him back the Earldom of Northumberland and making him the Warden of the East March.

Married to the Woodvilles, 1464-6

In 1464 Richard Neville, 16th Earl of Warwick, was negotiating a royal marriage between Edward IV and King Louis XI's sister-in-law Bona, which would have united England and France. However, the king had already wed Elizabeth Woodville, the widow of a Lancastrian soldier, in secret. He may have married her for love, for lust, or even to block Warwick's plans. Whatever the reason, Neville was offended when he found out. He was appalled that the king had sabotaged his plans for a mighty alliance by marrying a woman of low status and he left court.

The established earls were then disgusted to see Edward shower honours on Elizabeth's family, especially when her father Richard was created Earl Rivers, Lord Treasurer and Constable. Elizabeth's young sister Catherine was married to the infant Henry Stafford, 2nd Duke of Buckingham. Stafford would grow up to hate Edward IV for two reasons: his wife had a lowly status, and the king had taken part of his inheritance.

Neville was once more negotiating in 1466, this time it was a French marriage to Edward's sister Margaret. But Richard Woodville interfered with his plans by suggesting a Burgundian alliance, which Edward signed in secret in October. Richard Woodville was then made treasurer, replacing George Neville. Edward also objected to the marriage of his brother George, Duke of Clarence, to Richard Neville's daughter Isabel. It all amounted to one thing: the upstart Woodvilles were replacing the Nevilles at court.

Jasper Tudor, 1468-9

Jasper Tudor had raised his nephew Henry Tudor, because his father had died before he was born. Edward IV had defeated Jasper at the battle of Mortimer's Cross in February 1461 so he left for France. He returned to North Wales in 1468 only to be defeated again, this time by William

Herbert who was rewarded with the title of Earl of Pembroke and Pembroke Castle.

Jasper's fortunes changed for the better when Edward IV was captured following the battle of Edgecote Moor in 1469. Henry VI was reinstated as king and he gave Jasper the Earldom of Pembroke. But Edward IV returned from exile two years later and both Henry and Jasper had to escape from Tenby in south-west Wales. Storms forced them to land at Le Conquet in Brittany and Edward tried to convince Francis, Duke of Brittany, to return them to England. But Henry and Jasper remained safe in exile until Edward died in April 1483.

The Battle of Edgecote Moor, 1469

There were rumours that the Captain of Calais, Richard Neville, Earl of Warwick, was sympathetic to the Lancastrian cause after his deputy John Wenlock was found to be involved in a conspiracy in 1467. Neville was indeed working on behalf of the Lancastrians and he organised a rebellion in Yorkshire, led by Robin of Redesdale. Neville then persuaded Edward's 19-year-old brother George Plantagenet, the ambitious Duke of Clarence, to marry his daughter Isabel in Calais. They then returned to Kent and gathered an army before meeting John de Vere, 13th Earl of Oxford, another Lancastrian plotter.

Humphrey Stafford, 1st Earl of Devon, and William Herbert, Earl of Pembroke, intercepted Robin of Redesdale's rebels near Banbury in Oxfordshire. But Stafford left following an argument and Herbert was defeated at the battle of Edgecote the next day, 26 July 1469. The bloodletting against the Yorkists started immediately. William Herbert, 1st Earl of Pembroke, and his brother Richard were executed. The king's father-in-law Richard Woodville, 1st Earl Rivers, and brother-in-law John, were captured at Chepstow and beheaded at Kenilworth on 12 August 1469. Stafford was lynched by the mob at Bridgwater in Somerset five days later. Then Richard Neville captured the greatest prize of all: the king. Edward IV was held at his Warwick Castle before he was then taken north to blood-letting in Yorkshire.

The Percys are Given the North, 1469

Richard Neville, 16th Earl of Warwick, soon found it was impossible to rule without the king and so he released Edward from Middleham Castle in September 1469. Attempts to reconcile Neville and the king failed so he took the Earldom of Northumberland from John Neville and gave it to his bitter rival Henry Percy.

The dishonour to John was too much for his brother Richard so he organised a private feud in Lincolnshire to draw the king out of London.

But Edward discovered the plot when Robert, Lord Welles, was captured at the battle of Losecoat Field on 12 March 1469 and he confessed the plan to the Yorkists.

Neville and George Plantagenet returned to Calais but this time the garrison would not let them in and they had to be given shelter by King Louis XI of France. The reconciliation between Neville and Margaret of Anjou resulted in the marriage of Henry and Margaret's son Edward, Prince of Wales, and Neville's daughter Anne. Neville had achieved his plan to become influential in the House of Lancaster and he now planned how to restore Henry VI to the throne of England.

Henry Returns, 1470

John Neville was created the Marquess of Montagu as compensation for taking Northumberland from him but he had few estates and little income. So he joined his brother Richard Neville, 16th Earl of Warwick, and they organised another uprising in the north in support of Henry VI. The Nevilles headed south in September 1470 with George Plantagenet, 1st Duke of Clarence, and John de Vere, 13th Earl of Oxford. Many joined them as they marched towards London and Edward IV fled to Flanders with his brother Richard, Duke of Gloucester, at the beginning of October. Henry IV was crowned again on 9 October after London had been taken; Richard Neville, the 'Kingmaker', was his lieutenant.

Rewards for Henry's supporters followed while his enemies were punished. Clarence was awarded the Duchy of York and John Courtenay, 15th Earl of Devon, was given his estates back. The deposed Edward was attainted and John Howard, 1st Duke of Norfolk, was sacked as Earl Marshal. The cruel Lord High Constable, John Tiptoft, 1st Earl of Worcester, was also accused of treason; he asked his executioner to chop off his head with three blows, for the sake of the Trinity.

The Stanleys and the Nevilles, 1469-72

Thomas Stanley and his brother-in-law Richard Neville, Earl of Warwick, had campaigned together against the Lancastrian forces. Edward IV had confirmed Stanley's offices when he came to the throne in 1461, hoping he would secure the north-west on his behalf. But a series of Lancastrian victories and the break-up of the Yorkist coalition during the 1460s severely tested his loyalty.

Stanley waited for Neville to visit him in Manchester, after Edward was captured in 1469, before he pledged his allegiance to Henry. Stanley would be forgiven when Edward was restored in 1471 and he was appointed a steward of the king's household and a member of the royal council. But the death of Stanley's wife Eleanor ended his connection with the Nevilles. His marriage to Henry Tudor's mother Margaret Beaufort, Countess of Richmond, in 1472 bound him to the House of Lancaster.

De Vere Rebels, 1470-1
John Tiptoft, Earl of Worcester, had many executed for supporting Margaret of Anjou including John de Vere and his son Aubrey in 1462. Tiptoft was known as the Butcher of England while Henry Holland, 3rd Duke of Exeter, tortured many in the Tower. His favourite instrument was the rack which caused immeasurable pain by stretching victims; it became known as the 'Duke of Exeter's daughter'.

Edward IV allowed John de Vere to inherit the Earldom of Oxford, in the hope of securing his loyalty. It failed because he was soon imprisoned in the Tower in 1469 for plotting with the Lancastrians. He was released after he confessed but immediately joined Richard Neville, Earl of Warwick, and George, Duke of Clarence. He then had to go into exile in the court of Henry VI's wife Margaret of Anjou after the Yorkists lost the battle of Edgecote in July. He joined Warwick and Clarence when they returned to England to restore Henry VI to the throne in September 1470. As Lord High Constable, Vere condemned John Tiptoft, 1st Earl of Worcester, to death; he was the ex-Lord High Constable who had condemned his own father and brother to death eight years earlier.

The Battle of Barnet, 14 April 1471
Richard Neville, 16th Earl of Warwick, had allied with Margaret of Anjou through marriage in May 1470 and he agreed to help her restore her husband to the throne. But Henry VI had been on the throne for less than six months when Neville attacked Burgundy, where John Howard, 1st Duke of Norfolk, had recently arranged the marriage of Edward IV's sister Margaret to Charles, Duke of Burgundy. King Louis XI of France objected and he declared war on Burgundy, so Charles gave his brother-in-law the troops he needed to invade England.

Henry's son Prince Edward landed with French troops at Ravenspurn in Yorkshire on 14 March 1471 with the consent of his old ally Henry Percy, Earl of Northumberland. Neville had expected Queen Margaret and her son Edward to bring reinforcements to help but bad weather stopped them crossing the English Channel. George, Duke of Clarence, initially supported his brother Edward, but he soon realised he had made a mistake. Any child of Prince Edward and Neville's daughter Anne would be first in line for what he wanted for himself: the crown.

So George defected to the Yorkists, weakening Neville's support, but he went looking for Edward and found him at Barnet, north of London, on 14 April 1471. The battle went well for the Lancastrians to begin with as John de Vere, 13th Earl of Oxford, overcame Lord Hastings' men. But his troops became disoriented in the fog and they mistook the de Vere star for Edward's sun. Lancastrian fought Lancastrian until Vere's men fled.

An injured Henry Holland, 3rd Duke of Exeter, was imprisoned and Earl Marshal Thomas Howard, 1st Earl of Surrey, was also severely wounded. Both Richard Neville, 16th Earl of Warwick, and John Neville, 1st Marquess of Montagu, were killed and their bodies were displayed in London's St Paul's Cathedral to prove they were dead. The battle of Barnet had ended Henry VI's brief return to power and his supporters were deprived of their titles, appointments and estates.

Vere fled via Scotland to France and then captured St Michael's Mount Castle in Cornwall in 1473. He was forced to surrender after a five-month siege and was imprisoned in Hammes Castle near Calais. But Vere had had enough by 1478 and he jumped into the moat and drowned, either attempting to escape or committing suicide.

A Disenfranchised Earl, 1470-5
Nine-year-old George Neville was created Duke of Bedford in 1470 so he could be betrothed to Elizabeth of York. But George's father and uncle Richard Neville, 16th Earl of Warwick, rebelled against Edward IV and they were both killed at the battle of Barnet in 1471. George's inheritance was given to Warwick's son-in-law Richard, Duke of Gloucester, in 1475, leaving him in debt and his title was taken from him. The Dukedom of Bedford would be given to Edward IV's third son the infant George Plantagenet.

The Battle of Tewkesbury, 1471
Following the disaster at Barnet, Edward IV and Richard, Duke of Gloucester, intercepted Edmund Beaufort, 4th Duke of Somerset, as he marched towards Wales looking to get help from Jasper Tudor. They fought at Tewkesbury in Gloucestershire on 4 May 1471 and Beaufort was routed after foolishly leaving his hilltop position to attack the Yorkists' flank.

Henry's son and heir Edward, Beaufort's brother John, and John Courtenay, 15th Earl of Devon, were killed. Edmund took refuge in Tewkesbury Abbey with other Lancastrian leaders but they were tried and executed in the town a few days later. Henry died in the Tower of London on 21 May 1471, some say of depression after hearing about the defeat at Barnet in 1471. Others say he was murdered on Edward IV's orders. Whatever the truth, Edward IV was recrowned the following morning.

Henry's death left Edmund's aunt Margaret Beaufort and her 14-year-old son Henry Tudor heads of the House of Lancaster. The unpredictable Henry Holland, 3rd Duke of Exeter, also had a claim to the throne but he had little support. Edward did not forget he had a rival. Holland served on Edward's 1475 expedition to France only to drown on the return voyage; it is possible he was thrown overboard on the king's orders.

The Neville Inheritance, 1470-8
George Plantagenet, Duke of Clarence, had married Isabel, daughter of Richard Neville, 16th Earl of Warwick, in 1469, an important union. Neville supported Edward IV's claim to the throne until his father-in-law switched his allegiance to Henry VI and Margaret of Anjou. George joined them in France where he was made second in line after Edward of Westminster.

The plan was to exclude Edward IV from the line of succession, either through accusing him of treason or declaring him illegitimate. But the rules changed when Neville married his daughter Anne to Henry VI's son Edward of Westminster in December 1470. George realised he would never be allowed to replace Edward so he deserted Neville and went back to supporting Edward IV.

Neville's attempt to return Henry VI to the throne ended with his death at the battle of Barnet in April 1471. Edward died at the battle of Tewkesbury a month later. Richard Plantagenet, Duke of Gloucester, asked to marry Edward's widow Anne. His brother George agreed but only after making him surrender the Earldoms of Warwick and Salisbury, the office of Great Chamberlain and most of his estates before he gave his consent.

Despite the deal, the brothers continued to fight over their father-in-law's inheritance. Edward IV would favour his brother George and he gave him the Earldom of Warwick. But George was still not satisfied and he resumed his plotting against his brother; he would be executed for treason in 1478. The complicated inheritance was eventually divided between cousins, with George's son Edward taking the Earldom of Warwick while Richard's son, also Edward, took the Earldom of Salisbury.

Poor Anne would become queen of England when her husband Richard seized the throne in 1483. She became a widow when he was killed at the battle of Bosworth in 1485 and died in obscurity in Beaulieu Abbey after her daughters and sons-in-law had disinherited her.

The Execution of the King's Brother, 1478
George Plantagenet, 1st Duke of Clarence, had married Isabel Neville, daughter of Richard Neville, 16th Earl of Warwick, in 1469. His father-in-law had been killed at the battle of Tewkesbury in 1471 and George was created Earl of Warwick the following year. Isabel's sister Anne married Richard, Duke of Gloucester, after handing over most of Anne's lands and the office of Great Chamberlain to George. The brothers-in-law would still argue over the Neville inheritance.

Isabel died in 1476 and George had her lady in waiting hanged, believing she had poisoned her. But Clarence was discovered to be plotting against his brother Edward again after his servant John Stacey was imprisoned in the Tower. Stacey confessed under torture that he and Thomas Burdett had practiced black magic to imagine the king's death and they were executed. George was found guilty of treason and 'privately executed' in the Tower on 18 February 1478. It was rumoured that he had been drowned in a barrel of wine.

Edward's Children, 1483
Edward IV had ten children with Elizabeth Woodville and seven outlived him. Edward, Prince of Wales, was 13 and Richard, Duke of York, was 10 when their father died, but George, 1st Duke of Bedford, did not survive childhood. Edward possibly also had several illegitimate children with numerous mistresses, the best known was Elizabeth (or Jane) Shore.

The End of Edward's Reign
The Lancastrian claim to the throne had ended through death in battle and execution; ended apart from one man, the exiled Henry Tudor. Edward had declared war on France and his troops landed at Calais in June 1475. He was expecting support from Charles the Bold, Duke of Burgundy but it never came, so Edward agreed the Treaty of Picquigny and accepted the bribe to withdraw his troops.

Edward then supported Alexander Stewart, 1st Duke of Albany, when he tried to seize the Scottish throne from his brother King James III in 1482. The king's brother Richard, Duke of Gloucester, captured Edinburgh and the King of Scots, but Albany backed out of the deal, forcing King Edward and Richard to withdraw.

Edward became ill soon afterwards and he named his brother Protector. The king died as a result of his unhealthy lifestyle on 9 April 1483 but the rest of his family had met bloody ends. His father and brother had been killed at the battle of Wakefield while his grandfather and another brother had been executed for treason; his two young sons would disappear after being held in the Tower. Edward's youngest brother, Richard III, would be killed on Bosworth Field in 1485, ending the Plantagenet's rule.

Chapter 18

Edward V
1483

The Princes in the Tower

Edward IV died suddenly on 9 April 1483. Queen Elizabeth instructed her brother Anthony Woodville, 2nd Earl Rivers, to escort her young son Edward and the king's half-brother Richard Grey to London. The king's brother Richard, Duke of Gloucester, had been named Lord Protector but he planned to seize the throne for himself. Gloucester and Henry Stafford, 2nd Duke of Buckingham, intercepted the prince and his escort and took them to Pontefract Castle.

The Bishop of Bath and Wells, Robert Stillington, testified that Edward IV had agreed to marry Eleanor Talbot in 1461. Eleanor had been alive when Edward had secretly married Elizabeth Woodville in 1464, so the regency council concluded that Edward had committed bigamy. Edward's marriage to Elizabeth was invalidated on 25 June 1483 and both King Edward V and his brother Richard of Shrewsbury, 1st Duke of York, were declared illegitimate and removed from the line of succession. Anthony Woodville and Richard Grey were beheaded at Pontefract Castle while 13-year-old Edward was taken to the Tower of London where he was joined by his 10-year-old brother.

Young Richard had been married to the wealthy heiress Anne de Mowbray, 8th Countess of Norfolk, when he was only 5 but she had died at the age of 9. An Act of Parliament had disinherited her cousin William, Viscount Berkeley, and Edward IV had given his estates to Richard. William gave his support to the Lord Protector and Richard rewarded him with the Dukedom of Norfolk and returned half his estates back.

With the princes locked away, the way was clear for Richard, Duke of Gloucester, to be crowned King Richard III. The princes were rarely seen and they were believed to be murdered on the orders of their uncle Richard. Henry Stafford, 2nd Duke of Buckingham, was the chief suspect.

Chapter 19

Richard III
1483–85

Stafford's Rebellion, 1483

With the Princes declared illegitimate and locked in the Tower, Richard could crown himself king. But Henry Stafford, 2nd Duke of Buckingham, and Bishop John Morton of Ely, soon became disillusioned with his rule. They were joined by Edward IV's brother-in-law Richard Woodville, 3rd Earl Rivers, who had seen his lands confiscated and his brother Anthony executed.

Their plan to release young Edward V ended when they heard rumours that the Princes were dead. Stafford then plotted to return Henry Tudor from exile and marry him to Elizabeth of York, uniting the Houses of Lancaster and York. But his plan was thwarted when a storm stopped his ships reaching England.

King Richard sent Thomas Howard, 1st Earl of Surrey, and Thomas Stanley to confront the rebels when he heard about the plot and they scattered. Stafford was arrested at Beaulieu Abbey in the New Forest, convicted of treason and beheaded on 2 November 1483 at Salisbury. His widow Catherine was married to Jasper Tudor, Duke of Bedford, and his post of Lord High Constable was given to Stanley.

The Death of the King's Heir, 1484

Edward of Middleham, Prince of Wales, Duke of Cornwall and Earl of Salisbury and Chester, was the only child of Richard III and Anne Neville. His sudden death from illness in 1484 at the age of 10 was seen by the king's enemies as divine retribution for the disappearance of Edward IV's sons, Edward and Richard.

Richard appointed his nephew John de la Pole, 1st Earl of Lincoln, heir to the throne following Edward's death. Edward IV's nephew Edward Plantagenet had a superior claim but he had been attainted since his father George, Duke of Clarence, had been executed for treason in 1478. Richard

William the Conqueror with his half-brothers, Odo and Robert, on the Bayeux Tapestry, 1066.

The fall of Simon de Montfort at the Battle of Evesham, 1265.

The capture of Dolwyddelan Castle brought an end the 200 year conquest of Wales.

Edward III defeats the French at the Battle of Crecy, 1346.

The Coronation Chair made by Edward I, so he could sit on the Scone of Scotland.

The coronation of Henry Bolingbroke as Henry IV after deposing Richard II in 1399.

The Tower of London where so many nobles were executed; Traitor's Gate is at the bottom.

Henry V's archers prepare to defeat the French Dauphin at Agincourt in 1415.

Edward IV watches the execution of Edmund Beaufort, Duke of Somerset, at Tewkesbury, 1471.

Stanley hands Richard III's crown to Henry Tudor at the end of the Battle of Bosworth, 1485.

Fountains Abbey was one of the many houses of worship closed down by Henry VIII.

Oliver Cromwell's headquarters during the Parliamentarian victory at the Battle of Naseby, 1645.

Huge crowds watch the execution of King Charles I in 1649.

The decadence of Charles II summed up in John Michael Wright's portrait circa 1661.

Dutch warships destroy the English navy in the River Medway.

King William defeating
James II at the Battle of
the Boyne in 1690.

A replica of Edward the Confessor's original
crown.

Charles II's elaborate version of the
crown.

III had also declared Edward's marriage invalid making his children illegitimate and disqualifying them from the line of succession.

Henry's Supporters

A number of supporters with different motives gathered around Henry Tudor, 2nd Earl of Richmond, while he was in exile in Brittany. Philibert de Chandée entertained Henry and Francis, Duke of Brittany, and recognised Henry as the heir to the English throne. Philibert and Francis would command Henry's French contingent during the invasion of England.

John de Vere, 13th Earl of Oxford, escaped from Hammes Castle, near Calais, and he persuaded the castle commander, James Blount, to join him. Henry was 'ravished with joy incredible' when he heard. Jasper Tudor, Duke of Bedford, taught Henry, his nephew, battle tactics while he organised the invasion.

The King and Stanley Argue

Henry Tudor's stepfather Thomas Stanley had immense power across the north-west. Stanley had demanded a balance of power between the Lord Protector, Richard, Duke of Gloucester, and his mother's family, the Woodvilles, following the death of Edward IV. But Richard had attacked Stanley's supporters at a council meeting in June 1483; a wounded Stanley was imprisoned while Lord Hastings was executed. Stanley was released, but the new King Richard insisted he left his son George behind as a hostage before he returned to his northern estates.

Richard discovered that Edward Courtenay, 1st Earl of Devon, was passing messages between Stanley's wife Margaret Beaufort and Edward IV's widow Elizabeth Woodville. So he confiscated her titles and instructed Stanley to keep her under house arrest. The exiled Henry Tudor had also been in contact with Thomas Stanley, looking for cooperation because he planned to land in Wales.

Henry landed at Milford Haven in Pembrokeshire on 7 August and William Herbert, 2nd Earl of Pembroke, reported the news to the king. Stanley was supposed to raise troops and join Richard but he excused himself saying he was too ill. George Stanley was also caught trying to escape. He confessed that he and his uncle William had conspired with Henry Tudor so Richard called him a traitor and took him hostage.

The Battle of Bosworth, 1485

The armies of Richard and Henry met near Market Bosworth in Leicestershire on 22 August 1485. Thomas Stanley had recovered sufficiently to raise troops but he deployed them independently rather than alongside Richard's. The king allegedly threatened to execute his son

George if he did not join him on the battlefield, but Thomas replied, 'sire, I have other sons'.

The battle did not go well for Richard because Henry's French mercenaries fought off his early attacks. John Howard, 1st Duke of Norfolk, commander of his vanguard was struck down in front of the king, and his son Thomas, Earl of Surrey, was wounded and taken prisoner. The tide of the battle was turning against the king but Henry Percy, 4th Earl of Northumberland, would not or could not commit his reserve.

Thomas Stanley then made his decision and chose to support his stepson Henry Tudor, resulting in the defeat of the Yorkists; 'King Richard alone was killed fighting manfully in the thickest press of his enemies.' He would be the last English king to die in battle. Stanley would place Richard's crown on Henry's head before their cheering troops.

Chapter 20

Henry VII
1485–1509

The King Rewards his Supporters, 1485
Henry Percy, 4th Earl of Northumberland, Ralph Neville, 3rd Earl of Westmorland and Thomas Howard, 2nd Duke of Norfolk, were arrested and asked if they would swear allegiance to Henry. They agreed and were allowed to keep their titles, estates and appointments. But the king was taking no chances with Neville and he was made to hand his son Ralph over to assure his loyalty.

John de Vere, 13th Earl of Oxford, had been a loyal supporter of Henry and he was 'immediately recognised as one of the great men of Henry VII's regime' as Lord Admiral and then Lord Great Chamberlain. He also created his father-in-law Thomas Stanley, the Earl of Derby, and appointed him High Constable and High Steward of the Duchy of Lancaster. Jasper Tudor, Earl of Pembroke, was pardoned and elevated to Duke of Bedford. The Earldom of Wiltshire was returned to the young Henry Stafford, son of the executed Duke of Buckingham, and he was handed to King Henry's mother Margaret Beaufort so she could raise him.

Uniting the Houses of Lancaster and York, 1485
Henry Tudor, 2nd Earl of Richmond, had won his throne on the field of battle, the last king of England to do so. The next step was to restore stability in the kingdom and end the thirty years of bloody civil war. Margaret Beaufort arranged the marriage between her son Henry Tudor and Edward IV's daughter Elizabeth of York, uniting the two warring families. It allowed Henry to work on maintaining the peace and restoring the power of the English monarchy. The death of Richard and being crowned queen was retribution for Elizabeth, in memory of her brothers who had been murdered in the Tower.

The Imposter Lambert Simnel, 1487
Henry VII imprisoned the Yorkist heir to the throne, 10-year-old Edward

Plantagenet, 17th Earl of Warwick, in the Tower after Bosworth. The claimants John de la Pole, 2nd Duke of Suffolk, and his son, also John, Earl of Lincoln, both submitted to Henry VII after Bosworth but John junior was soon plotting against the king. In 1487 he promoted Lambert Simnel, who bore a likeness to Edward, but he planned to seize power for himself if the rebellion was successful.

John acquired money from his aunt Margaret, Duchess of Burgundy, and then sailed to Ireland with Simnel and mercenaries where Gerald FitzGerald, Earl of Kildare, welcomed him. FitzGerald wanted a return of Yorkist rule because Richard III had allowed him to govern Ireland as its 'uncrowned king'. Simnel was proclaimed Edward VI and was crowned king in Dublin but Henry VII countered by parading Edward Plantagenet in St Paul's Cathedral, to show that he was still alive.

Pole landed in Lancashire and Henry VII was concerned his step-father Thomas Stanley, 1st Earl of Derby, would hedge his bets before committing himself, as he had done at the battle of Bosworth. Pole marched to York, but the traditionally Yorkist stronghold refused to open its gates to him. He then defeated a small Lancastrian force at Bramham Moor in Yorkshire and marched south towards London. John and most of the other Yorkist supporters were killed at the battle of Stoke Field in Nottinghamshire on 16 June 1487.

The Percys' Loyalty, 1489

Thomas Howard had declined an opportunity to escape from the Tower during the Simnel rebellion so Henry VII returned his Earldom of Surrey and a few of his estates. He was sent north to put down a rebellion against taxation, after Henry Percy, 4th Earl of Northumberland, was murdered in York. Twelve-year-old Henry Percy would be raised at court and the king chose husbands for his sisters. Henry was eventually appointed to the traditional family post of the Warden of the Eastern Marches in 1503.

Dubious Inheritances

Henry Daubeney's father wanted to be connected to the Basset family so he could claim Beaumont's huge inheritance. So he took in Basset's two daughters and let his son choose one. Henry's father died when he was only 15 but the teenager still fought to get the Basset fortune.

Henry Stafford, 1st Earl of Wiltshire, paid the king for permission to marry Cecily Bonville, hoping to get his hands on her inheritance. But Cecily's son Thomas Grey, 2nd Marquess of Dorset, acquired the right to be his father's executor, leaving Stafford with an aging wife and fourteen irate step-children.

The Pretender Perkin Warbeck, 1499

Edward Plantagenet, 17th Earl of Warwick, was kept in the Tower for many years because of his claim to the throne. Some say he had a mental disability but his long imprisonment 'out of all company of men and sight of beasts' could not have helped and 'he could not discern a goose from a capon.' In 1499 Perkin Warbeck impersonated Richard of Shrewsbury, Duke of York, one of the princes who disappeared in the Tower in 1483. King James IV of Scotland declared his support for Perkin Warbeck and the powerful Ralph Neville, 3rd Earl of Westmorland, headed north to join him.

There was even talk of a plot to free Edward as a figurehead for a rebellion in November. So he was put on trial and Lord High Steward John de Vere, 13th Earl of Oxford, heard him plead guilty. He was beheaded, the final male member of the House of Plantagenet with a claim to the throne. William, brother of Thomas Stanley, 1st Earl of Derby, was executed for treason at the same time.

While Edward had been a figurehead for those wishing to challenge Henry VII, he may have been executed to appease new allies, Ferdinand II of Aragon and Isabella I of Castile. Their daughter Catherine of Aragon was due to marry Henry's heir Arthur, and Henry VII wanted no one to challenge his succession.

The Pole Conspiracy, 1501

The Poles were the leading Yorkist contenders following Richard III's death at Bosworth. Margaret of York was married to Henry VII's cousin Richard Pole in 1487 to stop conspirators using her as a figurehead for a rebellion. The couple were then kept at court where they served Prince Arthur and his wife to be, Catherine of Aragon.

John de la Pole, 2nd Duke of Suffolk, had submitted to Henry VII after Bosworth and while he served the king faithfully, Edmund de la Pole was not so loyal after he was demoted to Earl of Suffolk in 1491. He was determined to seize the throne and escaped from England in 1501 only to find the Holy Roman Emperor, Maximilian, refused to support him. James Tyrrell was executed for helping Edmund escape while William Courtenay, 1st Earl of Devon, was imprisoned in the Tower for supporting him.

In 1506 Maximilian's son Philip of Burgundy was sailing to Castile to claim the throne on behalf of his wife when a storm drove his ship ashore and he became a guest of Henry VII. Philip was allowed to continue on his journey but only after Maximilian had handed over Pole, with a guarantee he would not be executed. While Henry VII stuck to his word, his son Henry VIII would not feel bound by the agreement and he beheaded Pole in 1513.

The Heirs to the Throne, 1502
The birth of Henry VII and Elizabeth's first son unified the House of Tudor and the House of York in blood. The boy was named after the legendary King Arthur and he was created Duke of Cornwall. Eleven-year-old Prince Arthur was betrothed to Catherine of Aragon, daughter of Ferdinand and Isabella, creating an Anglo-Spanish alliance against France. They married in November 1501 but Arthur would die only five months later, aged 15.

Henry VII was anxious to maintain the Treaty of Medina del Campo so he discussed marrying Catherine to his second son Henry, Prince of Wales. Ten-year-old Henry had been raised out of the spotlight of the royal court and was 'untrained in the exacting art of kingship'. Catherine claimed her marriage to Arthur had not been consummated so a papal dispensation was only needed to silence the 'impediment of public honesty'. But Henry VII and the Spanish ambassador both wanted the stronger dispensation called an 'affinity' from the pope, in case the teenage princess was lying.

Thomas Boleyn, Viscount Rochford, escorted the king's daughter Margaret to Scotland in 1503, as part of the Treaty of Perpetual Peace. She was betrothed to James IV of Scotland in an attempt to break the Auld Alliance between Scotland and France.

Meanwhile, Henry and Catherine were betrothed in June 1503. But the situation in Spain became complicated when Isabella died in 1504, leaving the kingdom of Castile to her daughter Joanna the Mad. Ferdinand was anxious for Catherine to stay out of the political turmoil, so he made his daughter an ambassador to England. Matters were further complicated when Prince Henry declared he did not want to marry Catherine as soon as he turned 14. The relationship between Ferdinand and Henry VII deteriorated but young Henry eventually married Catherine when the king died in 1509, declaring the union was his father's wish.

Chapter 21

Henry VIII
1509–47

Stafford's Execution, 1510
Edward Stafford, 3rd Duke of Buckingham, belonged to the Plantagenet line and Richard III had executed his father for treason in 1483. In 1510 he discovered his sister Anne was having an affair so William Compton was forced to take the sacrament to prove they had not committed adultery. An angry Stafford then discovered the king was having an affair with Anne so she was sent to a convent to repent of her sins.

Stafford was one of twelve challengers chosen to joust against Henry VIII and his companions in 1517 but he excused himself from the contest. He said he did not want to be responsible for hurting the king but some viewed his attitude as contempt for the king. He was in trouble again the following year for failing to keep the Welsh rebels in check in South Wales.

But all the time Stafford was plotting to assassinate Henry VIII and take the throne for himself because he was a direct descendent of Edward III. He was arrested and held in the Tower in April 1521, accused of listening to prophecies of the king's death and intending to kill the king. Lord High Steward Thomas Howard, 2nd Duke of Norfolk, 'pronounced the sentence of death with tears streaming down his face' and Stafford was executed on Tower Hill on 17 May.

Trouble in East Anglia, 1511-3
Twelve-year-old John de Vere married Anne, daughter of Thomas Howard, 2nd Duke of Norfolk, in 1511, uniting the two wealthiest families in East Anglia. John inherited the Earldom of Oxford when his uncle John died in 1513, making the union even more powerful. A concerned Henry VIII declared the marriage invalid on the grounds that John had been underage and he offered him a new bride instead. John refused the offer of Margaret Courtenay, so Henry fined him.

The Invasion of France, 1512-3

George Talbot, 4th Earl of Shrewsbury, was the lieutenant general of the army which invaded France in 1512. Henry Bourchier, 2nd Earl of Essex, routed the French gendarmes at the Battle of the Spurs in August 1513 and he was appointed the Chief Captain of the king's forces. Talbot went on to capture Thérouanne and Tournai with the help of Charles Brandon, 1st Duke of Suffolk, Henry Algernon Percy, 5th Earl of Northumberland, and Henry Stafford, 1st Earl of Wiltshire.

Victory against the Scottish, 1513

Thomas Howard, 2nd Earl of Surrey, and his sons Thomas and Edmund, faced another Auld Alliance invasion in 1513. They defeated the Scots and killed King James IV at the battle of Flodden on 9 September. Thomas senior was elevated to Duke of Norfolk while his son Thomas became the Earl of Surrey. The lion of Scotland pierced through the mouth with an arrow was added to the Howard coat of arms to celebrate the victory.

The King's Sister, 1514

Earl Marshal Thomas Howard, 2nd Duke of Norfolk, had escorted Henry VIII's sister Princess Mary to France in 1514 for her marriage to King Louis XII. But Louis died soon afterwards and Charles Brandon, 1st Duke of Suffolk, was sent to Paris to congratulate the new King Francis I and to bring back the king's sister and her dowry. Henry VIII knew Charles was in love with his sister but so did Francis and he accused him of wanting to marry his mother-in-law. The matter jeopardised the negotiations and Henry forced Charles to pay a huge fine when he found out Brandon and Mary had married in secret.

Cardinal Thomas Wolsey, 1520-5

Francis I had been crowned king of France in 1515 and Charles was crowned king of Spain in 1516; Charles also became the Holy Roman Emperor in 1519. Cardinal Thomas Wolsey negotiated the Treaty of London in 1518, an attempt to unite Western Europe against the Ottoman sweeping across Eastern Europe. Henry would entertain Francis at a lavish event near Calais called the Field of the Cloth of Gold in June 1520 but he still favoured Charles.

France, 1522-5

The peace ended when the Holy Roman Empire attacked France the following year. Charles Brandon, Duke of Suffolk, recrossed the Channel in 1522 and his army conducted a scorched earth campaign across the north of France. Henry VIII then welcomed the news that King Francis I had been captured by Charles V, Holy Roman Emperor, at the battle of Pavia in 1525. Henry VIII sent Henry Courtenay, 1st Marquess of Exeter, to meet the Regent Louise of Savoy and he secured a promise that Francis would be freed. Henry withdrew from the war soon afterwards under the Treaty of the More.

Gamblers and Drunks, 1524-7

Richard Grey, 3rd Earl of Kent, had to sell most of his property to the crown to pay off gambling debts. His half-brother Henry inherited the title in 1524 but he failed to get the properties back so he had to live on a modest income and never formally took the title.

John de Vere, 14th Earl of Oxford, was described as an 'incompetent wastrel' and Henry VIII ordered him to 'moderate his excessive hunting, drink less wine, not stay up late, eat less meat, and forbear excessive and superfluous apparel.' He also banned him from his offices, stopped his pensions and he was told to 'discharge his household, act lovingly towards his wife and live with his father-in-law.' But Vere's excessive lifestyle caught up with him and he died in 1525 aged only 26.

Henry Stafford had been imprisoned briefly in the Tower, suspected of treason, when Henry VIII came to the throne. Stafford soon become one of the king's favourite courtiers, 'sharing his taste for lavish entertainments, tournaments, and hunting' and he was created Earl of Wiltshire. But his extravagant lifestyle cost him dearly and he ended up in debt to the crown.

Henry Percy was described as 'a proud, presumptuous, and unthrift waster' but he still became the 6th Earl of Northumberland in 1527. He often complained about his wife Mary Talbot, daughter of the Earl of Shrewsbury, and her spiteful behaviour. Percy bequeathed his inheritance to the king when it was clear Mary was not going to produce an heir, to stop his wife claiming it; not surprisingly she petitioned for a divorce.

The Howard Marriages, 1530

Ralph Neville, 4th Earl of Westmorland, was originally betrothed to Elizabeth, eldest daughter of his guardian Edward Stafford, 3rd Duke of Buckingham. But politics meant she had to marry Thomas Howard, Earl of Surrey and heir to the Dukedom of Norfolk, so Neville was married to Stafford's second daughter and they had eighteen children. But the Howard marriage did not go so well and Elizabeth moved out when Thomas moved his mistress Elizabeth Holland into their home.

Thomas's sister Katherine married Edward Stanley, 3rd Earl of Derby, without the king's permission. While Henry allowed the marriage, Katherine died of the plague only a few weeks later. The Stanleys and Howards were anxious to maintain the union so Edward married Thomas's half-sister Dorothy.

A Royal Divorce, 1529-33

By 1527 Queen Catherine of Aragon had only had one daughter, Mary, but she had had a number of miscarriages. It was doubtful if she could have any more children so Henry VIII wanted his marriage annulled. The king had been pursuing Anne Boleyn and her uncle Thomas Howard, 3rd Duke of Norfolk, had been encouraging the romance. Anne's father Thomas Boleyn, 1st Earl of Wiltshire, was sent to speak to Pope Clement VII and Holy Roman Emperor, Charles V, to seek support for the Henry's 'Great Matter' in 1529.

Many supported the king during the protracted negotiations to get his marriage annulled but Catherine defiantly refused to cooperate, stating, 'God never called me to a nunnery. I am the King's true and legitimate wife.' Thomas Howard, 3rd Duke of Norfolk, and William Paulet, 1st Marquess of Winchester, would join King Francis I of France in an audience with Pope Clement VII but he refused to grant a divorce.

Catherine was banished from court in 1531 but she still refused to an annulment and was supported by Bishop John Fisher, Lord Chancellor John More, and King Henry's sister Mary. Henry VIII eventually took matters into his own hands and appointed lawyers to seek his own solution. They declared that the Bible implied Henry's marriage was void because he had been forced to marry the widow of his long dead brother Arthur.

Henry and a pregnant Anne Boleyn married in secret on 14 November 1532 and Henry and Catherine's marriage was declared null in May 1533. Mary lived in relative hardship and she was not allowed to see her daughter Mary because both refused to acknowledge Anne Boleyn. Although she always considered herself to be the Queen of England, Henry titled her the 'Dowager Princess of Wales' because she was his brother's widow. Catherine died in January 1536 and some believed she had been poisoned on the king's orders. Anne Boleyn miscarried her baby boy on the day of the funeral.

Cardinal Wolsey's Downfall, 1529-30

Henry believed his marriage was void but Pope Clement would still not grant him a divorce and Catherine refused to cooperate. Cardinal Wolsey was made the scapegoat for the failure and Henry sent Thomas Howard, 3rd Duke of Norfolk, and Charles Brandon, 1st Duke of Suffolk, to get his great seal in October 1529. Wolsey was later charged with treason and Henry Percy, 6th Earl of Northumberland, arrested him at Cawood in Yorkshire in November 1530. He fell ill during the journey south and died in Leicester.

The King's Illegitimate Son, 1525-33

Henry had an affair with her lady in waiting, Elizabeth Blount, while

Catherine was in her last confinement. The queen gave birth to a stillborn daughter born in November 1518, but Elizabeth's pregnancy went full term. Elizabeth was taken to St Lawrence Priory in Essex and in June 1519 she gave birth to the son Henry was desperate for. Henry was the only illegitimate offspring the king ever acknowledged and was given the surname FitzRoy to signify he was the king's son.

Henry VIII had young Henry raised as if he were a prince and he was created Earl of Nottingham, the first time an illegitimate son had been honoured for 400 years. He was also appointed Lord High Admiral of England, Lord President of the Council of the North and Warden of the Scottish Marches, and Lord-Lieutenant of Ireland. He was later invested as the Duke of Richmond and Somerset.

During the discussions concerning Henry VIII's divorce from Catherine it was suggested that young Henry could marry his half-sister Mary. It would make an annulment unnecessary and would strengthen Fitzroy's claim to the throne. Even the Pope would allow the marriage because he was anxious to prevent the royal divorce. But the discussions came to nothing and Henry Fitzroy married Mary, daughter of Thomas Howard, 3rd Duke of Norfolk, in 1533 when he was 14.

The king obtained his divorce and married Anne Boleyn at the beginning of 1533 but she too gave birth to a daughter. The marriage quickly turned sour and Anne was executed in May 1536 while Henry married Jane Seymour. Henry had an Act of Parliament introduced to disinherit Anne's daughter Elizabeth. It also allowed the king to designate his successor, legitimate or not, meaning young Henry could have been heir to the throne. However, everything changed in the king's favour a few months later. Henry Fitzroy died and Queen Jane gave birth to a son, Edward.

The King's Nephew, 1533

The king's sister Mary died in 1533, leaving Charles Brandon, Duke of Suffolk, facing a dilemma. His young son Henry, Earl of Lincoln, was betrothed to marry his ward, 14-year-old Catherine Willoughby. Forty-nine-year-old Brandon was worried he would lose her wealthy inheritance if he waited for his son to grow up, so he married her himself.

Anne Boleyn's Courtship, 1533-6

Thomas Boleyn and Elizabeth, daughter of Thomas Howard, 2nd Duke of Norfolk, had three children, Mary, Anne and George. A teenage Henry Percy, 6th Earl of Northumberland, had wanted to marry Anne Boleyn in 1523 but his father refused permission because he was betrothed to the daughter of George Talbot, 4th Earl of Shrewsbury. The love affair would later come back to haunt them.

Anne's father, Thomas, was always busy at King Henry's court and he served as ambassador to France, arranging the spectacular Field of the Cloth of Gold meeting with the king of France. He then served as an envoy to the Holy Roman Emperor, Charles V. Anne was lined up to wed James Butler, 9th Earl of Ormond, to resolve a dispute with the Boleyn's over the Earldom of Ormond, but Thomas had his eye on greater things.

Boleyn encouraged his daughters to flirt with Henry VIII, hoping to raise his profile at court. The king initially had an affair with Mary but ignored her as soon as she fell pregnant. There were rumours Boleyn had allowed his wife to have an affair with the king but Henry's reply was, 'never with the mother'.

It was Anne's turn next but she was encouraged to make the king fall in love with her, starting in 1525, to avoid the situation Mary had found herself in. The plan worked but Henry had problems convincing Pope Clement VII to allow him to divorce Catherine. Meanwhile, Thomas was first created Viscount Rochford and then Earl of Wiltshire and Earl of Ormond in 1529 as his daughter exercised increasing control over the king. Three years later Henry granted Anne the Marquessate of Pembroke, giving her great powers in court. He would also appoint her uncle Thomas Howard, 3rd Duke of Norfolk, his Earl Marshal for helping him to arrange the marriage.

But sibling rivalry resulted in Mary accusing Henry Percy and Anne of promising to get married when they were teenagers. Mary told her father and he informed Thomas Howard, 3rd Duke of Norfolk. But Anne used her new powers to order an inquiry in which Percy denied the accusation.

After prolonged theological discussions, Henry finally split with Rome and declared he was head of the English Church. He then committed bigamy (although he did not think it was) when he secretly married the pregnant Anne in January 1533. The obedient Thomas Cranmer was consecrated Archbishop of Canterbury and he declared the king's marriage to Catherine unlawful, allowing Anne to be crowned queen in June.

Everyone had to swear oaths which accepted the legitimacy of the marriage and the Act of Succession which declared Catherine's daughter Mary illegitimate. But Thomas More and John Fisher, Bishop of Rochester, refused to comply so they were imprisoned in the Tower and executed.

Reforming the Church, 1536
Henry VIII appointed Thomas Cromwell Royal Vicegerent and Vicar General, with instructions to carry out the desired reforms to the churches and monasteries. He was also in control of the king's legal and parliamentary affairs when he denounced the clerical abuses and the power of the ecclesiastical courts. He described Henry as 'the only head, sovereign lord, protector and defender' of the Church, but not everyone agreed. The

resignation of Thomas More as Lord Chancellor in May 1532 had increased Cromwell's influence over the king and he was given appointments in the royal household, the Chancery and the Exchequer.

Cromwell replaced Thomas Boleyn as Lord Privy Seal and he conducted a detailed census of the church's properties so they could be taxed appropriately. His inspectors found corruption and immoral practices so he organised the dissolution of the monasteries starting in 1536. The king also endorsed Ten Articles which explained the Church's new doctrines and ceremonies and injunctions for their enforcement followed.

Confiscated church goods helped pay for the king's extravagant projects while forfeited estates were given to the nobility to ensure their loyalty. Anne Boleyn had wanted the proceeds of the dissolution of the monasteries to be used for educational and charitable purposes but Cromwell routed the money into the crown's coffers instead. The Queen took it upon herself to oppose the Vicar General, making him her enemy.

Anne's Marriage 1533-6
Anne had promised Henry she would provide a male heir to the throne but she gave birth to a daughter, Elizabeth, and suffered two miscarriages. She became increasingly paranoid and desperate when the king found a new love interest, Jane Seymour. Thomas Cromwell concocted evidence against Anne, with the king's approval, and Archbishop Cranmer declared the king's marriage illegal, making their daughter illegitimate.

Anne's uncle, Thomas Howard, presided at Queen Anne's trial in May 1536 while John de Vere, 15th Earl of Oxford, acted as Lord Great Chamberlain. Many earls lined up to hear the unpopular queen found guilty. Anne's first love, Henry Percy, 6th Earl of Northumberland, was on the jury and he was horrified to hear her confess their pre-contract of marriage as she tried to save her life. He was a sick man and collapsed when the verdict was announced.

William FitzWilliam, 1st Earl of Southampton, had used torture to extract confessions. His victims accused each other, resulting in Anne being accused of outrageous multiple cases of adultery and incest. The musician Mark Smeaton, the king's groom of the stool, Henry Norris, the king's friend, Francis Weston, William Brereton and her brother George were also accused of plotting to kill the king and they were executed on 17 May 1536. Two days later, Anne was executed, while her conniving father was lucky to escape with his life. The king was then free to marry Jane Seymour on 30 May.

The Pilgrimage of Grace, 1536-7
The economy of the north of England was heavily reliant on the

monasteries. Ralph Neville, 4th Earl of Westmorland, and Henry Percy, 6th Earl of Northumberland, had to stop outbreaks of violence as Thomas Cromwell's agents went about their work. The first ever Privy Council was held to discuss stopping the Pilgrimage of Grace and the committee of royal advisors replaced Cromwell's one-man rule.

By October 1536 the rebels had become more organised and, while Neville and Percy's brothers Thomas and Ingelram were sympathetic, Henry remained loyal to the king. The rebel leader Robert Aske asked an ill Percy to hand his command of the Scottish Marches over to his brothers or join the rebels. He refused, so Aske sent him to York to stop the rebels executing him. The Pilgrimage of Grace then moved south, gathering support on the way. But not everyone supported the rebellion. Edward Stanley, 3rd Earl of Derby, and John Dudley, 1st Duke of Northumberland, stopped it gathering momentum in their areas and Henry Clifford, 1st Earl of Cumberland, was besieged in Skipton Castle when he refused to join it.

Meanwhile, news of the rebellion had reached an outraged King Henry in London and he ordered his barons to march north and confront the rebels. Henry Courtenay, 1st Marquess of Exeter, and Charles Brandon, 1st Duke of Suffolk, failed to defeat them in Yorkshire and they withdrew. George Talbot, 4th Earl of Shrewsbury, raised troops on his own authority and stopped the rebels at Ampthill, Bedfordshire. Later it was stated that 'his courage and fidelity on this occasion perhaps saved Henry's crown.' Thomas Howard, 3rd Duke of Norfolk, then joined Talbot and they met Robert Aske and his 30,000 strong army at Doncaster. Howard promised the rebels a pardon and persuaded them to disperse so the king and parliament could consider their grievances.

King Henry ignored Howard's promise and instead planned his revenge against those who had challenged his measures. William FitzWilliam, 1st Earl of Southampton, acted as the king's enforcer and the Percy brothers were arrested for supporting the rebellion; Thomas was executed but Ingelram was released and went into exile. Robert Radcliffe, 1st Earl of Sussex, and Edward Stanley, 3rd Earl of Derby, were instructed to restore order in Lancashire but Ralph Neville, 4th Earl of Westmorland, refused to be the Warden of the Middle and East Marches because his men had supported the rising.

The Reformation Continues, 1537-42
The northern revolt re-erupted in January 1537, when the rebels heard the king planned to continue the dissolution of the monasteries. This time Henry ordered his barons to carry out brutal reprisals and hundreds were executed, including many innocent people.

The suppression of the risings spurred further Reformation measures and Cromwell organised the removal of statues, rood screens and images from churches in 1538. He also had an English language Bible placed in every church. But there was continued resistance to these extra religious reforms and even the king was getting uncomfortable about them. Even so, Henry sanctioned the destruction of saints' shrines, the remaining monasteries were dissolved, and their property transferred to the crown in 1542.

Married to the Royals, 1537
Henry Clifford, 2nd Earl of Cumberland, was married to Eleanor Brandon, daughter of Charles Brandon, 1st Duke of Suffolk, and Mary Tudor, Henry VIII's sister, in 1537. The marriage gave Henry great influence at court but the expensive lifestyle he was expected to lead put him in great debt. Clifford was forced to retire to the country following Eleanor's death.

The Exeter Plot, 1538-41
Margaret Pole, Countess of Salisbury, had seen her brother Edward Plantagenet, 17th Earl of Warwick, imprisoned when Lambert Simnel impersonated him in 1487. She then saw him executed in November 1499 when there was another rebellion centred on Perkin Warbeck.

Margaret served as Catherine of Aragon's lady-in-waiting and as governess to Princess Mary. Margaret refused to return Mary's gold and jewels when she was declared a bastard in 1533, so Henry dismissed her. Margaret's son Reginald was the Plantagenet claimant to the throne and he had gone into exile in Padua after warning of the dangers of Henry marrying Anne. He had also suggested he could marry Princess Mary, so they could combine their claims to the throne.

Reginald continued to oppose King Henry, issuing a pamphlet which denied Henry's royal supremacy and urged the princes of Europe to depose Henry. Pope Paul III made him a cardinal in 1537 and instructed him to organise support for the Pilgrimage of Grace, but neither Francis I of France nor Emperor Charles V would help. Henry's agents failed to assassinate Reginald but they did arrest his brother Geoffrey in August 1538 when they discovered they were in contact.

Meanwhile, Thomas Cromwell's rival Henry Courtenay, 1st Marquess of Exeter, was in trouble. His devotedly Catholic wife Gertrude Blount was accused of supporting the 'Nun of Kent', Elizabeth Barton, who had been executed for threatening the king would die if he married Anne Boleyn. Gertrude was banished from court and later charged with writing to Catherine of Aragon.

A furious Cromwell struck back at his enemies when Geoffrey Pole warned there could be a Catholic uprising. He arrested Geoffrey and

Margaret, Henry Courtenay, 1st Marquess of Exeter, and Henry Montagu in November 1538. Courtenay was released due to a lack of evidence but he joined the Poles while the Cornish rebels called for Henry Courtenay to be named the heir apparent.

Courtenay was arrested again, in what became known as the Exeter Plot, and the king relied on William FitzWilliam, 1st Earl of Southampton, to gather the evidence. John de Vere, 15th Earl of Oxford, presided over the trials and while Geoffrey was pardoned, Henry Courtenay and Henry Montagu were executed for treason. Edward Neville and Nicholas Carew were also executed on Geoffrey Pole's evidence.

But the king had not done with the Poles. Margaret and her young grandson Henry were arrested in May 1539 and a tunic with the Five Wounds of Christ, the symbol of the Pilgrimage of Grace, was discovered at Margaret's house; the tunic was probably planted. An inexperienced executioner took a dozen blows to decapitate the 67-year-old Margaret on 27 May 1541. Henry was deprived of a tutor and died in the Tower, possibly starved to death.

Henry Courtenay's other son, Edward, 1st Earl of Devon, had also been imprisoned. He had not been involved in the plot but he was still kept in prison because he was an heir of the House of York.

Anne of Cleves, 1539-40
By 1539 Thomas Howard, 3rd Duke of Norfolk, and his son Henry Howard, Earl of Suffolk, were challenging Thomas Cromwell's religious reforms. Matters came to a head when they were dining with the king and Cromwell as guests of Archbishop Cranmer in June. Cromwell accused the Howards of being disloyal to the king and Thomas retaliated by calling Cromwell a liar.

Queen Jane gave birth to the son, Edward, Henry desperately wanted in October 1539, but she died a few days later. Cromwell took the initiative in looking for a new wife for the grieving king straight away. King Francis of France and Emperor Charles had been in an alliance since the beginning of the year, so Cromwell was looking to organise a useful union for England.

Cromwell suggested Anne of Cleves and Henry accepted, but his decision was only based on a miniature painted by Hans Holbein in October. William FitzWilliam, 1st Earl of Southampton, captained the ship which carried Anne from Calais and she arrived in Dover on 27 December. The king could not wait and he rode to meet her at Blackheath, near Rochester, accompanied by John de Vere, 15th Earl of Oxford, and Robert Radcliffe, 1st Earl of Sussex.

The king was not impressed with his new bride and he left immediately, leaving Anne's lord chamberlain, Thomas Manners, 1st Earl of Rutland, to escort her to Greenwich Palace. Henry was forced to marry Anne, to prevent upsetting his new ally, but he refused to consummate the marriage. Cromwell was granted the Earldom of Essex but the furious king felt he had been misled into marrying.

Cromwell's enemies, headed by Thomas Howard and Bishop Gardiner, worked to undermine him and he was arrested at a Privy Council meeting in June 1540. Howard personally 'tore the St George from his neck' before he was led away for treason. Cromwell was condemned to death without trial and was beheaded on Tower Hill on 28 July 1540.

Catherine Howard, 1540-2

The royal marriage was annulled, with Anne's agreement, in July 1540 and Thomas Howard, 3rd Duke of Norfolk, immediately made his young niece Catherine available to the king. Henry VIII wed Catherine Howard, as his fifth wife, the same day Cromwell was executed and Howard received his rewards. The king was happy, but his marriage to his teenage bride would not last long.

Archbishop Cranmer revealed Catherine's premarital sexual indiscretions with Francis Dereham, and Henry accused the Howard family of covering up her misconduct. Catherine's alleged adultery with Thomas Culpeper was also revealed during investigation. Dereham was hung drawn and quartered and Culpeper was beheaded. Catherine was executed on 13 February 1542 and several members of the Howard family were imprisoned in the Tower.

A New War with Scotland, 1542-4

Earl Marshal Thomas Howard, 3rd Duke of Norfolk, and Edward Stanley, 3rd Earl of Derby, invaded Scotland in 1542 and they defeated the Scots at the battle of Solway Moss in November. John Dudley, 1st Duke of Northumberland, was appointed Warden of the Scottish Marches and William FitzWilliam, 1st Earl of Southampton, was appointed Lieutenant and Captain General of the North after the battle. An ill FitzWilliam was reluctantly carried to Newcastle in a litter where he died on his arrival.

Edward Seymour, 1st Earl of Hertford, crossed the border again in 1544 while Dudley and Edward Fiennes de Clinton, 1st Earl of Lincoln, sailed their fleet up the coast. Their combined forces captured and burnt Edinburgh.

A New War with France, 1543-6

Earl Marshal Thomas Howard, 3rd Duke of Norfolk, declared war on France in the king's name in 1543. He besieged Montreuil, near Calais, the following year while the king and Charles Brandon, 1st Duke of Suffolk, captured Boulogne. But Howard complained he was being left short of provisions and munitions and the king criticised him after he withdrew his troops to Calais. John Dudley, 1st Duke of Northumberland, would join the peace negotiations in 1546.

Unfaithful Wives, 1543-7
Anne, daughter of Henry Bourchier, 2nd Earl of Essex, was unfaithful, so William Parr, 1st Marquess of Northampton, brother of Henry VIII's sixth wife Catherine Parr, had his marriage annulled by an Act of Parliament in 1543. Parr was given his wife's estates and her inheritance, the Earldom of Essex, while Anne's children were disinherited and declared bastards.

Edward Seymour, Earl of Hertford and brother of the late Queen Jane, accused his wife Catherine of being unfaithful and questioned the paternity of his two sons. They were excluded from his will but they remained faithful to their father and were imprisoned with him in the Tower of London at the end of Henry VIII's reign. Edward was released but John died in prison.

The Fall of the Howards, 1543-7
Henry VIII married his final wife, Catherine Parr, in 1543, and she was known to favour the reformed religious faith. The leader of the reform party, Edward Seymour, 1st Earl of Hertford, clashed with the conservative Thomas Howard, 3rd Duke of Norfolk, even though Hertford's brother Thomas was married to Howard's daughter Mary.

Thomas's eldest son Henry Howard, Earl of Surrey, included the royal arms of Edward the Confessor in his coat of arms to signify his opposition, a treasonable offence. Father and son were imprisoned in the Tower in December 1546 and Thomas offered the king his lands, hoping for his forgiveness. But father and son were doomed when Thomas's estranged wife, his daughter Mary, and his mistress Elizabeth Holland, all gave evidence against him. Henry was beheaded in January 1547 but Thomas's execution was delayed because Henry VIII died on 28 January. The removal of the Howards from court would allow the Protestants to continue their reforms with a passion.

Chapter 22

Edward VI
1547–53

Seymour's Rise, 1547

Henry VIII's will named sixteen executors who would act as young Edward's advisors until he reached the age of 18. They were assisted by a twelve-man council who would carry out his wishes. But Henry had added a controversial clause just before he died. The executors were allowed to reward themselves and the council members with lands and honours. It was a recipe for nepotism and corruption.

John Dudley had been one of Henry's advisors in his final years and a leader of the religious reform party. He was created Earl of Warwick and appointed Lord Great Chamberlain. Edward's uncle Edward Seymour was appointed Governor of the King's Person and created Duke of Somerset. Seymour's son was created Earl of Hertford and he was raised along with the young Prince Edward.

The Regency Council was supposed to be a democratic body which ruled by majority decision but it had soon appointed Seymour the Lord Protector of the Realm. He obtained permission to appoint members to the Privy Council but he rarely consulted them and used proclamations to run the realm. Chancellor Thomas Wriothesley was charged with selling off some of his offices and was dismissed from his post when he protested.

No Bloodshed, 1547

Thomas Howard, 3rd Duke of Norfolk, was due to be executed for treason when Henry VIII died on 28 January. Edward VI's regency council decided not to begin the new reign with bloodshed so they confiscated his estates instead. They also announced an amnesty on all prisoners of the previous regime. That was all except Edward Courtenay, 1st Earl of Devon, a great-grandson of Edward IV and an heir to the House of York.

A War with Scotland, 1547-8

Lord Protector Edward Seymour, 1st Duke of Somerset, immediately restarted the war in Scotland. To begin with the campaign went well and John Dudley, 1st Duke of Northumberland, was described as 'one of the key architects of the English victory' at the battle of Pinkie Cleugh in September 1547.

But Mary, Queen of Scots, renewed the Auld Alliance and she was escorted to France to marry Henry II's son Francis. The arrival of French reinforcements in Scotland stalled Somerset's campaign and he found it too expensive to maintain military garrisons. Henry Manners, 2nd Earl of Rutland, was soon forced on the defensive in his role as Warden of the Scottish Marches and a French attack on Boulogne in August 1549 forced Somerset to withdraw his troops from Scotland.

The Worm in the Bud, 1549

Edward Seymour, 1st Duke of Somerset, may have been Lord Protector of the Realm but he had a problem: his younger brother. He had given Thomas appointments when he demanded the post of Governor of the King's Person. Thomas then smuggled pocket money to King Edward, telling him Edward was refusing to give him more, earning him the title, 'the worm in the bud'. He also advised the king to dismiss his brother and 'bear rule as other kings do' but Edward was too young to do anything.

In 1547 Thomas secretly married Henry VIII's widow Catherine Parr and she was soon pregnant. But he was sacked from her household when she caught him kissing the teenage Princess Elizabeth the following summer. Catherine died in childbirth and the brazen Thomas Seymour asked the council for permission to marry Elizabeth.

This time the worm had turned too far and Thomas was arrested on various charges, including embezzlement, in January 1549. Edward VI gave evidence against Seymour and he was also accused of discussing a marriage between the king and Jane Grey, daughter of Henry Grey, soon to be the 1st Duke of Suffolk. The lack of any evidence ruled out a trial but Thomas Seymour was still beheaded on 20 March 1549.

Seymour's Fall, 1549

Edward Seymour, 1st Duke of Somerset, had complete control of the kingdom but his uncoordinated proclamations caused unrest. Commissioners sent out to implement the decrees often encountered hostility because of their contradictory terms. Unrest turned into two armed rebellions in April 1549. The decision to hold all church services in English resulted in the Prayer Book Rebellion. Then Robert Kett rebelled at Norwich when landlords were given permission to take over common grazing ground. William Parr, Marquess of Northampton, was unable to crush the Norfolk rebellion so John Dudley, 1st Earl of Warwick, and his son Ambrose, offered Kett a pardon if he disbanded his army of peasants.

He refused and Dudley's troops massacred 2,000 rebels; another 300 were rounded up and executed.

The privy councillors blamed Seymour for the violence and they wanted him removed. Paget went so far as to say, 'every man of the council has misliked your proceedings...' Henry FitzAlan, 19th Earl of Arundel, and Thomas Wriothesley, 1st Earl of Southampton, met at John Dudley's home in October 1549 to discuss how to remove the Protector. Seymour failed to raise enough troops to counter them when they made their move so he took the king to Windsor Castle where he wrote, 'me thinks I am in prison'.

The Council published details of Somerset's mismanagement after persuading Dudley and Archbishop Cranmer to surrender. The 12-year-old king finally stood up for himself and personally ordered his uncle's arrest, accusing him of 'ambition, vain glory, entering into rash wars... enriching himself of my treasure, following his own opinion, and doing all by his own authority...'

Then Thomas Wriothesley accused the Lord President of the Council and co-conspirator John Dudley of working with Somerset during the early years of Edward's reign. Dudley took no chances when he answered the charge, sword in hand, with the words, 'my lord, you seek his [Somerset's] blood and he that seeketh his blood would have mine also'.

Duke for an Hour, 1551
Henry Brandon succeeded his father as the 2nd Duke of Suffolk in 1545. The Brandon brothers were taken to the country during an epidemic of sweating sickness in 1551 but Henry died first, age 16. 14-year-old Charles died an hour later and he holds the unenviable record for the shortest tenure as an English peer. They had no more siblings so the title became extinct.

Seymour's Return, 1552
Lord President John Dudley pushed forward his religious reforms and dismissed two religious conservatives, Henry FitzAlan, 19th Earl of Arundel, and Thomas Wriothesley, 1st Earl of Southampton, from the council. He also placed FitzAlan under house arrest on trumped-up embezzlement charges.

Edward Seymour, 1st Duke of Somerset, was released from the Tower and restored to the Privy Council in February 1550. Dudley married his son John to Seymour's daughter Anne to seal their new alliance and Seymour created Dudley the 2nd Earl of Warwick.

Despite the outward show of friendship, Seymour wanted to overthrow Dudley and retake control of the kingdom. But Dudley struck first and both Seymour and FitzAlan were arrested, accused of planning a 'banquet massacre'. Seymour was acquitted of treason due to a lack of evidence but

Lord High Steward William Paulet, 1st Marquess of Winchester, found him guilty of felony. This second charge related to the time he raised an unlicensed group of armed men to escort the king to Windsor Castle. He was executed in January 1552. FitzAlan would be pardoned a year later and was readmitted to the Privy Council.

William Paulet, 1st Marquess of Winchester, and the king's 'beloved uncle' William Parr, 1st Marquess of Northampton, joined Dudley and they 'ruled the court' on behalf of Edward VI. They would continue to pursue religious reforms across the country, persecuting both Roman Catholics and religious conservatives.

The Grey Ladies, 1533

Thomas Radclyffe, 3rd Earl of Sussex, was working to arrange Edward VI's marriage to a daughter of King Henry II, to secure a peace with France. Meanwhile, John Dudley, 1st Earl of Warwick, had elevated himself to Duke of Northumberland and had promoted his wife's half-brother Henry Grey to Duke of Suffolk. Henry Grey, 3rd Marquess of Dorset, had three daughters who became well known in court. More importantly, they were the granddaughters of Henry VIII's sister Princess Mary and of royal blood.

The teenage Edward VI had been seriously ill since January 1553 but Dudley continued his manipulating ways. He acquired permission to betroth his son Guildford to Henry's daughter Jane. They married on 25 May 1553 and Jane's sister Catherine married Henry Herbert, son of William Herbert, 1st Earl of Pembroke, the same day.

A Protestant Successor, 1553

It was clear 15-year-old Edward was dying by the beginning of June and there were plans to place a Protestant monarch on the throne, ahead of Mary, the Catholic daughter of Catherine of Aragon. Guildford Dudley had just married Jane Grey, daughter of Henry Grey, 1st Duke of Suffolk. His father John Dudley, 1st Duke of Northumberland, was also considering forcing his eldest son John Dudley, 2nd Earl of Warwick, to divorce so he could marry Mary's half-sister, 19-year-old Princess Elizabeth.

The Imperial ambassador Jehan de Scheyfve was convinced Dudley senior had some 'mighty plot' to seize the crown and he was right. Young Edward added a controversial clause, called, 'My Devise for the Succession' to his will on his deathbed. It nominated Lady Jane Grey as his successor and over one hundred signatures confirmed his decision.

Edward VI died on 6 July and Henry Grey, 1st Duke of Suffolk, and John Dudley, 1st Duke of Northumberland, were joined by other members of the Privy Council when they proclaimed Jane Queen of England. It was an unpopular announcement.

Chapter 23

Mary I
1553–58

The Struggle for the Throne, 1553

John Dudley, 1st Duke of Northumberland, planned to place his Protestant daughter-in-law Jane Grey on the throne. He sent his son Robert, 1st Earl of Leicester, and 300 soldiers to arrest Mary in Norfolk while he dealt with matters in London. But the Dudleys had underestimated the support for Mary because she was assembling a much larger army at Framlingham Castle.

The Privy Council received Mary's demand to be recognised as queen on 10 July, the same day Jane Grey was proclaimed queen. Dudley hesitated over what to do next but he eventually headed for Cambridge, with more troops and his sons John and Ambrose, on 14 July. Henry Grey, Duke of Suffolk, remained in London with Queen Jane at his daughter's request.

Dudley's indecision had given Mary time to amass a large army, while the navy had donated cannons to her cause. Dudley was forced to withdraw while the barons declared for Mary, one by one, when they heard the news. William Herbert, Earl of Pembroke, Francis Talbot, 5th Earl of Shrewsbury and John Bourchier, 2nd Earl of Bath, were just a few of those who joined the groundswell of support for Henry VIII's daughter.

Henry FitzAlan, 19th Earl of Arundel, sent the Privy Council's letter of submission and the royal great seal to Mary on 19 July. They also instructed the Dudleys to disband their army and send their men on their way. The Dudleys also proclaimed Mary their queen but John senior was arrested and taken to London where the hostile crowds made it clear they thought he had poisoned King Edward. Princess Mary was met on the outskirts of London by John Dudley, 2nd Earl of Warwick, and the Lords of the Council welcomed her 'as if she had been Queen of England'. Young Jane had only been queen for nine days when she was deposed.

Mary had Thomas Howard, 3rd Duke of Norfolk, released from the Tower, restored and appointed Earl Marshal. She also had all the Dudleys imprisoned in the Tower. Their trials were held in August in Westminster Hall but only John junior pleaded guilty. All were sentenced to death and John senior begged for mercy for his sons. The execution of John Dudley senior was delayed for a day so he could renounce his faith, take the confession and the Holy Communion. Dudley's words were then distributed to the people, in a Catholic propaganda coup, and he was executed the following day. Jane's husband Guildford was also executed but Robert and Ambrose were released.

The Queen's Suitor, 1554

Henry VIII had imprisoned the Courtenays in the Tower following the Exeter conspiracy in 1538. Henry Courtenay had been executed in 1539 but his teenage son Edward had been kept in prison because he was a great-grandson of Edward IV and an heir to the House of York.

Edward's mother Gertrude had remained friends with Mary, and she pleaded with her to release her son when she came to the throne. He was released after fifteen years in the Tower and soon became a favourite of his royal cousin who restored his Earldom of Devon. Edward considered himself a potential suitor for Mary but she rejected him in favour of Prince Philip of Spain, son of Charles V, and heir apparent to vast territories in Europe and the New World.

Wyatt's Rebels, 1544

The spurned Edward Courtenay, Earl of Devon, repaid Mary by deciding to seize the throne for himself and he organised a rebellion in Kent in February 1544. Earl Marshal Thomas Howard, 3rd Duke of Norfolk, William Herbert, 1st Earl of Pembroke and Edward Fiennes de Clinton, 1st Earl of Lincoln, quickly put down Thomas Wyatt's rebellion and the reprisals followed.

Henry Grey, 1st Duke of Suffolk, was arrested and beheaded on 23 February 1554. The surviving Dudleys, John, Ambrose, Robert and Henry, were again imprisoned in the Tower. The rebellion led to the executions of Jane Grey and her husband Guildford Dudley. William Herbert also threw his daughter-in-law and Jane's sister Catherine Grey out of his house. Queen Mary then persuaded Herbert to end his marriage and distance himself from the Grey family.

Edward Courtenay, 1st Earl of Devon, was imprisoned in the Tower before he was moved to Fotheringhay in May. Mary's half-sister Elizabeth was also held in the Tower for a time and she blamed Courtenay for her imprisonment. The ambassador of Spain, Simon Renard, reminded Mary that the two 'great persons' posed a threat and he made it clear he would advise Philip to stay in Spain until Courtenay and Elizabeth had been tried.

Mary did rush their trials into court but there was a lack of evidence to convict them.

Philip still decided to travel to England and he married Mary on 25 July 1554. Elizabeth was held under house arrest until the end of the year and Courtenay was exiled at Easter 1555. He met several Protestant exiles in Venice and they discussed how he could marry Elizabeth and take the throne of England. But Courtenay refused to change his wet clothing after being caught in a storm in Padua in 1556; he died of a fever but some believed he had been poisoned. It left Henry Manners, 2nd Earl of Rutland, senior male descendent of Richard, 3rd Duke of York, and heir presumptive of the House of York.

Burning Heretics, 1554-5
Mary initially announced she would not force anyone to follow her religion but she soon changed her mind and began imprisoning leading Protestant churchmen. Catholicism was reinstated with King Philip's support, but the estates confiscated by Henry VIII were not returned to the Church. Pope Julius III approved the compromise in 1554 and the Heretic Laws returned.

Mary I confirmed William Paulet as Marquess of Winchester after he converted to Catholicism and he began persecuting Protestants. Around 800 wealthy Protestants chose exile rather than convert but many did not have the means to escape. Mary considered her false pregnancy in 1555 to be divine punishment for tolerating heretics and she stepped up the persecutions. Nearly 240 Protestants would be executed over the next three years, earning the Queen the title 'Bloody Mary'. Ex-Archbishop of Canterbury Thomas Cranmer made a last minute conversion to Catholicism after watching Bishops Ridley and Latimer burn but Mary refused to reprieve him. He retaliated by withdrawing his recantation just before he too died at the stake.

The Dudleys, 1555-6
The Dudley brothers had been released in October 1553, and while John died soon afterwards, Robert and Henry were only allowed at court if King Philip was there. Ambrose Dudley was allowed to inherit the Earldom of Warwick but Mary still did not trust him and he was ordered out of London at the end of 1555. The Dudley brothers were forced into exile when a conspiracy by their distant cousin Henry was uncovered in 1556. King Philip was now also King of Spain and they joined his army fighting in France. All three fought at the battle of St Quentin, where Henry was killed. Robert and Ambrose would return when Elizabeth I came to the throne and Robert would become her favourite.

Plantations in Ireland, 1556

Thomas Radclyffe, heir to the Earldom of Sussex, was appointed Lord Deputy of Ireland in 1556. But English statesmen were ignorant of Irish matters and the chieftains continued to fight each other. Radclyffe worked to reverse the strategy to promote Protestantism across Ireland. The new policy was to move English settlers across the Irish Sea so they could start model plantations in the Irish midlands where Laois and Offaly were renamed King's County and Queen's County.

Radclyffe stopped further Scottish immigration into Ulster after defeating the O'Neills and the MacDonnells. He declared Mary I queen of the kingdom of Ireland and then fought Shane O'Neill and the Donough O'Conor before attacking the Scottish settlements along the Antrim coast.

The Percys Return to Favour, 1557

Henry VIII had executed Thomas Percy in 1537 for leading the Pilgrimage of Grace rebellion in the North of England. His sons Thomas and Henry were only 8 and 5 at the time. Thomas Percy recaptured Scarborough Castle from rebels in 1557 and was rewarded with the return of the Earldom of Northumberland. He was also named Warden General of the Marches, with Henry as his deputy.

Chapter 24

Elizabeth I
1558–1603

A New Style of Religion, 1559

After King Edward's Protestant regime and Mary's Catholic regime, Elizabeth adopted a compromise religion called Anglicanism. It was a Protestant Church with the Queen at its head but it kept many Catholic doctrines and ceremonies, in an attempt to appease everyone. Henry Percy, 8th Earl of Northumberland, and Thomas Young, Archbishop of York, were commissioned to administer the Protestant oath of supremacy to the priests in the pro-Catholic north in 1559. But not everyone agreed and Henry Clifford, 2nd Earl of Cumberland, was accused of protecting priests.

Lord Treasurer William Paulet, 1st Marquess of Winchester, always switched to the latest religious trend and his conversion to Anglicanism was his fifth change of religion. When asked how he kept his position, he answered, 'by being a willow, not an oak'. Paulet was one of Elizabeth's favourites and she once joked, 'if my lord treasurer were but a young man, I could find it in my heart to have him for a husband before any man in England.'

The Queen's Favourite, 1558-78

The Dudleys' attempt to put Jane Grey on the throne had ended with the executions of John Dudley, 1st Duke of Northumberland, and his son Guildford. Queen Mary had exiled the surviving Dudley brothers but Robert became Elizabeth's constant companion. The Queen's affection for Dudley created jealously and there were rumours they were having an affair; some even plotted to kill him.

Robert Dudley's career at court interfered with his private life and he rarely saw his long suffering wife Amy Robsart. She died after falling down the stairs at her home near Oxford in September 1560 and there were rumours Elizabeth had arranged her death. But the Dudleys' influence increased when Robert's brother Ambrose was created Earl of Warwick and given his father's Northumberland estates in 1561. Elizabeth said he was not as handsome or graceful as his brother but he was less of an intriguer and became known as 'the Good Earl of Warwick'.

Robert remained at the queen's side; she even stopped him leaving England in the spring of 1561. Elizabeth asked the Privy Council to make Dudley Protector of the Realm when she fell ill in October 1562 but they refused. She then decided he could marry her rival, the recently widowed Mary, Queen of Scots, and created him the Earl of Leicester to make him a suitable spouse. Mary accepted the offer but Dudley refused. After Mary's escape to England in 1568, Leicester wanted to restore her as the queen of Scotland with a Protestant English husband; only not him.

Dudley's closeness to the queen helped his career but it hindered his love life. He was moved into an apartment next to the queen and she became more possessive and jealous of his behaviour as the years passed. He dared not remarry for many years but he fathered a son with his mistress Douglas Sheffield, and then pursued Lettice, wife of Walter Devereux, 1st Earl of Essex. Some even believed he had poisoned Devereux when he died in 1576. Robert and Lettice married in secret but he dared not tell the Elizabeth and she was furious when she found out nine months later. She banished Lettice from court, calling her a 'she-wolf' and referred to Dudley as a 'traitor' and a 'cuckold'.

The Scottish Threat, 1560

Elizabeth opposed the French presence in Scotland because she thought they might invade England, hoping to put Mary, Queen of Scots, on the English throne. Earl Marshal Thomas Howard, 4th Duke of Norfolk, was the Queen's Lieutenant in the North. He invaded Scotland in 1560, after negotiating the Treaty of Berwick with the Scottish Protestants who called themselves the Lords of the Congregation. The clumsy campaigning resulted in the Treaty of Edinburgh but it stopped the French. Mary returned to Scotland the following year and was horrified to find that her kingdom had a Protestant church and was being run by Protestant nobles. She refused to confirm the treaty with England, infuriating Elizabeth.

A Dangerous Liaison, 1560

Edward Seymour, 1st Earl of Hertford, secretly married Catherine Grey, sister of the executed Jane Grey, in December 1560 without the queen's permission. It was a dangerous liaison because he was Elizabeth's close relative and she was a potential claimant to the throne. A heavily pregnant Catherine confided in Elizabeth's favourite Robert Dudley in August and he immediately told the queen.

Edward and Catherine were imprisoned and questioned to determine the legitimacy of the unborn child. Both claimed to have forgotten the date of the marriage and the conception but the interrogators decided they had married in November. It would make their son illegitimate, so he was removed from the line of succession; Edward was fined for 'seducing a virgin of the blood royal'.

The couple continued their marital relations even though they were in the Tower and she soon fell pregnant again. She gave birth to a second son in 1563 and he too was declared illegitimate. Edward was finally released when Catherine died in 1568.

Continuing the Irish Plantations, 1562

Lord Lieutenant of Ireland Thomas Radclyffe, 3rd Earl of Sussex, worked to extend English control beyond the area around Dublin, known as the Pale. He continued to introduce settlers into the King's and Queen's County plantations in 1562, despite objections from the Dublin administration. But the Master of the Rolls, John Parker, accused Radclyffe of having Catholic sympathies because he had served Queen Mary loyally. He was replaced by Gerald FitzGerald, 11th Earl of Kildare, after failing to deal with Shane O'Neill.

A delegation submitted to Elizabeth on behalf of O'Neill but they returned to their rebellious ways as soon as they returned to Ireland. Radclyffe was sent back to put down the rebellion but he failed once again. Parker had been busy examining the administration and he accused Radclyffe of embezzling soldiers' wages. He was imprisoned when he refused to repay the money and was eventually ordered back to England.

The Fight for Le Havre, 1563

Elizabeth refused to let Robert Dudley lead an army to recapture Calais from the French in 1558. Instead Ambrose Dudley, 3rd Earl of Warwick, crossed the Channel and took command of the Le Havre garrison. He assisted the Huguenots in the First French War of Religion before making a deal to exchange Le Havre for Calais in 1563. But the French attacked and the Queen allowed Dudley to surrender after the plague decimated the garrison. Ambrose was shot in the leg while attempting to parley and he was seriously ill by the time he returned to England.

The Imprisonment of Mary Queen of Scots, 1565-72

Mary, Queen of Scots, married Henry Stuart, Lord Darnley, in 1565, a claimant to the English throne. But Darnley soon became unpopular and he was found murdered after his house was blown up in February 1567. Mary then shocked everyone by marrying James Hepburn, Earl of Bothwell, even though many suspected him of killing Darnley.

The Scottish nobility forced Mary to abdicate in favour of her infant son James and she was imprisoned while he was raised a Protestant. Mary eventually escaped in 1568 and fled across the border following the disastrous battle of Langside. Elizabeth decided against fighting to reinstate Mary and she did not want to exile her in case she assembled France support. So she imprisoned Mary and Thomas Howard, 4th Duke of Norfolk, and headed the York commission which heard evidence against her.

George Talbot, Earl of Shrewsbury and Waterford, was appointed to guard Mary; he would be her guardian for the next fifteen years. She was held at Tutbury Castle and then moved to Wingfield Manor in 1569. She was back at Tutbury following a rescue attempt by Leonard Dacre where the spy, Henry Hastings, 3rd Earl of Huntingdon, joined her household.

Almost immediately there was a Catholic rising in the north of England. The rebels planned to free Mary, marry her to Howard, and then replace Elizabeth with the Catholic couple. Charles Neville, 6th Earl of Westmorland, and Thomas Percy, 7th Earl of Northumberland, wrote to Pope Pius V asking for advice but they captured Durham and held Mass in November 1569 before their letter arrived. Thomas Radclyffe, 3rd Earl of Sussex, organised local resistance while Edward Fiennes de Clinton, 1st Earl of Lincoln, and Ambrose Dudley, 3rd Earl of Warwick, led the army north to crush the rebellion.

Neville and Percy failed to rescue Mary because she had been moved to Coventry. Howard was arrested and over 750 rebels were executed but Neville and Percy escaped into Scotland. The Queen hired Robert Constable and he tracked down his cousin Neville to Ferniehurst Castle in 1572. He escaped but was forced to live in poverty in Flanders and would never see his family again. Percy was captured by the Scottish noble the Earl of Morton and was handed over in exchange for money three years later. He refused to renounce Catholicism and was executed in York in August 1572.

Pope Pius V mistakenly thought the rebellion had succeeded and he issued a bull calling Elizabeth 'the pretended Queen of England and the servant of crime'. The Queen was also excommunicated, leaving Catholics to choose between their religion and their sovereign. The bull gave Catholics a reason to want Mary on the throne and plots followed, keeping Elizabeth's spymaster Francis Walsingham busy.

Talbot moved Mary to Chatsworth in Derbyshire in May 1570 where he foiled another rescue attempt. Henry Percy, 8th Earl of Northumberland, and Bishop John Lesley, planned another escape attempt over Easter 1571. But Henry was betrayed and the pair were sent to the Tower where Lesley incriminated Henry Wriothesley, 2nd Earl of Southampton, and he too was confined to the Tower.

Thomas Howard was again arrested in 1572 for his involvement in the Ridolfi plot with King Philip II of Spain. Initially Henry Howard, 1st Earl of Northampton, had been wrongly accused of being put forward as Mary's husband. His brother Thomas was executed for treason when it turned out he had been the planned bridegroom. Henry would retire from public life but he stayed in touch with Mary and would advise and keep her informed during her fourteen-year stay in Sheffield Castle.

A Royal Marriage
There were several attempts to marry the 'Virgin Queen' but they all failed. Thomas Radclyffe, 3rd Earl of Sussex, tried to negotiate the queen's marriage to the Archduke Charles in 1566. Thomas Sackville, 1st Earl of Dorset, also discussed a possible union with the French king's brother the Duke of Anjou in 1571. But Elizabeth refused to accept anyone.

Colonising Ulster, 1573
Walter Devereux, 1st Earl of Essex, offered to colonise part of Ulster but his fleet was scattered by a storm in 1573. Most of his men died or deserted from their winter camps around Belfast but the survivors massacred the O'Neills. Devereux arrested MacPhelim at a meeting in Belfast and executed him, his wife and brother in Dublin. The queen ordered him to 'break off his enterprise' but he first defeated Turlough O'Neill and then massacred Sorley Boy MacDonnell's Scottish settlers.

Devereux returned to England in 1575 only to be appointed Earl Marshal of Ireland. He died as soon as he landed in Ireland and the Queen's favourite Robert Dudley, Earl of Leicester, was accused of poisoning him; even more so when he married Devereux's widow.

The Howard Martyrs, 1582-9
Elizabeth had executed Thomas Howard, 4th Duke of Norfolk, in 1572 for planning to marry Mary, Queen of Scots. His wayward son Philip succeeded as 20th Earl of Arundel in 1580 and attended a religious debate soon afterwards. He was so impressed by the Catholic argument that he renounced his excessive lifestyle and reconciled with his wife.

Henry Howard, 1st Earl of Northampton, made the mistake of arguing with his cousin Edward de Vere, 17th Earl of Oxford, in 1582 so he had him arrested for heresy and treasonable correspondence with Mary. The charges were dropped and Howard retired to write a book only for it to be denounced for its heretical and treasonable content. Philip Howard refused to support de Vere's allegations and the Howards joined forces, accusing him of everything from atheism to heresy, from treason to assassination, and from sexual perversions to alcoholism. A weary Privy Council eventually cleared all three men.

Philip Howard, 20th Earl of Arundel, tried to leave England without permission in 1585 but he was betrayed by a servant and arrested. Henry Herbert, 2nd Earl of Pembroke, accused Henry Howard of treason in April 1589, and de Vere retaliated by announcing that 'the Howards were the most treacherous race under heaven' and 'the Lord Howard was the worst villain that lived in this earth.'

Although Elizabeth never signed Philip Howard's death warrant he was under the impression she had. When he asked if he could see his wife and his newborn baby, the Queen replied, 'if he will but once attend the Protestant Service, he shall not only see his wife and children, but be restored to his honours and estates with every mark of my royal favour.' Philip possibly replied, 'tell Her Majesty if my religion be the cause for which I suffer, sorry I am that I have but one life to lose.' He never saw his family and died of dysentery in October 1595. It was some consolation for his family that the Church would later proclaim Philip a saint.

The Demise of Mary Queen of Scots, 1582-7

Henry Percy and Henry Howard were again arrested in September 1582 for conspiring with Francis Throckmorton. Although they were released, Percy met Mary's agents the Paget brothers in September 1583 to advise them where to land French troops. His companion William Shelley was arrested a few months later and he confessed Percy's intentions under torture. Percy was sent to the Tower for a third time and six months later was found dead in his cell. The jury returned a verdict of suicide but it was noted that Vice Chamberlain Sir Christopher Hatton had ordered the Lieutenant of the Tower, Sir Owen Hopton, to place the prisoner under the care of a new warder only the day before. Although no one dared say openly that Percy had been murdered, many thought it.

In 1586 Francis Walsingham exposed Anthony Babington's plot to organise a Spanish invasion of England and put Mary on the throne. There was now enough evidence to bring Mary to trial for treason and she was found guilty of being involved in 'things tending to the hurt, death and destruction of our royal person'. Around twenty conspirators were hung, drawn and quartered in September while Mary was imprisoned in Fotheringhay Castle.

Thomas Sackville, 1st Earl of Dorset, told Mary she had been sentenced to death and Elizabeth signed the death warrant with the proviso that it must not be carried out until she said so. But the Queen's Secretary of State, William Cecil, Lord Burghley, and the Queen's favourite Robert Dudley,

1st Earl of Leicester, went ahead with Mary's execution. She was beheaded at Fotheringhay Castle on 8 February 1587; Elizabeth was outraged.

Bad Marriages

William Knollys, 1st Earl of Banbury, was married to Dorothy who was twenty years his senior. But he took in Mary Fitton, a family friend's daughter, and fell in love with her. He was subjected to ridicule in court after she refused his advances.

Edward de Vere, 17th Earl of Oxford, was accused of fathering a child with Anne Vavasour, one of the Queen's maids of honour in 1581. Both parents and the child were imprisoned in the Tower for a time and there were brawls between the two families after they were released.

George Talbot, 6th Earl of Shrewsbury, married Bess of Hardwick in 1567 and Talbot's son Gilbert married Bess's daughter Mary a year later. Gilbert sided with his mother-in-law (who was also his stepmother) when George and Bess argued. But Gilbert refused to give Bess her part of her husband's inheritance when George died in 1590 and they too fell out.

Secret Seymour Marriages

Edward Seymour, 1st Earl of Hertford, wanted his marriage to Frances Howard annulled in 1595 because it was clear Queen Elizabeth was never going to marry. He planned to get his sons legitimised so they could make a claim to the throne. Elizabeth had Edward arrested when she found out his plans and Frances died soon afterwards.

Seymour secretly married (his third secret marriage) the wealthy widow Frances Prannell in 1601. The couple even employed a priest prepared to marry them without reading the banns or the necessary license. The priest was suspended for three years but the Seymour family tradition of secret marriages would continue.

Dudley's Influence Continues, 1584-8

Dudley's increasing influence over the Queen was viewed with suspicion and jealousy and a libellous document titled 'Leicester's Commonwealth' appeared in 1584, describing Dudley as Elizabeth's unscrupulous 'master courtier'. Dudley wanted a military expedition to Flanders to help William of Orange's rebels. But there was chaos when William was murdered and the Duke of Parma captured Antwerp in August 1585. Dudley led an English army to support the Dutch revolt and he was appointed Governor General of the United Provinces.

Elizabeth refused to be the sovereign of the United Provinces but she wanted the Dutch to follow Dudley's advice. She told him to avoid decisive action with Parma but he executed Grave's governor when the town of

Grave surrendered unexpectedly, infuriating his allies. Elizabeth was angry the war was costing too much and she delayed sending more money and troops, leaving Dudley powerless to do more. She did, however, order him to place a ban on trade with Spain, angering Dutch merchants. He then introduced economic reform, infuriating the Dutch members of the State Council.

Dudley returned to England in December 1586 and William Stanley and Rowland York immediately defected and handed over their fortresses to the Duke of Parma. Dudley was sent back to restore the situation the following summer but he lost the port of Sluis and was forced to negotiate with the Duke of Parma. He returned to England and resigned, having spent his fortune on the war. But Dudley then infuriated Elizabeth when he supported the Privy Council's decision to execute Mary, Queen of Scots, in the interests of the state against the Queen's instructions.

Dudley was appointed Lieutenant and Captain General of the Queen's Armies and Companies when the Spanish planned to invade in 1588. The English army was in no fit state to stop an invasion so it was fortunate that the Spanish Armada was scattered by a storm. Robert Dudley died soon afterwards and Elizabeth was deeply affected by the death of her close friend who she had lovingly nicknamed 'Eyes'. His brother Ambrose died two years later after having his gangrenous leg amputated.

The War with Spain, 1585-1604

Elizabeth did her best to avoid fighting on the continent until 1585. But an alliance between King Philip II of Spain and the French Catholic League undermined France's ability to stop Spanish control of the Netherlands. So the Spanish influence along the French coast threatened England while the Duke of Parma's siege of Antwerp resulted in the Treaty of Nonsuch between Elizabeth and the Dutch.

In July 1588 Spain sent an armada to attack England while Charles Neville, 6th Earl of Westmorland, gathered a force of English fugitives in Flanders and joined the Duke of Parma's army. The plan was to land in the west of England, protected by the armada. Robert Dudley, 1st Earl of Leicester, was appointed 'Lieutenant and Captain General of the Queen's Armies and Companies' as the Spanish Armada approached and he found disorganisation everywhere.

Faulty planning, poor weather and bad luck scattered the Spanish fleet and many ships were lost off the Irish coast. Meanwhile, militias assembled across England unaware the threat had passed. Henry Stanley, 4th Earl of Derby, tried to negotiate an end to the Anglo-Spanish War but he failed. Francis Drake and Robert Devereux, 2nd Earl of Essex, sailed to Spain in an unsuccessful attempt to take advantage of the Spanish disaster. Devereux and Thomas Howard, 1st Earl of Suffolk, would distinguish themselves by capturing Cádiz in 1596. The Anglo-Spanish War would last until the Treaty of London was agreed in 1604 but most of it was fought at sea.

The Hesketh Plot, 1593-6
The Stanley family were lawful heirs to the throne of England through Henry VIII's sister Mary Tudor, and Ferdinando Stanley inherited the claim when he succeeded his father as the 5th Earl of Derby in 1593. Soon afterwards Elizabeth's chief minister Lord Burghley received reports that exiled 'Papists' supported Ferdinando's claim.

Richard Hesketh was sent to talk to Ferdinando about his claim to the crown and the pair went to London to see his mother. But Ferdinando rejected the rebels' plan and he handed Hesketh over to the authorities even though he had been warned he would die if he rejected the offer. Hesketh was interrogated and executed while Ferdinando mysteriously died a few months later. Ferdinando's brother William inherited the earldom but his three nieces claimed their father's estates. Anne Stanley would become heir presumptive to the throne when Ferdinando's mother died in 1596.

Gamblers and Drunks
Despite having huge incomes from their estates, some earls fell into debt due to their excessive lifestyles. Henry Radclyffe, 4th Earl of Sussex, had succeeded his brother Thomas in 1583 but the estates were burdened by debt to the crown. So much so that Robert Radclyffe, 5th Earl of Sussex, petitioned the queen to cancel the liability in 1603.

Henry Wriothesley, 3rd Earl of Southampton, was exiled for fighting one of the queen's esquires in court in 1598. He returned briefly to secretly marry his pregnant mistress Elizabeth Vernon and then returned to Paris to gamble away his fortune, ignoring the Queen's calls to return to London. He eventually came back when he ran out of money and turned over the administration of his estates to trustees before he was thrown into prison.

George Clifford, 3rd Earl of Cumberland, was an accomplished jouster and a champion of the queen. However, he lost all of his money betting on jousting and horse racing and had to sell his lands. William Paulet, 4th Marquess of Winchester, fell into debt after entertaining the queen at his Basing House. Edward de Vere, 17th Earl of Oxford, died in 1604, presumably a happy man after eating, drinking and gambling his fortune away.

The Nine Years War, 1595-1603
Robert Devereux, 2nd Earl of Essex, was appointed Lord Lieutenant of Ireland in 1597 and he took a large army to Ireland to crush the O'Neills'

rebellion. But he failed to draw them into battle and the Irish rebels joked, 'he never drew sword but to make knights'. All Devereux could do was to agree an unpopular truce and return to England in 1599, against the Queen's instructions. He was briefly imprisoned in the summer of 1600 after William Cecil accused him of deserting his duty.

Devereux was anxious to explain his case and he marched into London accompanied by his supporters in February 1601 to request an audience with the queen. But Cecil proclaimed him a traitor so he withdrew and surrendered. He was found guilty of treason and executed on 25 February 1601, the last royal prisoner to be beheaded on Tower Green.

Devereux's brothers Francis and George were also imprisoned and fined; Roger would be fined three times more than any other conspirator. Henry Wriothesley, 3rd Earl of Southampton, had his death sentence commuted to life imprisonment while Roger Manners, 5th Earl of Rutland, was imprisoned for several months.

Chapter 25

James I
1603–25

King of England and Scotland, 1603
When it was clear Elizabeth I was going to die without an heir, Henry Percy, 9th Earl of Northumberland, sent Thomas Percy on three secret missions to Scotland. He visited the Protestant King James VI, her first cousin twice removed, to assure him that the English Catholics would accept him as their king if he did not persecute them.

Elizabeth died on 24 March 1603 and Robert Carey, 1st Earl of Monmouth, immediately rode to Holyrood to give James the news; he was appointed a Gentleman of the Bedchamber. The Privy Council deemed Monmouth's self-serving mission to be 'contrary to all decency, good manners and respect' so he was dismissed as soon as James arrived in London.

A Peace with Spain
One of the first acts of James's reign was to make peace with Spain. Henry Howard, 1st Earl of Northampton, and Admiral Thomas Howard, 1st Earl of Suffolk, negotiated the treaty in 1604 but Howard's wife became a Spanish informant, in return for an annual pension.

The King's Favourites
James I became well known for having favourites and he met his first, Philip Herbert, 4th Earl of Pembroke, while hunting in 1603. But Herbert was a heavy gambler and James had to pay off his debts when he got into financial difficulties. He also paid the debts of another favourite, James Hay, 1st Earl of Carlisle, and secured him a rich bride, Honoria, heir of Edward Denny. The next favourite was Robert Carr, who James helped nurse back to health after he broke his leg at a tilting match in 1607. He was given estates, made a Privy Councillor, and Secretary of State; James even wanted him to be his secretary when he tried to act as the Chief Minister of State.

The government was controlled by the Howards: Henry Howard, 1st Earl of Northampton; Thomas Howard, 1st Earl of Suffolk; his son-in-law William Knollys, 1st Earl of Banbury; Charles Howard, 1st Earl of Nottingham; and Sir Thomas Lake. They objected to Carr's interference and they saw their opportunity to replace him when James took a shine to 21-year-old George Villiers while out hunting in 1614.

Different Half-Brothers, 1605
Robert Cecil was described as having a gift for politics while his half-brother Thomas was said to be hardly fit to govern a tennis court. It did not stop James creating either of them earls in 1605; Robert the Earl of Salisbury and Thomas the Earl of Exeter.

The Gunpowder Plot, 1605
The repression of Catholics led to a plot to blow up the king and the Houses of Parliament during the state opening on the night of 4-5 November 1605. A letter warned William Parker not to attend (some believe he wrote it himself). He in turn showed it to Robert Cecil, 1st Earl of Salisbury, and then joined Thomas Howard, 1st Earl of Suffolk and Salisbury, as they searched the parliament cellars. Guy Fawkes was arrested and then the Keeper of the Palace, Sir Thomas Knyvet, found barrels filled with gunpowder. Parker was richly rewarded for exposing the plot.

Fawkes confessed under torture and the conspirators were soon rounded up. Thomas Percy had been shot dead while escaping but Fawkes and the rest were executed. Henry Percy, 9th Earl of Northumberland, was spared because he planned to attend Parliament on the fateful night, meaning he did not have direct involvement or knowledge of the plot. Even so he was fined a huge sum and held in the Tower for seventeen years.

Problem Marriages
William Herbert, 3rd Earl of Pembroke, was imprisoned after refusing to marry his pregnant mistress Mary Fitton. He was released when Mary's baby died but they were both barred from court. Herbert's punishment was to be forced to marry another Mary, the dwarfish and deformed daughter of Gilbert Talbot, 7th Earl of Shrewsbury, in 1604. He had no children with his unwelcome wife but he did have two illegitimate children with his cousin, yet another Mary.

Roger Manners, 5th Earl of Rutland, had contracted syphilis and his wife Elizabeth refused to consummate their marriage. She was further humiliated in 1605 when a goldsmith had her arrested for her husband's debts. He would die an early death from the disease.

Troubles in Ireland, 1603-8

There was serious disorder in Ireland when several towns refused to proclaim the Protestant James I their King. The ailing George Carew, 1st Earl of Totnes, worked to restore order before he returned to England. Matters took a turn for the worse when James Ley, 1st Earl of Marlborough, Ireland's Lord Chief Justice, had the English Book of Common Prayer translated into Irish so each church could possess a copy. He then tried to make it compulsory for all the Irish lords to attend a Protestant church. Meanwhile, the plantation of Protestant settlers in Ulster continued unabated.

A Secret Tudor Marriage, 1610

Gilbert Talbot, 7th Earl of Shrewsbury, had raised his orphaned niece Arbella Stuart, the daughter of Charles Stuart, 1st Earl of Lennox. Gilbert's wife helped her marry William Seymour, 2nd Earl of Hertford, in secret in 1610, an unusual match because Arbella was thirteen years his senior. But there was a motive because they were two distant Tudor claimants to the throne.

James I disapproved of the marriage and he sacked Gilbert from the Privy Council while his scheming wife was sent to the Tower. William was condemned to life imprisonment, the fourth of five generations of Seymours to spend time in the Tower. Seymour and Arbella escaped soon afterwards and while he reached Ostend, a storm stopped her sailing. Arbella was recaptured and would die in the Tower in 1615.

The Overbury Case, 1613-5

Thirteen-year-old Robert Devereux, 3rd Earl of Essex, was married to 14-year-old Frances Howard, the Earl of Suffolk's daughter, in 1604. He went on a European tour and she had an affair Robert Carr before he returned to consummate the marriage. Frances sought an annulment, stating Devereux was impotent, but he replied he was capable of performing with other women, adding that she 'reviled him, and miscalled him, terming him a cow and coward, and beast'.

Thomas Overbury persuaded Carr not to marry Frances, so Thomas Howard told James I that Overbury had been disrespectful to the queen. Overbury refused a position in the Russian court, to get him out of London, so he was imprisoned in the Tower in April 1613. Henry Howard, 1st Earl of Northampton, helped Frances obtain a divorce while subjecting Devereux to ridicule in court. Frances could finally marry Carr, who was now Earl of Somerset, but Frances had not finished with Overbury. Frances arranged for the Lord Lieutenant of the Tower, Gervase Helwys, to poison Overbury; her husband and father then interfered in the murder investigation.

Four conspirators were hanged after the facts came to the notice of the king's favourite, George Villiers in 1615. Henry Howard was already dead but Robert and Frances Carr and Thomas Howard were brought to trial. Devereux made sure he was on the jury and he pressured the king to execute his ex-wife. But the king was worried Robert Carr might implicate him in the case and he offered him a pardon if he pleaded guilty. He refused so both Carr and Howard were imprisoned in the Tower and condemned to death. But the sentences were never carried out and the two were released a few years later when the fuss had died down.

The King's New Favourite, 1614-24

Those opposed to Robert bought George Villiers new clothes and made him the royal cupbearer so he could talk to the king; he was soon infatuated. George became the king's constant companion and was nicknamed 'Steenie' after Saint Stephen because he had 'the face of an angel'.

In 1618 Thomas Howard, 1st Earl of Suffolk, tried in vain to groom another young man to succeed Villiers, to raise his profile with the king. He also spent huge amounts on naval ventures and built extravagant buildings to get the king's notice, but all it did was get him into debt. Howard worked for the Treasury and his wife helped him extort bribes from creditors of the crown until Villiers found out and he was suspended and fined for corruption.

Meanwhile, Villiers was showered with appointments, rising to Earl, Marquess, and then Duke of Buckingham in 1619 before he was appointed Lord Admiral of the Fleet. By 1623 Villiers was negotiating abroad on the king's behalf, inviting criticism from his rivals. Of course, his enemies suspected the king and George of being lovers.

Villiers had helped Francis Bacon become the Lord Chancellor in 1618 and he then used him to advance his relatives and friends. George's brother Christopher (or Kit) was an 'unattractive and unintelligent' man and his Earldom of Anglesey was delayed while the king persuaded him to give up his mistress. In short, Villiers' behaviour 'summed up all that was unsavoury and corrupt with the court of James'. Bacon was later convicted of corruption and forced to retire and Villiers did not speak up to save him, in case he was implicated.

Villiers became involved in the Irish plantations but his corrupt policies were subjected to an inquiry in 1621. He countered by starting arguments between the king and parliament over the proposed marriage of Prince Charles to the Spanish Princess Maria Anna, forcing Parliament to be dissolved. It ended the investigation into his malpractices in Ireland. But his Irish reforms were nullified when the Lord Treasurer, Lionel Cranfield, 1st Earl of Middlesex, was impeached. Cranfield reluctantly married

Villiers' relative Anne Brett to get his support but he was still found guilty of corruption. James was unimpressed with Villiers and warned Prince Charles that he would regret using impeachment as a parliamentary tool to get his own way.

Another of the king's favourites was the Scottish aristocrat John Ramsay, but they fell out when he did not get the Earldom of Montgomery in 1619. He retired to France until James lured him back with money and the Earldom of Holderness. The king then paid off Ramsay's debts and gave his new wife an annual grant.

The Main Plot and the Bye Plot, 1618

Henry Percy, 9th Earl of Northumberland, was passionate about science and was nicknamed the Wizard Earl. But some thought his experiments were linked to the occult and Robert Cecil, 1st Earl of Salisbury, warned Henry Howard, Earl of Northampton, about Percy and his acquaintances Henry Brooke and Walter Raleigh. Howard in turn warned King James that Percy intended to marry Arbella Stuart and then place her on the throne. The three of them were arrested in 1603 in what became known as the Main Plot and the Bye Plot. Brooke and Raleigh were imprisoned but Percy was appointed to the Privy Council. Raleigh would be executed after thirteen years in the Tower.

In another occult case around the same time, Francis Manners, 6th Earl of Rutland and owner of Belvoir Castle in Leicestershire, lost his two young sons, Henry and Francis. Three women were accused of causing their deaths through witchcraft and the 'Witches of Belvoir' were condemned to death.

The Colonies

England's colonies around the world developed and expanded during James I's reign. Philip Herbert, Earl of Pembroke and Montgomery, James Hay, 1st Earl of Carlisle, Edward Sackville, 4th Earl of Dorset, Robert Rich, 2nd Earl of Warwick, and William Cavendish, 1st Earl of Devonshire, were all involved in the Virginia Company. Henry Wriothesley, 3rd Earl of Southampton, worked to make Jamestown a permanent colony but the king 'roundly and soundly' criticised all the colonists for their mismanagement and the company folded in 1624.

There were other colonies in the Americas. Ludovic Stewart, 2nd Duke of Lennox and 1st Duke of Richmond, helped colonise Maine in New England. Henry Howard, 1st Earl of Northampton, established the London and Bristol Company in 1610 to exploit Newfoundland, while Philip Herbert, Earl of Pembroke and Montgomery, invested in the Northwest Passage Company in 1612. Sackville and Cavendish took part in the colonisation of the Bermuda Islands while Hay bought the Caribbean interests of James Ley, 1st Earl of Marlborough. In the east, Philip Herbert,

Earl of Pembroke and Montgomery, and Robert Rich, 2nd Earl of Warwick, were members of the Honourable East India Company.

The Veres and the Villiers Argue, 1617-23

Edward Coke wanted to improve his status in court so he offered his daughter Frances's hand to John Villiers, brother of the king's favourite, George. King James approved of the match but Frances's mother, Hatton, was against it and she wanted her to marry Henry de Vere, 18th Earl of Oxford, instead. But Frances was already married to Villiers by the time Henry returned from his European tour in 1617. Arguments followed until Villiers got his brother to post de Vere to a ship guarding the English Channel in 1621.

De Vere was later imprisoned in the Tower after stopping Christopher Villiers marrying his cousin Elizabeth Norris. His statement summed up the situation at court because he 'hoped the time would come when justice would be free and not pass only through Buckingham's hands.'

De Vere was freed in 1623 and he married Diana, daughter of William Cecil, 2nd Earl of Exeter, a beautiful bride with a huge dowry. But he had not forgotten his quarrel with his first love rival and refused to reconcile with Villiers.

Bribers and Gamblers

Richard Sackville, 3rd Earl of Dorset, was described an 'accomplished gambler and wastrel' but he managed to marry Lady Anne Clifford. In 1617 he made her sign away her claim to her ancestral lands, to clear his gambling debts. His brother Edward had to sell off more estates to pay off debts when he succeeded as the 4th Earl of Dorset in 1624. William Cavendish had the opposite experience. He came into money when his mother and older brother died and he paid the crown £10,000 for the Earldom of Devonshire in 1618.

The Spanish Match, 1623

Henry, Prince of Wales, was a tall, strong man but he died in November 1612 aged 18. His brother, the weak, stammering 11-year-old Charles became heir apparent and was raised by Robert Carey, 1st Earl of Monmouth, with his wife Elizabeth.

Charles had been baptised a Protestant and parliament was against him marrying a Catholic princess when James started negotiating an alliance with Spain in 1621. James insisted the royal match was nothing to do with parliament while Charles thought they were interfering with a royal privilege. Henry de Vere, 18th Earl of Oxford, was even imprisoned in the Tower for speaking out against the matter.

Charles and George Villiers, Duke of Buckingham, travelled anonymously to Spain in February 1623 with the diplomat John Digby, 1st Earl of Bristol. Robert Carey, 1st Earl of Monmouth, William Feilding, 1st Earl of Denbigh, and Edward Montagu, 2nd Earl of Manchester, also accompanied them on the important visit. Tough negotiations followed in which King Philip IV of Spain wanted toleration for English Catholics and asked Charles to convert to Catholicism before he married his daughter. He also wanted the princess to remain in Spain for a year to make sure Charles stuck to his promises.

The mood of the meeting worsened when Villiers argued with the Count of Olivares, the Spanish chief minister. Princess Maria Anna was also not impressed with her suitor and Charles returned to London in October empty-handed. King Philip went so far as to ask for the disrespectful Villiers to be executed, so he retaliated by calling for a war with Spain. An embarrassed Charles asked Digby to take the blame and he was imprisoned in the Tower when he refused. His trial was halted when the House of Lords asked to hear Digby's defence first.

King James was ill by 1624 and Charles was ruling the country in all but name. Of course, Villiers was at his side and he led the negotiations for a marriage with Princess Henrietta Maria of France. Charles's marriage by proxy to a Catholic bride was unpopular but no one could stop it. She became queen when James died in March 1625 and Charles became king.

Chapter 26

Charles I
1625–41

Opposing the King, 1626-8

Charles immediately introduced unpopular policies. He started in 1626 by imposing a 'forced loan' on the nobility to pay for a war against France. He imprisoned anyone who refused to pay, like Oliver St John, 1st Earl of Bolingbroke, and Thomas Wentworth, 1st Earl of Strafford. Theophilus Clinton, 4th Earl of Lincoln, was then imprisoned in the Tower after circulating a pamphlet accusing the king of trying to overthrow parliament. Thomas Wentworth, 1st Earl of Strafford, and William Seymour, 2nd Earl of Hertford, were just two of many who supported the Petition of Right to curb the king's powers in 1628.

Villiers Loses Popularity, 1627-8

Charles supported George Villiers, 1st Duke of Buckingham, the only man from James's court who kept his position. But Villiers was blamed when he could not to recover the Electorate of the Palatinate and for failing to capture the Spanish port of Cádiz in 1625. He then failed to intercept a fleet carrying a huge amount of silver from the New World to Spain.

Villiers also negotiated a deal in which English ships would fight the Huguenots and Parliament was horrified that English Protestants were fighting French Protestants. He would see his army defeated when they tried to help French Protestants at the siege of La Rochelle in 1627. James Hay, 1st Earl of Carlisle, called for peace with Spain and a new war with France when the siege failed but his advice was ignored so he withdrew from public life.

Algernon Percy, 10th Earl of Northumberland, headed the faction opposing Villiers in the House of Lords and the king had to intervene to stop parliament prosecuting him on two occasions. Public opinion took a hand in matters when the mob murdered his advisor Doctor Lambe. Villiers was stabbed to death in a Portsmouth pub in August 1628 by John Felton, an army officer, and the public applauded his actions. Villiers' son would be raised in the royal household alongside the princes Charles and James.

Problem Marriages, 1626-30

William Knollys was created Earl of Banbury in 1626 and he remarried even though he was aged 82. His wife had two children but the House of Lords doubted their legitimacy and refused to let them keep the earldom.

Algernon Percy, 10th Earl of Northumberland, chose to marry Anne, daughter of William Cecil, 2nd Earl of Salisbury, in 1629 against his father's wishes. Henry Percy blamed William for his seventeen-year imprisonment in the Tower following the 1605 Gunpowder Plot and warned that 'the blood of a Percy would not mix with the blood of a Cecil if you poured it on a dish.'

There was a scandal when Emanuel Scrope, 1st Earl of Sunderland, died in 1630. His four children had all died young so he left his estates to the illegitimate children he had had with his maid Martha, rather than his legitimate relatives.

The Tyranny, 1629-40

Charles opened the second session of Parliament in January 1629 but there was opposition to his taxation policies. He soon wanted an adjournment but the members pinned the speaker in his chair until their resolutions had been read out. Charles had nine parliamentary leaders arrested and dissolved Parliament. He then ruled for eleven years without recalling it, in a period known as the 'Personal Rule' or the 'Tyranny'. Thomas Wentworth, 1st Earl of Strafford, headed the royal advisors, called the Thorough Party, but only parliament had the legal right to raise taxes. It left the treasury short of money and Charles had to make peace with France and Spain.

The Scottish Covenanters, 1637

The Scottish Covenanters opposed the introduction of the Book of Common Prayer into Scotland in 1637. George Villiers, 2nd Duke of Buckingham, supported an alliance with the Scottish Presbyterians and accompanied the king to Scotland in June. But the war was opposed by some, including Algernon Percy, 10th Earl of Northumberland, who knew his northern estates were vulnerable to attack. Philip Herbert, Earl of Pembroke and Montgomery, Henry Rich, 1st Earl of Holland, and William Cecil, 2nd Earl of Salisbury, also urged the king to accept the Scots' terms but he ignored their warnings. He ordered Pembroke to return to London to raise funds for a new war with Scotland.

Drunks and Gamblers

Charles I's court became notorious for self-indulgent behaviour but some took their antics too far. Robert Dormer, 1st Earl of Carnarvon, was addicted to gambling and hunting, while Christopher Villiers, 1st Earl of Anglesey, was banned from court because of his drunken behaviour. James Hay, 1st Earl of Carlisle, ran up huge debts entertaining, spending all the money the king loaned to him.

Thomas Howard, 21st Earl of Arundel, inherited large estates in Nottinghamshire, Yorkshire and Derbyshire when he married Alatheia, daughter of Gilbert Talbot, 7th Earl of Shrewsbury. He acquired a taste for art while acting as an envoy around Europe and became known as the 'Collector Earl'. He also invested in new buildings but his activities left him heavily in debt.

The Bishops' Wars, 1638-40

Charles I wanted uniformity between the churches on the Anglican model. He stirred up opposition when he imposed the Book of Common Prayer in Scotland but the General Assembly of the Church of Scotland abolished it in November 1638. Skirmishes along the border resulted in the Pacification of Berwick.

Charles also wanted a church government ruled by bishops in Scotland but another General Assembly abolished the bishops and declared itself free from royal control. After eleven years of ruling alone, Charles called parliament in April 1640 hoping to get its support. Instead parliament made several demands Charles would not agree to and he dissolved the Short Parliament.

Thomas Wentworth, Earl of Strafford, organised a second invasion of Scotland but the Scots won the battle of Newburn on 28 August. Lieutenant General Henry Wilmot, 1st Earl of Rochester, was captured but George Monck, 1st Duke of Albemarle, saved the English artillery. The Scots then seized Northumberland and Durham and Francis Leigh, 1st Earl of Chichester, had to agree the peace under the Treaty of Ripon. Charles was forced to recall parliament in October 1640, to raise money to pay the Scottish expenses. This time the Long Parliament would sit for eight years and it would impeach Wentworth; he would eventually be executed. Charles had to accept what the General Assembly and the Scottish Parliament wanted in the autumn of 1641.

An Irish Army, 1640-1

Thomas Wentworth had been appointed Lord Deputy of Ireland in 1632 and he set about reforming the administration. He planned to break the power of the Irish Catholic gentry by appointing juries to identify defective titles. They then set about confiscating land and raising extra customs duties but the money went to the crown instead of being spent in Ireland. Richard Burke, 1st Earl of St Albans, Governor of Connaught, opposed Wentworth's actions and the arguments were said to have accelerated his death in 1635. Wentworth sarcastically retorted by saying he was not to blame for the death of a man over 60. Wentworth was recalled to England in September 1639 and was created Earl of Strafford.

Charles raised an army to fight the Scottish Covenanters but the House of Commons called for peace. Wentworth was given command of the English army but fell ill and Charles sued for peace under the Treaty of Berwick. In November 1640 the Long Parliament accused Strafford of 'high misdemeanours' in Ireland and imprisoned him in the Tower. His crime had been to tell the king that there was 'an army in Ireland you may employ here to reduce this kingdom'; he argued that carrying out the king's wishes was not a treasonable act.

The impeachment failed but Wentworth was attainted following the Army Plot in May 1641. General Henry Wilmot, 1st Earl of Rochester, was imprisoned in the Tower and Henry Jermyn, 1st Earl of St Albans, fled to France when the plot was discovered. William Cavendish, 1st Duke of Newcastle upon Tyne, was also involved but he remained loyal to the king because he believed the monarchy 'was the foundation and support of his own greatness'.

Oliver St John, 1st Earl of Bolingbroke, made his 'foxes and wolves' speech in favour of the attainder. Meanwhile, George Digby opposed Strafford's attainder and spoke out about the weakness of the evidence. But Digby was accused of stealing the prosecution notes and the House of Commons protested by having the hangman burn his speech. Colonel Lord Goring then warned the Master of Ordnance, Mountjoy Blount, 1st Earl of Newport, of a Royalist plot to capture London, seize the Tower and rescue the king. Wentworth's fate was sealed and Charles refused to support him because he dared not oppose parliament.

Wentworth's sentence split opinion and Charles became angry when Philip Herbert, Earl of Pembroke and Montgomery, encouraged a crowd to jeer at the condemned man. Algernon Percy, 10th Earl of Northumberland, had given evidence against Wentworth but he still helped his brother Henry try to rescue Wentworth from the Tower. Edward Hyde, 1st Earl of Clarendon, and William Cavendish, 3rd Earl of Devonshire, opposed Wentworth's conviction while John Digby, 1st Earl of Bristol, and John Holles, 2nd Earl of Clare, were just two of those who tried to save his life. They all failed and Wentworth was eventually executed in January 1645.

The Royal Marriage, 1641

Edward Sackville, 4th Earl of Dorset, was described as 'beautiful, graceful and vigorous: his wit pleasant, sparkling, and sublime'. He used his charms to arrange the marriage of the Princess Mary to the Prince of Orange in 1642 and then accompanied her to the marriage.

The Run up to War, 1641-2

The Long Parliament passed the Dissolution Act in May 1641. It formalised the king's means to raise taxes, attacked the bishops and demanded that parliament would be summoned at least once every three years. Charles's supporters countered the 'wicked counsels' of government by issuing the 'Protestation'; they also had Wentworth arrested. There was an uneasy stand-off between the royalists and the parliamentarians in England but many, including John Robartes, 1st Earl of Radnor, were worried by Charles I's determination to impose his religious policy and autocratic rule, believing he was being misled by wicked councillors. But it was the Irish Catholics who rebelled first because they were worried about an increase of Protestant rule.

Charles went to the House of Commons accompanied by troops at the beginning of January 1642, expecting to arrest five members for treason, including Edward Montagu, 2nd Earl of Manchester. But Robert Devereux, 3rd Earl of Essex, had warned them and they had already left when the soldiers entered the chamber. The Speaker, William Lenthall, told the king 'I have neither eyes to see nor tongue to speak in this place but as the House is pleased to direct me, whose servant I am here.' A few days later Charles left London with his family, fearing for their safety.

Different areas of the country declared their loyalties during the spring and summer and local grievances often decided which side they chose. Most urban areas wanted a balanced government and they favoured Parliament while most rural communities wanted a traditional government and supported the king. While there were views across the spectrum, virtually everyone wanted the king to stay on the throne. There were only small numbers of troops involved to begin with but some areas formed local militias to protect their communities from ill-disciplined soldiers.

Charles received an early setback when Sir John Hotham, the military governor of Kingston upon Hull, refused to hand over the cache of weapons used for the recent Scottish campaign. George Digby fled to the Dutch Republic after being ordered to appear in the Lords to answer a charge of high treason for an armed attempt to seize the port. Charles later moved to Nottingham and raised the royal standard on 22 August 1642. His next move was to march south-west, and en route he made the Wellington Declaration to uphold the 'Protestant religion, the laws of England, and the liberty of Parliament'.

The nobility raised regiments under the ancient system called the Commission of Array. General Henry Wilmot, 1st Earl of Rochester, had raised a regiment of horse for the king and he was wounded at the battle of Powick Bridge near Worcester on 23 September. It was the first major skirmish of the war.

Chapter 27

Civil War
1642–49

Conflict in Devon, 1642

Henry Bourchier, 5th Earl of Bath, secretly moved his household to Devon when war threatened in June 1642. He then headed there when Charles I issued a commission of array to organise, arm and train forces in July. Bourchier rejected a summons to attend the House of Lords but his 'sour-tempered unsocial behaviour' hindered his recruitment attempts. His cavaliers were driven off by an angry mob when they entered South Molton. Parliament imprisoned Bourchier in the Tower for a year. After his release he refused to go into exile on the Continent and joined the royal court at Oxford. He was appointed Commissioner for the Defence of Oxford but abandoned it and left for Devon as soon as the Parliamentarian army approached.

Lancashire, 1642-3

James Stanley, 7th Earl of Derby, wanted to secure Lancashire but the king banned him from raising troops on his estates because he was jealous of his power. Later on he was defeated at Chowbent and Lowton Moor and while he seized Preston in 1643, he could not capture Bolton and Lancaster from the Parliamentarians.

The Battle of Edgehill, 1642

Edward Hyde, 1st Earl of Clarendon, summed up the Royalists' next move by saying, 'it was considered more counsellable to march towards London, it being morally sure that Essex would put himself in their way.' King Charles's dynamic nephew Prince Rupert, Count Palatine of the Rhine, Duke of Bavaria, Duke of Cumberland and Earl of Holderness, made a forced march to take the high ground at Edgehill where the armies clashed on 23 October 1642.

Robert Bertie, 1st Earl of Lindsey, then wanted to deploy their troops in the Swedish fashion, to maximise their firepower, but Rupert would only take orders from the king. So Bertie Lindsey resigned and was replaced by Jacob Astley. Lieutenant General Henry Wilmot, 1st Earl of Rochester, made an impressive charge against the Parliamentarians but his cavalry then scattered, throwing away the victory. A badly injured Bertie was rescued by his son Montagu. The battle was inconclusive but the highest-ranking member of the government on Parliament's side, Algernon Percy, 10th Earl of Northumberland, was appalled by the violence.

There was then a stand-off at Turnham Green and John Digby, 1st Earl of Bristol, was one of the 'moderate party' who persuaded Charles to withdraw to Oxford, his base for the rest of the war. If he had marched to London, it could have ended the war.

The Savages Ravaged, 1643
The Civil War affected all families in different ways but Elizabeth Savage, Countess Rivers, suffered more than most. She was cross-examined for supporting Charles I and Parliamentarian troops attacked and then seized her lands. Although they were restored, her tenants refused to pay rent and she had to go into exile when they were taken a second time. A destitute Elizabeth would return home when the war ended.

The Battles of Hopton Heath, Roundway Down and First Newbury, 1643
In March, Spencer Compton, 2nd Earl of Northampton, failed to take Lichfield so he headed to Stafford and engaged the Parliamentarians at Hopton Heath on the 19th. He routed Parliament's cavalry and captured eight guns but he charged too far forward and became surrounded. He was executed after refusing quarter. The Royalists defeated Henry Grey, 1st Earl of Stamford, at the battle of Stratton on 16 May 1643. He withdrew to Exeter and was charged with cowardice when he surrendered three months later.

The Royalists gained control of Yorkshire after the battle of Adwalton Moor on 30 June and there was a Royalist victory at Lansdowne in Somerset on 5 July. Lieutenant General Henry Wilmot, 1st Earl of Rochester, then defeated William Waller at the battle of Roundway Down on 13 July. It secured the royalist position in the west, allowing Prince Rupert to capture Bristol. Around the same time, Oliver Cromwell won the battle of Gainsborough for Parliament with his disciplined troop of 'Ironsides'.

Robert Pierrepont, 1st Earl of Kingston-upon-Hull, was captured at Gainsborough. He had declared himself neutral at the start of the war, saying, 'When I take arms with the king against Parliament or with the

Parliament against the king, let a cannon-ball divide me between them.' He later became a general of the royalist forces in the eastern counties. He was being taken by boat along the River Trent to Hull when a royalist cannon ball killed him, fulfilling his prophesy.

By the early autumn, Royalist control was at its peak but things were about to change. It started when Robert Devereux, 3rd Earl of Essex, forced the king to raise the siege of Gloucester. He then defeated the Royalists at the First Battle of Newbury on 20 September 1643 and returned to London. In the north Parliamentary forces had won the battle of Winceby, allowing them to take Lincoln.

George Digby was appointed secretary of state in September 1643. His decision to support Queen Henrietta's ideas to use Irish troops and look to form foreign alliances embarrassed the king, but Charles was feeling the pressure because he was losing areas to Parliament so he negotiated a ceasefire in Ireland, releasing troops to fight for him in England.

The Parliamentarians were also looking for help elsewhere and they offered concessions to the Scots in return for assistance. But some, like Henry Rich, 1st Earl of Holland, John Holles, 2nd Earl of Clare, and William Russell, 1st Duke of Bedford, were in the parliamentary 'peace party' which wanted a settlement. Russell switched sides when Robert Devereux, 3rd Earl of Essex, rejected the idea and while Charles pardoned him, the king's advisors refused to work with him. He returned to the Parliamentary side only to find they too were wary of him, so he went home after being refused entry to the House of Lords.

The Battles of Cheriton, Marston Moor and Second Newbury 1644
Parliament's power was increasing but the king had arranged reinforcements from Ireland. But the Irish army was defeated at the battle of Nantwich on 25 January and George Monck, 1st Duke of Albemarle, was captured by Thomas Fairfax; he would spend two years in the Tower.

Rupert had taken over the Northern Command but it faced the Scottish army marching south to support Parliament's cause. Rupert was running out of time and although he raised the siege of Newark in March, he could not be everywhere at once. Charles was also hoping for help in the north after promising James Graham the Marquisate of Montrose, so he would bring his Scottish troops south of the border.

The Royalists were defeated at Cheriton in Hampshire on 29 March and Charles withdrew to Oxford. There was a small Royalist victory at Cropredy Bridge on 29 June but while events were inconclusive in the south, they had reached a decision in the north. The Parliamentarian victory at Marston Moor on 2 July meant they held York and had secured their position, while Oliver Cromwell was becoming an important military leader. But it was a different story in the south where Robert Devereux, 3rd Earl of Essex, tried to capture the West Country. The Royalists forced Parliament's troops to surrender at Lostwithiel in Cornwall on 2 September and Devereux had to escape in a fishing boat. The battle of Newbury on 27 October was indecisive but it gave Parliament another check.

The war was dragging on; Parliament held the north and the Royalists were dominant in the south. While nepotism and privilege ruled the Royalist cause, Parliament knew it had to reform its army, proposing that 'no member of either house shall have or execute any office or command'. While the first 'self-denying ordinance' was turned down in December 1644, a second attempt succeeded four months later. At last Parliament could start to form a professionally organised and competently led military force.

Personal Feuds, 1644

Sometimes the war started personal rivalries. Lieutenant General Henry Wilmot, 1st Earl of Rochester, advised the king to dismiss Lord Digby and the Chancellor of the Exchequer, Sir John Culpeper, and then march on London in June 1644. He contacted the Parliamentarian commander-in-chief, Robert Devereux, when the king ignored him so Digby and Culpeper accused him of treason.

Wilmot was imprisoned in Exeter but was released after officers petitioned on his behalf and he joined the court of Queen Henrietta Maria in France. But it did not end there because Digby defeated Wilmot in a duel in Paris three years later.

The Battle of Naseby and the End of the First War, 1645

Parliament formed its New Model Army, promising regular wages in return for serving wherever it was ordered, but it would take time to organise units and instil discipline in the new recruits. The Royalists had campaigned in the west but their sieges were indecisive and when Rupert marched north, the Parliamentarian forces converged and forced him back.

There was a general war-weariness across the kingdom but the Royalist diehards were fighting for survival while the Parliamentarians were determined to defeat them. Rupert tried to move north again in April only to be stopped by Cromwell's cavalry so the king concentrated all his forces around Oxford. The New Model Army were slow to react and the main Royalist army had marched north by the time it invested the king's capital.

Charles reached the Midlands and then turned east, so Fairfax was told to abandon the siege of Oxford and track down the Royalist army. While Cromwell joined the New Model Army, an insubordinate George Goring, 1st Earl of Norwich, refused to reinforce the king. The two armies clashed at Naseby on 14 June and the New Model Army annihilated their opponents.

A complete Royalist defeat was only a matter of time and their last large field army was destroyed at Langport on 10 July.

The king headed to South Wales hoping to raise a new army, only to discover that Irish levies serving under Charles Gerard, 1st Earl of Macclesfield, had been on the rampage in the area. Charles had to sack Gerard before anyone would join him and he then had to head for Chester because Bristol had fallen. One by one the Royalist strongholds of Hereford, Dartmouth, Chester, Exeter, and Newark fell, and the final battle in the open was at Stow-on-the-Wold on 21 March 1646. Charles surrendered to the Scottish army on 5 May and then Oxford and Worcester fell. Wallingford and Raglan castles were the last two Royalist garrisons to surrender.

The King in Custody, 1646-7
Charles escaped from Oxford, a city under siege, disguised as a servant in April 1646 and he joined the Scottish Presbyterian army as it marched north. Algernon Percy, 10th Earl of Northumberland, was guardian of the king's three young children but Edward Hyde, 1st Earl of Clarendon, took the king's heir Charles, Prince of Wales, to Jersey to escape the Parliamentarian soldiers.

After nine months of negotiations the Scots handed Charles over in return for money in January 1647 and he was held under house arrest in several locations. While Parliament and the New Model Army argued over how the country should be ruled, Charles escaped from Hampton Court in November. He met Colonel Robert Hammond, Governor of the Isle of Wight, thinking he was a supporter, only to find himself being handed in. In December Charles took the desperate step to sign a secret treaty with the Scots called the 'Engagement'. They would invade England and put him back on the throne on the promise he would restore Presbyterianism in England for the next three years.

The Second Civil War, 1648
The end of the Civil War left the Presbyterians, the New Model Army and the remaining Royalists at odds over who would rule the country. But they all needed the king to make their cause viable and he knew it. For two years the Army and Parliament argued until the Presbyterians combined with the Scots and the Royalists and launched a rebellion in South Wales in February 1648, sparking a Second Civil War.

By April the Scots were arming while some Royalists had taken Berwick and Carlisle. But most Royalists had promised not to bear arms against the Parliament and they faced harsh treatment if they were captured because they had served 'Charles Stuart, that man of blood'. For example, George Villiers, 2nd Duke of Buckingham, was lucky to escape when his force was overwhelmed at St Neots. But Henry Rich, 1st Earl of Holland, was captured and was told he 'may spend time as well as he can and have leisure to repent his juvenile folly.' He was put on trial in February 1649, condemned as a traitor and executed.

Kent rose in revolt in May and then the Navy defected, placing itself under the command of the Prince of Wales. Maidstone was stormed on 1 June and then attention turned to the South Downs. Thirty Flemish ships arrived with 1,500 mercenaries on 16 July but the Royalists could not pay them so they deserted. The deadlock in the south was broken on 23 August when a message containing news of Cromwell's victory at Preston was fired into Deal Castle tied to an arrow. Deal and Sandown surrendered, ending the Kentish rebellion.

A Scottish Engager army had assembled on the border in July 1648, but the English uprisings were coming to an end. The Kirk party had refused to sanction 'The Engagement' so James Hamilton, Duke of Hamilton, could not rally experienced men to his cause. On 17 August Cromwell's New Model Army scattered the much larger Scots militia army near Preston; they were then driven south until they surrendered on 25 August. Arthur Capell, 1st Earl of Essex, was defending Colchester so Lord Fairfax's soldiers took his teenage son to the town and carried him around the works to persuade his father to surrender. He eventually did at the end of August, bringing the Second Civil War to an end.

The Trial and Execution of a King, 1649
Although Parliament wanted to try to negotiate with Charles, Oliver Cromwell and the army opposed the idea. In December the dissenters were either arrested or excluded by Colonel Thomas Pride in Pride's Purge. Some stayed away leaving the remaining members to form the Rump Parliament.

The king was indicted on a charge of treason in January 1649. All the courts rejected it as unlawful, so the Rump Commons created their own court. But not everyone agreed because only 68 out of 135 commissioners attended the trial. Charles was charged 'for accomplishment of such his designs, and for the protecting of himself and his adherents in his and their wicked practices, to the same ends hath traitorously and maliciously levied war against the present Parliament, and the people therein represented.'

Witnesses were produced to back the charge that 'wicked designs, wars, and evil practices of him, have been, and are carried on for the advancement and upholding of a personal interest of will, power, and pretended prerogative to himself and his family, against the public interest, common right, liberty, justice, and peace of the people of this nation.' King Charles was found 'guilty of all the treasons, murders, rapines, burnings, spoils, desolations, damages and mischiefs to this nation, acted and committed in the said wars, or occasioned thereby.'

Charles refused to plead, insisting the court was illegal and it had no jurisdiction over a monarch. The court replied that 'the King of England was not a person, but an office whose every occupant was entrusted with a limited power to govern by and according to the laws of the land and not otherwise.' Charles was condemned to death and fifty-nine commissioners signed his death warrant. The king had few friends left but William Seymour, 2nd Earl of Hertford, remained with him until he was led out to his death. He was executed in front of the Palace of Whitehall's Banqueting House on 30 January in front of a huge crowd; the only time a monarch was publically executed.

Many were horrified by the execution, including Edward Hyde, 1st Earl of Clarendon, who thought the king had been led astray by his favourites. Some took it very seriously, like Francis Leke, 1st Earl of Scarsdale, who dressed himself in sackcloth and laid in an open grave every Friday in commemoration of his dead king.

Chapter 28

The Cromwells
1649–59

An Invasion of Ireland, 1649-50

George Monck, 1st Duke of Albemarle, had experience of fighting in Ireland so he was sent across the Irish Sea to fight the rebels. He swore loyalty to the Parliamentary cause and his conscience allowed him to face the Irish because he was not taking arms against the king. But Monck was unable to suppress Owen Roe O'Neill and while he agreed an armistice, Parliament refused to accept it.

The Scottish Covenanters agreed to the Solemn League and Covenant, an agreement to preserve their reformed religion. Monck responded by joining the Royalist cause, under the command of Hugh Montgomery, 1st Earl of Mount Alexander. Parliament quickly rejected the truce he had made.

James FitzThomas Butler, 1st Duke of Ormonde, commanded the Irish Confederates and English Royalist troops in Ireland. Cromwell's troops landed in Ireland in 1649 and routed the Confederates at the battle of Rathmines in August. The New Model Army's brutal sack of Drogheda convinced some towns to surrender but others fought on despite fearing a massacre. By May 1650 Charles II had given up on the Irish Confederates and he allied with the Scottish Covenanters. FitzThomas's Protestant troops switched to Cromwell and he left Ireland soon afterwards. Heber MacMahon's Ulster army was defeated at the battle of Scarrifholis in June and then Limerick and Galway were taken.

The Catholic Confederates had lost their trust in FitzThomas, so he was exiled to France and his lands were confiscated as organised fighting came to an end. Guerrilla warfare followed and the rebels were known as 'Tories' from the Irish for pursued man (*tóraidhe*). Famine and the plague swept Ireland as the rebels were executed and soldiers exiled. Cromwell confiscated lands from Catholics and either sold them to raise the army's wages or gave them to soldiers in lieu of payment.

Scotland, 1650-4

George Monck, 1st Duke of Albemarle, fought alongside Oliver Cromwell at the victory of the battle of Dunbar in 1650. He was appointed commander-in-chief in Scotland and completed the defeat of the Scots. After spending time at Bath in England, restoring his health, Monck returned to Scotland and defeated a Royalist insurrection in the Highlands. He took the opportunity to remove dissidents, who were called 'enthusiasts', from the army after discovering his second in command, Robert Overton, was plotting a rebellion in 1654.

The Battle of Worcester, 1651

Prince Charles had spent the Second Civil War in exile in The Hague and his father was executed on 30 January 1649. Scotland's Covenanter Parliament proclaimed him king but refused to let him enter their territory until he accepted Presbyterianism. Oliver Cromwell defeated the Covenanters at the battle of Dunbar in September 1650 and Charles's attempt to join the royalist Engagers failed. Even so, he was crowned King of Scotland in January 1651.

Charles headed south across the border with an army and was met by George Villiers, 2nd Duke of Buckingham, in Lancashire. Lieutenant General Henry Wilmot, 1st Earl of Rochester, joined the king and James Stanley, 7th Earl of Derby, landed in Lancashire and swelled the numbers of the Royalist army marching south. But Charles was defeated at Worcester on 3 September 1651 and Thomas Wentworth, 1st Earl of Cleveland, had to help him escape the town. John Talbot, 10th Earl of Shrewsbury, led Charles to Shropshire and Wilmot took him on a six-week journey in disguise to escape England. He had several close escapes including the famous episode where he hid in an oak tree in the grounds of Boscobel House in Shropshire. Meanwhile, a new act of parliament declared those who contacted Charles guilty of treason.

The Protectorate, 1653

By 1653 the threats from Scotland and Ireland were over and it was time to consider what form Cromwell's rule should take. Many opposed the Rump Parliament but it also stopped the country becoming a military dictatorship. Oliver Cromwell was declared Lord Protector of the 'Commonwealth of England, Scotland and Ireland' following its dissolution in 1653. It heralded the start of the period of rule known as the Protectorate.

Members of the Council of State had differing views and while some wanted a republic, others wanted a type of monarchical government. For example, Anthony Ashley Cooper, 1st Earl of Shaftesbury, opposed Cromwell's attempt to rule without parliament, Edward Montagu, 1st Earl of Sandwich, was a member of the 'the kinglings' who urged Cromwell to proclaim himself King, and Charles Howard, 1st Earl of Carlisle, voted for the protector's assumption of the royal title.

Fined Royalists

The Parliamentarians set about charging the king's supporters for being 'Papists and delinquents', the terms for Catholics and Royalists. They drew up a list of crimes which included deserting the House of Lords, taking up arms against Parliament, raising troops for the king, lending money to the king, sitting in the king's Oxford assembly and accepting appointments from the king.

They imposed a range of punishments on the royalists; for example, Francis Leigh lost his Earldom of Chichester and was given a year to pay his fine, while Henry Bourchier, 5th Earl of Bath, was fined annually. John Paulet, 5th Marquess of Winchester, John Talbot, 10th Earl of Shrewsbury, William Craven, 1st Earl of Craven, and William Cavendish, 3rd Earl of Devonshire, were just some who had their lands confiscated. Some suffered personal loss like Philip Stanhope, 1st Earl of Chesterfield, whose son was killed and his house was burnt down; he eventually died in prison.

Some Royalists went into exile to avoid the Parliamentary punishments: George Villiers, 2nd Duke of Buckingham, escaped to Italy and John Digby, 1st Earl of Bristol, and Edward Somerset, 2nd Marquess of Worcester, left for Paris. Those who returned were imprisoned and would have to wait until Charles II's 1662 Act of Settlement until they received any compensation.

Royalist Plotters, 1652-9

The Royalist group known as the Sealed Knot made several attempts to restore the monarchy, all in vain, including one led by John Penruddock; Penruddock was beheaded. Lieutenant General Henry Wilmot, 1st Earl of Rochester, also led an uprising on the site of the Royalist defeat at Marston Moor near York in March 1655, but Colonel Robert Lilburne, Governor of York, put it down and Wilmot fled the country. He and James FitzThomas Butler, 1st Duke of Ormonde, would sign the Treaty of Brussels in April 1656, securing an alliance between the exiled Royalists and the Spanish King.

Charles Gerard, 1st Earl of Macclesfield, also encouraged his cousin John Gerard to assassinate Oliver Cromwell. But the conspiracy was discovered and John was executed.

Buckingham's Plot, 1657-60

George Villiers, 2nd Duke of Buckingham, escaped to Rotterdam after the battle of Worcester. He negotiated with Oliver Cromwell's government but his decision to give up the Church's interests upset the rest of Charles's supporters. Arguments over money and his courtship of the king's widowed sister Mary, Princess of Orange, completed his split with Charles.

Villiers' estates had been confiscated and given to Lord Fairfax so his plan to marry Fairfax's daughter in 1657 were viewed with suspicion. He was soon under house arrest, accused of organising a Presbyterian plot, but he escaped, was rearrested and was imprisoned in the Tower. He would join his father-in-law when Fairfax marched against General John Lambert in January 1660.

Richard Cromwell, 1660

Oliver Cromwell died on 3 September 1658 and Henry Somerset, 1st Duke of Beaufort, joined the party that demanded a 'full and free parliament' and the restoration of the House of Stuart. Charles Howard, 1st Earl of Carlisle, urged Richard Cromwell to defend his government against the army leaders but he refused and resigned; Howard was imprisoned.

It was soon clear his son Richard was incapable of running the government and he acquired the nicknames 'Tumbledown Dick' and 'Queen Dick'. Charles I's son, also Charles, made a tempting offer to take control of the kingdom in July 1659 and George Booth, 1st Baron Delamer, rebelled in Cheshire on his behalf. Henry Somerset, 1st Duke of Beaufort, Philip Stanhope, 2nd Earl of Chesterfield, and Charles Stanley, 8th Earl of Derby, were all arrested for taking part in the plot. Aubrey de Vere, 20th Earl of Oxford, and Francis Talbot, 11th Earl of Shrewsbury, were suspected of joining Booth.

A Regime Change, 1660

George Monck, 1st Duke of Albemarle, heard Charles Fleetwood and General John Lambert had declared against Parliament, so he secured Scotland and then crossed the border with his army. Monck was appointed commander-in-chief of the Parliamentary forces in November 1659 and he entered London on 3 February 1660. George Monck, 1st Duke of Albemarle, told the Rump Parliament to adjourn and some English garrisons announced their support, as did the navy and the army in Ireland. The Cromwell regime was over after only ten years.

Monck allowed Presbyterian members to re-enter Parliament on 21 February 1660 but it adjourned again on 16 March 1660 after preparing legislation for a new Convention Parliament. Meanwhile, Monck was keeping his options open. He was urging submission to the existing parliament while secretly encouraging the demands of Royalists in the City of London.

Chapter 29

Charles II
1660–85

A Bastard King, 1660

Charles II ended up in exile in Breda in the Low Countries after the battle of Worcester while his mother remained in Paris with Henry Jermyn. Henrietta Maria convinced her son to create him Earl of St Albans amidst rumours he had secretly married her. There were other rumours that Jermyn may have fathered at least one of her children. A report circulating in August 1660 stated that 'all the royal children were Jermyn's bastards'. Jermyn was appointed Lord Chamberlain, despite a reputation for compulsive gambling.

The King Returns, 1660

The king was accompanied by several of his supporters in exile, including Charles Stewart, 3rd Duke of Richmond, and Charles Berkeley, 1st Earl of Falmouth. Edward Hyde, 1st Earl of Clarendon, served as his Lord Chancellor. Charles was also accompanied by his favourite, Sidney Godolphin, 1st Earl of Godolphin, and his mistress Barbara Palmer.

Charles spent his nine years moving from France to the Dutch Republic to the Spanish Netherlands. Lieutenant General Henry Wilmot, 1st Earl of Rochester, was one of the king's principal advisers during the king's exile and he would visit Emperor Ferdinand III, Nicholas II, the Duke of Lorraine, and Frederick William, Elector of Brandenburg, on behalf of the king. Charles Gerard, 1st Earl of Macclesfield, also crossed Europe raising troops and chartering ships on behalf of the king.

James FitzThomas Butler, 1st Duke of Ormonde, attended Charles and the Queen Mother in Paris. He signed the Treaty of Brussels, securing a Royalist alliance with Spain in 1656, and two years later he went to England in disguise to see if it was possible to organise a rebellion.

Henry Somerset, 1st Duke of Beaufort, and Anthony Ashley Cooper, 1st Earl of Shaftesbury, were just two of the twelve members of parliament who met Charles in Breda. George Monck accepted the Declaration of Breda on

4 April 1660 under which Charles agreed an amnesty for all those who recognised him as the lawful king and a general pardon for any crimes committed during the Civil War. In return, Monck agreed to disband the New Model Army; he was created the Duke of Albemarle and the Earl of Torrington as a reward for his efforts.

Lionel Cranfield, 3rd Earl of Middlesex, George Berkeley, 1st Earl of Berkeley, and Aubrey de Vere, 20th Earl of Oxford, were just three of the six peers sent by the Convention Parliament to The Hague to petition for Charles's return in May 1660. John Granville took part in the negotiations which led to the Restoration of the Monarchy; he was created the 1st Earl of Bath.

Edward Montagu had been a 'diehard' Cromwellian but he was one of the first to contact the exiled Charles. He then commanded the fleet of twenty ships which took the royal supporters to Dover; Montagu would be created Earl of Sandwich. Dover Castle's guns fired a salute over the cheering crowds as Charles stepped ashore on 25 May 1660. Richard Sackville, 5th Earl of Dorset, then chaired the welcoming committee.

A Lustful Court in Exile

One of Charles II's many lovers was the wife of Charles Stanley, 8th Earl of Derby. In 1658 she gave birth to the king's son George and he was raised by an artilleryman named Swan. Although Charles II recognised his son he did not ennoble him, like all his other illegitimate children, and stated, 'I did not dare to make a duck of him, but I made a nobler bird.'

Mary, daughter of Lord Fairfax, jilted Philip Stanhope, 2nd Earl of Chesterfield, and married George Villiers, 2nd Duke of Buckingham. Stanhope started an affair with Barbara Villiers, one of Charles II's mistresses, so his wife flirted with the king's brother James, the Duke of York. Meanwhile George Villiers chased Charles's widowed sister Mary, Princess of Orange, irritating the king in the lewd world of the royal court.

Possible Heirs, 1660-1

The king's brother James, Duke of York, had made his mistress Anne Hyde pregnant before they were married. Henrietta Maria wanted to declare the unborn child illegitimate, because his mother was not of royal blood but Charles II approved of the marriage in September. Charles, the Duke of Cambridge, was born in October 1660 but the issue of his legitimacy ended when he died young from smallpox.

While Charles was unable to have any legitimate offspring with his queen, he was having plenty of illegitimate children with his mistresses. James's second son, also James, was born in 1661 and he was also created the Duke of Cambridge. He was treated as an heir to the throne until his death, at the age of 4, shocked the nation.

A Royal Marriage, 1660

George Villiers, 2nd Duke of Buckingham, had instructions to accompany Princess Henrietta to Paris to marry the Duke of Orléans in 1661. But Villiers made the mistake of making advances to the princess and was recalled to England in disgrace.

Queen Catherine, 1661-7

Edward Hyde, 1st Earl of Clarendon, helped organise Charles's marriage to the Portuguese Catherine of Braganza in 1661. But not everyone was happy with the match, particularly George Digby, 2nd Earl of Bristol. The ambassador to Portugal, Edward Montagu, 1st Earl of Sandwich, escorted the Queen to England the following year and he became her Master of the Horse. Charles later sacked him for 'showing attention to the queen of too ardent a nature'; she immediately appointed his brother Ralph.

While the king did not allow any man to pay attention to his wife, he had a string of mistresses. Hyde disapproved of the king's behaviour and Charles resented the interference, especially when Catherine failed to bear children. Meanwhile, Charles was busy having illegitimate ones, acknowledging at least twelve of them. But the lack of a legitimate heir to the throne was causing problems because the king's brother was a covert Catholic whose sons were dying young.

Charles was desperate to divorce but he wanted to do it legally, so he attended the parliamentary hearing of John Manners, heir to the Earldom of Rutland, and his wife Anne in 1667. She was accused of adultery and a Private Act of Parliament declared her children illegitimate and granted John permission to remarry. The king found it useful to attend debates in the House of Lords to learn about public opinion. But he only observed rather than contributing to the discussions, and the Lords said they were 'speaking to the fireside' when they were speaking to their king.

The King's Mistresses, 1660-74

Henry Bennet, 1st Earl of Arlington, was the keeper of the Privy Purse, and responsible for procuring and managing the royal mistresses. He was always kept busy. Roger Palmer's father correctly predicted his wife Barbara would make him one of the most miserable men in the world. They separated following the birth of her first illegitimate son, leaving her short of money. Barbara became Charles's mistress in exile in 1660 and the king created her husband the Earl of Castlemaine to keep him quiet. Barbara was appointed Lady of the Bedchamber, against the Queen's wishes, and she soon had more influence at the court than Catherine, causing arguments. When she converted to Catholicism in 1663, he said he was only interested in ladies' bodies, not their souls. Both the king and Barbara took other lovers but Charles created her Duchess of Cleveland and ennobled five of her six children.

Most members of court ignored the king's decadent lifestyle but some disapproved and advised him to stay faithful. Edward Hyde, 1st Earl of Clarendon, had played a key role in Charles's marriage to Catherine and the king resented his interference, especially when she failed to bear children. George Digby, 2nd Earl of Bristol, even went so far as to accuse Hyde of arranging a royal marriage to a barren woman.

Illegitimate Children

King Charles did not have any legitimate children with his Queen, Catherine, but he had plenty of children with many of his lovers and he gave titles to most of them. Lucy Walter had given birth to James Scott in 1649, when Prince Charles was only 19. There were rumours that Charles and Lucy had married secretly but they were untrue. In March 1658 Charles had young James kidnapped and taken to Paris when it was clear the Cromwell Protectorate was in trouble. He returned to England in 1663 and was created Duke of Monmouth at the age of 14. He married the heiress Anne Scott, 4th Countess of Buccleuch, and adopted her surname.

Roger Palmer, 1st Earl of Castlemaine, divorced his wife Barbara when she gave birth to her first illegitimate son with Charles II in 1662. The baby was baptised a Catholic but the king had him rechristened into the Church of England a few days later. Young Charles was betrothed to Henry Wood's daughter Mary when he was only 8 but Barbara abducted her after her father died; he was created the Duke of Southampton at the age of 13. Charlotte Fitzroy was another of the six children the king had with Barbara Palmer. Ten-year-old Edward Lee was created Earl of Lichfield in 1674 when he was betrothed to Charlotte but she went on to marry William Paston instead.

Clarendon's Rule, 1660-6

Edward Hyde was Charles II's chief advisor during his nine years in exile and he was appointed Lord Chancellor in 1658. He was created Earl of Clarendon following the restoration of the monarchy in 1660 and continued to advise the king. Hyde opposed the marriage of his daughter Anne to James, Duke of York, because he disliked her husband, upsetting the king. James and Anne would have two daughters, the future Queen Mary II and Queen Anne.

Hyde detested democracy but his autocratic style of government brought him many enemies. Chancellor of the Exchequer, Anthony Ashley Cooper,

1st Earl of Shaftesbury, opposed the imposition of the Clarendon Code, which was designed to overhaul the Church of England. Charles agreed, even though he favoured religious tolerance, and Hyde in turn supported the king's Declaration of Indulgence. While it promoted religious freedom for Catholic and Protestant dissenters, Parliament forced it to be withdrawn.

George Digby, 2nd Earl of Bristol, was one of those excluded from office because of his religion, and his accusations of high treason against Hyde were dismissed in 1663. Digby spent two years in hiding before he renounced Catholicism and declared himself a Protestant. But he still wanted the Lord Chancellor arrested and he accused the Lords of stirring up a rebellion when they refused to.

Hyde also dismissed George Villiers, 2nd Duke of Buckingham, from office in 1666 so he plotted his revenge. Villiers and Henry Pierrepont, 1st Marquess of Dorchester, were sent to the Tower for fighting in the House of Lords later in the year and although they were both released after apologising, Villiers' troubles were far from over. He was accused of intrigues and of forecasting the king's horoscope. After several months in hiding he gave himself up and was sent back to the Tower.

Plague and Fire, 1665-6

Plague swept through London in 1665 killing thousands and most of the nobility left the city and headed for the safety of their country homes. George Monck, 1st Duke of Albemarle, was one of the few exceptions and he remained in charge of the government during the disaster. He also stayed in the city during the Great Fire the following year, maintaining order in the wake of the tragedy. Edward Montagu, 1st Earl of Sandwich, was the ambassador to Spain when news of the fire reached Spain. He downplayed the damage to London to the Spanish government, claiming it had only destroyed the city's slums.

Treaties with Spain, 1665-7

The infant Charles II inherited a huge empire when he came to the Spanish throne in 1665. He also inherited a war with Portugal and soon became involved in another war with France. Edward Montagu, 1st Earl of Sandwich, took the opportunity to secure the Anglo-Spanish Commercial Treaty of 1667 which began a century of successful trading between the two countries. Montagu was also a mediator of the Treaty of Lisbon which ended the war between Spain and Portugal.

A Problem Marriage, 1665

Edward Montagu, 2nd Earl of Sandwich, was betrothed to the rich heiress Elizabeth Malet but she found him 'unexciting'. She found the impoverished but roguish John Wilmot, 2nd Earl of Rochester, more exciting; even more so when he abducted her. Wilmot was imprisoned until he apologised and he then joined the navy and served in the Second Anglo-Dutch War. John and Elizabeth eloped on his return but she had to endure his infidelities, his drunkenness, rudeness and 'extravagant frolics' as he partied with the infamous 'Merry Gang'.

Duelling

Edward Rich, Earl of Warwick and Holland, won a duel only to be tried for the murder of his opponent Richard Coote. He was found guilty of manslaughter but escaped punishment after pleading the privilege of peerage to evade justice.

James Douglas, 4th Duke of Hamilton, and Baron Charles Mohun both claimed they were heirs to Fitton Gerard, 3rd Earl Macclesfield. However, Macclesfield preferred Mohun because Hamilton had Tory sympathies and they spent a decade arguing over the inheritance in court. They finally settled their differences in a duel in which both men died of their injuries.

Francis Talbot, Earl of Shrewsbury and Waterford, had the misfortune of being married to the 'notorious' Anna Maria. He duelled with the equally infamous George Villiers, 2nd Duke of Buckingham, in 1668 while a disguised Anna Maria held Villiers' horse. Talbot's second son, John, was also killed in a duel after exchanging 'very unhandsome and provoking language' with Charles II's illegitimate son Henry FitzRoy, 1st Duke of Grafton.

The Second Anglo-Dutch War, 1665-7

George Monck, 1st Duke of Albemarle, headed the admiralty when James, Duke of York, commanded the fleet and both James Scott, Duke of Monmouth, and George Villiers, 2nd Duke of Buckingham, served under him. Edward Montagu, 1st Earl of Sandwich, was victorious at the battle of Lowestoft on 13 June 1665 but Charles Berkeley, 1st Earl of Falmouth, and James Ley, 3rd Earl of Marlborough, were killed. Edward Montagu, 1st Earl of Sandwich, was defeated at the battle of Vågen in Norway in 1665, but he was sacked for allowing his sailors to plunder captured ships in the 'Prize Goods Scandal'. While crews were allowed to take anything on a captured ship's deck, Montagu let them clear the holds and it was rumoured he had helped himself to a fortune. James, Duke of York, exploited the scandal but the king pardoned Montagu.

The Dutch made alliances with France and Denmark but the Dutch shipyards were making ships much faster than the English ones. Monck showed his skills at sea during the Four Days Battle in June 1666 and there was another English victory in the St James's Day battle in August. A raid by the Dutch which destroyed the English fleet anchored in the River Medway in June 1667 ended the career of Edward Hyde, 1st Earl of Clarendon, after he had agreed peace terms. Barbara Villiers shouted abuse as he left his office so he replied, 'Madam, pray remember that if you live, you will also be old.' He would be impeached for holding prisoners without trial and had to flee to France.

Alliances with the French and the Dutch, 1668-78

Sidney Godolphin, 1st Earl of Godolphin, had mediated between the king and his sister Henrietta Anne in 1668, paving the way for Charles to reject his Dutch allies in return for money from Louis XIV of France. Two years later Edward Montagu, 1st Earl of Sandwich, escorted Henrietta back to England to negotiate the Treaty of Dover between the English and French kings. The treaty was unpopular with some, including Thomas Osborne, 1st Duke of Leeds, and it would have been more unpopular if the secret clause, under which Charles II pledged to convert to the Roman Catholic faith, had been made public. Godolphin reassured Louis of Charles's allegiance before the French attacked the Dutch in 1672. He accompanied the French army into the field but was unimpressed by King Louis' skills as a general.

There would be a Third Anglo-Dutch War in 1672 and John Churchill, 1st Duke of Marlborough, and John Sheffield, Earl of Mulgrave and Normanby, fought a weakened Dutch fleet at the battle of Solebay off the Suffolk coast in June 1672.

Charles II's anti-French Parliament forced England to withdraw from the Franco-Dutch War in 1674 and Godolphin arranged the marriage between William and Mary without Louis knowing in 1677. There was a new alliance with the Dutch and John Churchill, 1st Duke of Marlborough, joined Godolphin as they negotiated the deployment of an English army in Flanders in April 1678. Churchill met William, Prince of Orange, unaware the king was dealing with Louis XIV behind his back. Instead he sued for peace under the Treaty of Nijmegen.

Ireland, 1669-75

James FitzThomas Butler, 1st Duke of Ormonde, recovered his confiscated Irish estates and Charles compensated him for the money he had spent on royal service. He was once again appointed Lord Lieutenant of Ireland in 1661 but he soon fell foul of the king's favourite, George Villiers, 2nd Duke of Buckingham. He was sacked in 1669 and Thomas Blood tried to assassinate FitzThomas Butler on Villiers' orders the following year.

Arthur Capell, 1st Earl of Essex, was the next Lord Lieutenant of Ireland and was against using Irish taxes to entertain the court. He challenged the donation of forfeited estates to the king's favourites and mistresses so he was recalled after his opponents disputed his accounts in 1675.

The Stop of the Exchequer, 1672

Thomas Wriothesley, 4th Earl of Southampton, was Lord High Treasurer but he had to work hard to balance the books of Charles II's economy. He was 'remarkable for his freedom from any taint of corruption and for his efforts in the interests of economy and financial order'. But declaration of a third war against the Dutch in 1672 was a step too far. Wriothesley had to announce a 'Stop of the Exchequer' before the country was bankrupted.

The Earl of Danby, 1673-7

Thomas Osborne was created Earl of Danby when he was appointed Lord Treasurer in 1673. He was soon running the government and he brought an end to the war with the Dutch Republic. But Osborne soon became known as 'the most hated minister that had ever been about the king' because of his corrupt and greedy administration. Anthony Ashley Cooper, 1st Earl of Shaftesbury, led the opposition to Osborne's policies and while they both resisted the growth of 'popery and arbitrary government', Cooper did not want England transforming into an absolute monarchy.

Osborne was against appointing Catholics to government posts but he often promoted friends ahead of able men, including appointing William Temple the Secretary of State ahead of Ralph Montagu, 1st Duke of Montagu. Eventually no one supported his 'weak, discredited, unpopular and unsuccessful' administration. Montagu was dismissed for arguing with the king's mistress Barbara Palmer, 1st Duchess of Cleveland, so he joined the opposition.

Osborne arranged the marriage between William and Mary behind the back of the French King in 1677, so an angry Louis XIV financed Montagu's plan to ruin Osborne. He was soon charged with assuming royal powers because he had been making decisions without the council's knowledge. But Charles Dormer, 2nd Earl of Carnarvon, warned everyone to 'mark the man who first dares to run down Lord Danby [Osbourne] and see what becomes of him.'

Osbourne was eventually forced to resign as Lord Treasurer after he was accused of murdering Sir Edmund Berry Godfrey, the man who had prosecuted the 'infamous' Philip Herbert, 7th Earl of Pembroke. Osbourne retaliated by revealing the Popish Plot to parliament only to be accused of having 'traitorously concealed the plot'. He would be pardoned by the king but he still spent five years in the Tower.

More Royal Mistresses, 1668-73

Barbara Villiers used money from the Privy Purse and took bribes from the Spanish and the French to finance her lavish lifestyle. She was not afraid of standing up to anyone and threatened to get Edward Hyde, 1st Earl of Clarendon, sacked when he challenged her. Charles created Barbara the Duchess of Cleveland in 1670 but her influence was waning because he was obsessed with a new woman. The king eventually advised Barbara to stop causing scandals and live a quiet life.

Charles Sackville, Earl of Dorset and Middlesex, had lured Eleanor Gwyn from the theatre and he introduced her into court in 1668 where she became one of the king's most notorious mistresses. Nell, as Eleanor was known, had two sons with the king, Charles and James Beauclerk.

Charles's attention soon drifted again, this time to Louise de Kérouaille. The French ambassador, Colbert de Croissy, and the secretary of state, Henry Bennet, 1st Earl of Arlington, encouraged the romance. The king's lovers could not have been more different: Louise was a sophisticated French noblewoman while Nell had been a street seller and actress with a dubious background.

Most people in court hated the promiscuous Louise because she was French and Nell Gwyn would call her 'Squintabella'. But Charles was fond of her and nicknamed her 'Fubbs', referring to her plumpness. Louise in turn understood Charles and her tact was rewarded when she was created the Duchess of Portsmouth and Aubigny.

More Illegitimate Children

Barbara Villiers, Countess of Castlemaine, was mother to Henry FitzRoy, Duke of Grafton, and George FitzRoy, who was elevated from Earl to Duke of Northumberland in 1683. Catherine Pegge was the mother of Charles FitzCharles, Earl of Plymouth, and Louise de Kérouaille was the mother of Charles Lennox who was given a string of titles including the Dukedoms of Richmond and Lennox and the Earldoms of March and Darnley; he was also appointed Lord High Admiral of Scotland.

Charles Beauclerk was Nell Gwyn's eldest illegitimate son. One story states that his mother said, 'come here, you little bastard, and greet your father,' and the king reprimanded her. So she replied, 'your Majesty has given me no other name to call him by,' and so he was created Earl of Burford. Another version says she threatened to drop him out of a window unless he was given a peerage and Charles shouted out, 'God save the Earl of Burford!' Beauclerk was elevated to the Duke of St Albans when he turned 14.

A Gambler and a Drunk, 1675

John Wilmot, 2nd Earl of Rochester, was a friend of Nell Gwyn and he became influential at court when she became one of the king's mistresses. He was also part of the notorious Merry Gang which included Henry Jermyn, Charles Sackville, the Earl of Dorset, John Sheffield, the Earl of Mulgrave, and George Villiers, the Duke of Buckingham.

Wilmot was famous for drunkenness, rudeness and 'extravagant frolics', until he was banned from court for punching Thomas Killigrew in front of the king in 1669. He was expelled a second time after correctly telling the king he was more interested in sex than the kingdom. The final straw came in 1675 when he made an outspoken rant about the king's behaviour. Wilmot ended up as a street hawker on Tower Hill, posing as a gynaecology expert named Doctor Bendo. He also dressed as a woman, calling himself Mrs Bendo, presumably so that he could inspect women in private. He died from venereal disease and alcoholism at the age of 33.

The Privilege of Peerage, 1677-80

Philip Herbert, Earl of Pembroke and Montgomery, was known as 'the infamous Earl of Pembroke' because he was a violent drunk. He was imprisoned in the Tower after seriously injuring a man in a duel in 1677 but the Lords petitioned for his release. He assaulted a man after only a few days of freedom and then murdered a man in a pub brawl. Although he was found guilty of manslaughter, he was discharged because he was granted the privilege of peerage.

Herbert attacked Charles Sackville, Earl of Dorset and Middlesex, because he had brought a lawsuit against him and Herbert's prosecutor, Edmund Godfrey, was then found murdered. The wave of anti-Catholic feeling that followed led to the uncovering of the Popish Plot, a fabricated plan to kill the king.

But Herbert refused to calm down and was again found guilty of murder in 1680 after murdering an officer of the watch in a drunken rage. Although he could not claim the privilege of peerage a second time, remarkably some felt that he had been unfairly treated and petitioned the king until he granted a royal pardon.

The Popish Plot, 1678-9

Titus Oates sent a message to Thomas Hickman-Windsor, 1st Earl of Plymouth, warning of a plot to assassinate the king in 1678. The so-called Popish Plot was blamed on five Catholics but it was a fake scheme designed to rouse anti-Catholic resentment. Charles did not believe the allegations but he still ordered his chief minister Thomas Osbourne, Earl of Danby, to investigate. Danby was also sceptical but he was accused of having 'traitorously concealed the plot' when he finally told parliament about it. He resigned as Lord and was imprisoned in the Tower for five years.

The Cavalier Parliament took the threat seriously and anti-Catholic hysteria swept the kingdom. Henry Howard, Earl of Norfolk, turned his back on his Catholic faith to save his family estates from confiscation. He even served on the jury of his cousin William Howard along with Henry Howard, 6th Duke of Norfolk. William was found guilty and executed.

William Herbert, 1st Marquess of Powis, spent six years in the Tower of London awaiting trial and his wife was nearly convicted after failing to set him free. She was also involved in the 'Meal-Tub Plot' another fake plan to assassinate the king, so called because the plans were found in a tub of meal (ground cereal grains). Charles Howard, 2nd Earl of Berkshire, fled to Paris and he died in exile while charges were brought against Thomas Savage, 3rd Earl Rivers.

The Exclusion Bill, 1679
The investigation into the Popish Plot revealed that Charles's brother and heir James, Duke of York, was a Catholic. James was exiled for three years and was accompanied by John Churchill, 1st Duke of Marlborough. Charles then faced a political storm led by Anthony Ashley Cooper, 1st Earl of Shaftesbury, over who would succeed to the throne of England. The Exclusion Bill was introduced to exclude James from the line of succession and some wanted to make Charles's illegitimate Protestant son James Scott, Duke of Monmouth, heir to the throne. But opinion in parliament was split. The Abhorrers opposed the bill and were called Tories (a name for dispossessed Irish Catholic bandits). The Petitioners supported the bill and were called Whigs (a name for rebellious Scottish Presbyterians).

Charles dissolved the parliament several times to stop the bill being passed and Arthur Annesley, 1st Earl of Anglesey, was dismissed as Lord Privy Seal after writing a protest about the 'true state of Your Majesty's Government and Kingdom'. But public opinion eventually swung in the king's favour. Lord Shaftesbury was prosecuted for treason so he fled to Holland, where he died. James would return in 1682, while Charles ruled until he died without a parliament.

The Duke of Monmouth, 1679-83
Many favoured the king's son James Scott, Duke of Monmouth, after the Popish Plot revealed the king's brother James, Duke of York, was Catholic but he was illegitimate and ineligible for the throne. So he had concentrated on soldiering and gained a good reputation at the Siege of Maastricht in June 1673. He took command of the Anglo-Dutch brigade, fighting for the United Provinces against the French in 1678, and improved his status at the battle of St Denis in August. He then took on the Scottish Covenanters, defeating them at the battle of Bothwell Bridge on 22 June 1679.

Monmouth went into exile in the Dutch United Provinces following the introduction of the Exclusion Bill. Charles Gerard, 1st Earl of Macclesfield, was sent to arrest him but he joined Monmouth's band of conspirators instead and even suggested murdering James, Duke of York, to terrorise the king. Monmouth was later identified as a conspirator in the Rye House Plot in 1683.

A Royal Dowry, 1680

England had acquired Bombay in India and Tangier in Morocco as part of the Portuguese dowry which came with Queen Catherine of Braganza. James Ley, 3rd Earl of Marlborough, took a squadron of ships to claim Bombay but the Portuguese stalled the handover and Marlborough was forced to land the garrison troops on tiny Anjadip Island, 200 miles to the south, and return home.

Tangier would have been a profitable Mediterranean trade centre but was under constant attack. The king was displeased with John Sheffield, 1st Duke of Buckingham, because he was too friendly with Princess Anne. So he was put in charge of an expedition sent to relieve Tangier in 1680, accompanied by Charles FitzCharles, 1st Earl of Plymouth and illegitimate son of Charles II. Some believe they were given a rotten ship in the hope that it would sink and drown them but they completed the voyage to North Africa. Charles died of dysentery and the English withdrew from the port soon afterwards, ending a twenty-year presence in Morocco.

The Rye House Plot, 1682-3

William Russell, Earl of Bedford, James Scott, 1st Duke of Monmouth, Arthur Capell, 1st Earl of Essex, and others met at Rye House in Hertfordshire, the home of Richard Rumbold in October 1682. They planned to kidnap Charles and James as they returned from the Newmarket races to London. But they missed their targets because a fire which destroyed the royal lodgings meant that they returned to London early. The plotters dispersed but the plan was uncovered in June 1683 and some of the conspirators, including Scott, escaped to Holland.

The rest were imprisoned. Charles Gerard, 2nd Earl of Macclesfield, was sentenced to death only to be pardoned by Charles II. Capell cut his throat, hoping his family could keep their inheritance, only for a regretful King to say he would have spared him 'for I owe him a life'. Ford Grey, 1st Earl of Tankerville, escaped from the Tower and headed to France.

It left Russell to be condemned to death for plotting to execute the king. He pleaded he knew nothing of the plot but was sentenced to be hung, drawn and quartered. The sentence was later commuted to beheading and he was executed on 21 July. Algernon Sydney was also executed.

Corruption, 1682

Laurence Hyde was appointed First Lord of the Treasury in 1679 and was then created Earl of Rochester. He was dismissed when Lord Halifax found that £40,000 was missing from the treasury in 1684. But to Halifax's disgust, Hyde was appointed Lord President of the Council, a more dignified but less lucrative office. Halifax's response to the promotion was 'I have seen people kicked downstairs but my Lord Rochester is the first person that I ever saw kicked upstairs'.

A Deathbed Conversion, 1685

Charles II suffered a fit on 2 February 1685 and died four days later, aged 54. His sudden death led many to believe he had been poisoned. His mistress Louise de Kérouaille was by his side as he lay dying. The Lord of the Bedchamber, Louis de Duras, 2nd Earl of Feversham, was also present during the king's deathbed conversion to Catholicism but it is doubtful if Charles was fully conscious at the time.

Chapter 30

James II
1685–88

The Monmouth Rebellion, 1685

James II came to the throne in February 1685 but the start of his reign was overshadowed by uprisings. The Earl of Argyll rebelled in Scotland and then Charles II's illegitimate son James Scott, Duke of Monmouth and Buccleuch, landed at Lyme Regis in Dorset on 11 June. He declared himself King but hesitated during his march to Bristol, giving Henry Somerset, 1st Duke of Beaufort, time to seize the port on 16 June. Somerset then imprisoned all the dissenters and threatened to set the city on fire if any of Monmouth's supporters entered.

John Churchill, 1st Duke of Marlborough, and James FitzJames Butler, 2nd Duke of Ormonde, intercepted and defeated the rebels at the battle of Sedgemoor in Somerset on 6 July. Richard Lumley, 1st Earl of Scarbrough, captured Scott in a ditch at Ringwood, Hampshire and he was taken to the Tower. Louis de Duras, 2nd Earl of Feversham, was cruel to the prisoners but he was rewarded with the colonelcy of the first troop of Life Guards. The king's illegitimate half-brother was executed on 15 July 'but the wretch made five chops before he had his head off'.

George and Anne, 1685

John Churchill, 1st Duke of Marlborough, had escorted Prince George of Denmark to England in 1683 so he could marry the 18-year-old Princess Anne, the Duke of York's youngest daughter and future Queen of England.

Princess Anne had married Prince George of Denmark and Norway in July 1683 and James welcomed the marriage because it reduced the influence of his son-in-law William of Orange. George was created Duke of Cumberland but he had no ambitions to be king, unlike William. Rivalries increased when Charles II died without any legitimate children in February 1685 and William refused to attend James's coronation because George took precedence over him.

Mistresses and Bastards

James FitzJames was the illegitimate son of King James and Arabella
Churchill, the 1st Duke of Marlborough's sister, who had been born before
his father came to the throne. He was created the Duke of Berwick when
he turned 17 but he had to go into exile with his father when he was
overthrown by William in December 1688. The exiled James would grant
his son the Dukedom of Albemarle and Earl of Rochford in 1696 but the
title was only recognised by Jacobites.

The king kept mistresses even after he became king, to the disgust of
some. Charles Sackville, Earl of Dorset and Middlesex, was forced to leave
court after ridiculing another of the king's mistresses, Catherine Sedley, the
Countess of Dorchester. Robert Spencer, 2nd Earl of Sunderland, advised
James to stop seeing her only to be told he was not the king's confessor. He
too was forced to leave court.

A Purge of Catholics, 1687-8

James started purging the government and the army of Protestants in 1687.
Richard Boyle, Earl of Burlington and Cork, was one of many who opposed
his attempts to restore Catholicism and he called on the king to call a
parliament 'regular and free in all its circumstances' in November 1688.

The purge caused many to struggle with their consciences. John Egerton,
3rd Earl of Bridgewater, was dismissed for refusing to produce a list of
Catholic officers who could serve in the militia. Earl Marshal Henry
Howard, 7th Duke of Norfolk, refused to replace Protestant magistrates in
his area and was forced into exile. Edward Noel, 1st Earl of Gainsborough,
was also dismissed as Lord Lieutenant of Hampshire in favour of the king's
illegitimate son James FitzJames, 1st Duke of Berwick.

Aubrey de Vere, 20th Earl of Oxford, refused to appoint Catholics to
public offices and was sacked as the Lord Lieutenant of Essex after stating,
'I will stand by Your Majesty against all enemies to the last drop of my
blood. But this is a matter of conscience and I cannot comply.' James
FitzJames was given de Vere's colonelcy of The Blues and he questioned
his officers to check their loyalty to the king.

Arthur Herbert, 1st Earl of Torrington, refused to vote in favour of
repealing the Test Act so the king reminded him he had a mistress by saying,
'but a man who lives as you do, ought not to talk about his conscience.'
Herbert replied, 'I have my faults, sir; but I could name people who talk
much more about conscience than I am in the habit of doing, and yet lead
lives as loose as mine.' His punishment was to be cashiered as a rear-admiral.

The king wanted all his officers to be Catholics but some, like Laurence
Hyde, 1st Earl of Rochester, was sacked when he refused to convert. Others
chose to convert so they could keep their appointments or advance their

careers. William Paston, 2nd Earl of Yarmouth, was appointed Treasurer of the King's Household after converting but not everyone was comfortable with their change of religion.

The purge resulted in plots and the home of Charles Talbot, 1st Duke of Shrewsbury, became a meeting place for the king's opponents. The Protestant William of Orange was interested in seizing the throne and one of his agents visited Thomas Osborne, 1st Duke of Leeds, to assure his support.

Planning the Glorious Revolution, 1688

William Nassau de Zuylestein, 1st Earl of Rochford, carried out his first spying mission in England while escorting the queen-consort to the funeral of her mother the Dowager Duchess Laura of Modena in August 1687. Seven men, later known as the 'Immortal Seven' met in June 1688 to sign an invitation to the Protestant Prince William of Orange, asking him to invade England and assume the throne. The group included Whigs, Tories, and the Bishop of London. Zuylestein then visited Mary Beatrice to congratulate her on the birth her son in August. Despite his seemingly good intentions, the real purpose of his visit was to learn more about the mood of the nation.

William landed at Torbay on 5 November 1688 and marched his small army towards Exeter accompanied by William Nassau de Zuylestein, 1st Earl of Rochford, and Arnold Joost van Keppel, 1st Earl of Albemarle. The well-known reprobate Richard Savage, 4th Earl Rivers, was the first nobleman to join William. William Courtenay funded a lavish reception for William at Forde House, Wolborough, but he did not attend because he did not want to associate himself too much with the new regime in case it failed. The Glorious Revolution had begun.

King James ordered Lord Feversham to move his army to Salisbury while he appointed a five-man council to represent him in London. But no one supported James for long, neither the nobility, the army nor Prince George, Duke of Cumberland. Thomas Osborne, 1st Duke of Leeds, occupied York in the north while Henry Booth, 1st Earl of Warrington, raised troops across Cheshire. John Churchill, Duke of Marlborough, had soon joined William at Axminster in Devon.

James headed to London hoping to meet William in December 1688 but Zuylestein explained he would not enter London while royal troops remained in the city. Henry Hyde, 2nd Earl of Clarendon, had planned to imprison James in the Tower but he had left after hearing Zuylestein's veiled threat. The king went into exile, taking his son with him; few joined them in France. Henry Mordaunt, 2nd Earl of Peterborough, and James Cecil, 4th Earl of Salisbury, were caught trying to reach him so they were imprisoned in the Tower accused of 'departing from their allegiance and being reconciled to the Church of Rome'.

Chapter 31

William and Mary
1689–1702

Completing the Glorious Revolution, 1689

The Glorious Revolution had succeeded but the first question was how they would deal with the king in exile. James FitzJames Butler, 2nd Duke of Ormonde, was one of the few who voted against declaring that James II had abdicated. The next question was, what role would William of Orange and Mary, James's eldest daughter, take? – and opinions were varied. Henry Somerset, 1st Duke of Beaufort, wanted a regency while Thomas Osborne, 1st Duke of Leeds, believed the succession fell to Mary and that William would not claim the crown. The Convention Parliament's majority decision was to put William of Orange and Mary on the throne in February 1689. Those like William Paston, 2nd Earl of Yarmouth, who refused to swear allegiance to William and Mary, lost all their offices.

The Nine Years War, 1688-97

John Churchill was created Earl of Marlborough in 1689 and he set about remodelling the army. William joined the League of Augsburg later in the year and Churchill took the army abroad. The king then spent every summer abroad during the Nine Years War with France while Mary depended on his advice to govern the kingdom.

Arthur Herbert, 1st Earl of Torrington, commanded the fleet in the English Channel and he was the first to use the term 'fleet in being', avoiding set battles except under favourable conditions. It forced the French to disperse their ships across a wide area, rather than concentrating their fleet to attack. But Herbert was imprisoned in the Tower after failing to support the Dutch during the defeat at the battle of Beachy Head on 30 June 1690. He was court-martialled but acquitted.

The allies ruled the high seas for a time after the Anglo-Dutch fleet defeated a French fleet at La Hogue off the Normandy coast in 1692. Ireland was also pacified by the Treaty of Limerick. But the Grand Alliance failed on the Continent as William lost Namur in the Netherlands in 1692 and was then defeated at the battle of Landen in 1693. James FitzJames Butler, 2nd Duke of Ormonde, was captured and was exchanged for James FitzJames, 1st Duke of Berwick, James II's illegitimate son, who had been captured while serving in the French army. The Treaty of Ryswick ended the Nine Years War in 1697.

James in Ireland, 1689-90

James had not given up on his crown. He landed with French troops in Ireland in March 1689 and the Irish Parliament declared he was still their king. He passed a bill of attainder against the Protestants who had rebelled against him and confiscated their estates. The Irish Parliament also passed an Act for Liberty of Conscience giving religious freedom for all Roman Catholics and Protestants.

James recruited an army in Ireland and was joined by Prince George of Denmark and Norway, Duke of Cumberland. But James distrusted him so he was excluded from command and banned from joining the navy. William sailed across the Irish Sea in June 1690 to take personal control of the campaign while John Churchill, 1st Duke of Marlborough, stayed behind in command of all troops in England.

William defeated James at the battle of the Boyne on 1 July 1690. James fled via Kinsale to France and became known as *Séamus an Chaca* or 'James the Shit' for deserting the Irish. Churchill crossed to Ireland in the autumn and captured the ports of Cork and Kinsale, cutting the Jacobite supply routes. The war was soon over and the Treaty of Limerick was signed in October. All Irish military units were banished to the continent but they would serve as mercenaries known as the Wild Geese.

Conspiracies, 1690

Henry Hyde, 2nd Earl of Clarendon, rejected the Whigs' assumption that King James had abdicated, so he contacted the Jacobite plotter, Richard Graham, 1st Viscount of Preston. Queen Mary had her uncle imprisoned in the Tower in June 1690 but his plotting resumed as soon as he was released. Lord Preston was arrested in December and he named Hyde among his accomplices, so he was again taken to the Tower. He retired when he was released.

George and Anne, 1692-4

There was mistrust between William and Anne's husband Prince George of Denmark and Norway, Duke of Cumberland, and George and Anne were banished from court following arguments in 1692. Charles Dormer, 2nd Earl of Carnarvon, was one of the few who stuck by Anne while she was away from court. Anne reconciled with William after Mary's death in 1694 and Dormer noted how the crowds gathered outside her house had ignored her for the past two years.

The Fenwick Conspiracy, 1691-7

John Churchill, 1st Earl of Marlborough, fought well in Flanders but he was unpopular with Queen Mary because he and his wife Sarah supported Princess Anne. Churchill was also frustrated he had not been rewarded for his overseas service while others had. By January 1691 he had had enough and he contacted the exiled James II asking for a pardon.

William and Churchill fought together in the Spanish Netherlands in the summer but Sarah continued to annoy Anne and both she and John were dismissed from court in January 1692. Matters went from bad to worse when a letter signed by Churchill, calling for the restoration of James II, was produced. He was imprisoned in the Tower in the spring of 1692 only to be released when it was proved the letter was a forgery.

The Camaret Bay letter accused Churchill of conspiring with the French during the disastrous Allied attack on Brest in 1694; it was just another attempt to frame Churchill. Tensions increased after Mary died in December 1694. In 1696 the Jacobite John Fenwick confessed about an attempted assassination of William III and he accused Churchill, Sidney Godolphin, 1st Earl of Godolphin, and William Russell, 1st Duke of Bedford, of plotting with James II. Fenwick was beheaded in 1697, Godolphin resigned and Charles Mordaunt, Earl of Monmouth, was imprisoned after he spoke out about the king.

The Jacobites, 1695

William Herbert, 1st Marquess of Powis, had taken Queen Mary and her infant son James, Prince of Wales, into exile in France and he was elevated to the Duke of Powis and created the Marquess of Montgomery. After serving as one of James's main advisers in Ireland, he settled with the exiled Jacobite Court at St Germain-en-Laye near Paris, as its Lord Steward and Lord Chamberlain.

Herbert's son, also William, stayed in England and was imprisoned in the Tower in 1689. He was then suspected of involvement in the Jacobite assassination plot in 1696 but he was freed from Newgate Prison following an outbreak of fever.

Thomas Bruce, Earl of Ailesbury and Elgin, had switched his support to William's new regime, but he was imprisoned for conspiring to restore James II to the throne in 1695. His wife Elizabeth died during a premature childbirth after hearing false rumours that her husband had been executed. Bruce was soon bailed and he went into exile in Brussels.

The King's Favourite
William became close to Arnold Joost van Keppel after he broke his leg in a hunting accident. There were rumours the two were having an affair, which increased when Keppel was created 1st Earl of Albemarle and appointed commander of the Life Guards.

Problem Marriages
The leading Jacobite, Lord Clancarty, escaped from the Tower over the winter of 1697-8. Robert Spencer, 2nd Earl of Sunderland, tracked down his daughter Elizabeth and persuaded her to consummate her marriage with Clancarty. But his servants alerted her brother Charles and saw to it that Clancarty was rearrested. Everybody teased William III about 'that little spark Clancarty' so he forced them to go into exile.

Charles Gerard, 2nd Earl of Macclesfield, used an Act of Parliament to divorce his wife Anna in 1698. It was the first time a divorce had been granted without needing permission from a Church court.

Gamblers and Drunks
Charles Gerard, 1st Earl of Macclesfield, was the Lord President of the Council of the Welsh Marches. But he was also described as a 'proud and violent man' whose 'rogueries and cheats' were notorious. Lieutenant General Henry Sidney, 1st Earl of Romney, was colonel of the First Regiment of Foot Guards (the Grenadier Guards) and he died 'a proud but drunken man'. He was remembered for introducing the family emblem, a broad arrow, onto prison uniforms and other government property. But the gambling and drinking could take its toll. Charles Granville inherited the Earldom of Bath in 1701 only to commit suicide a month later, allegedly overwhelmed by his father's debts.

The War of the Spanish Succession, 1701
King Charles II of Spain died in November 1700. He left no heir but he had planned to leave his huge empire to Louis XIV's grandson Philip, Duc d'Anjou. It would unite the Spanish and French kingdoms, making the House of Bourbon extremely powerful. England, the Dutch Republic and the Holy Roman Emperor, Leopold I, objected to the union and John Churchill, 1st Duke of Marlborough, represented his country during the negotiation of the Treaty of the Second Grand Alliance in September 1701. The treaty resulted in a struggle for Europe known as the Spanish War of Succession.

The Act of Settlement, 1701
The 1701 Act of Settlement restricted the succession to Protestants in England and Ireland but not in Scotland. It made Sophia of Hanover second in line to the throne ahead of fifty Catholics with a stronger claim. It was a popular Act and Robert Leke, 3rd Earl of Scarsdale, was one of only five peers to oppose it.

Chapter 32

Anne
1703–7

The Struggle to Produce an Heir

By 1700 Anne had been pregnant at least seventeen times. She had miscarried or had given birth to stillborn children twelve times. At least two of the five surviving children died within hours. Her grief must have been immeasurable.

Working for Anne

Anne was a difficult monarch to serve under. Her bad tempered uncle Laurence Hyde, 1st Earl of Rochester, advised the Queen but she dismissed him in 1703 following arguments. Edward Villiers, 1st Earl of Jersey, was dismissed as Lord Chamberlain in 1704 and he then became involved in the Jacobite plotting. Thomas Wharton, Earl of Wharton, was a fine public speaker and a 'political organiser of genius' who was one of the 'five tyrannising lords', or 'Junto' who led the Whigs. Anne hated the fact Wharton was 'void of moral or religious principles' and she enjoyed sacking the debauched and irreligious man when she had the chance.

The End of an Ancient Family, 1703

There have been many ancient and distinguished families in the English nobility. Aubrey de Vere was created the 1st Earl of Oxford by Empress Matilda in 1141 and members of the family have served twenty-seven monarchs. Aubrey de Vere, 20th Earl of Oxford, left no heirs when he died in 1703 ending over 550 years of unbroken line in his family.

Nobles in Trouble

Edward Montagu, 3rd Earl of Sandwich, was appointed Master of the Horse to Anne's husband Prince George of Denmark. But he suffered from mental illness and his wife had to keep him 'close confined' until his son was old enough to take over the family estates. The Queen dismissed him in 1704.

Lionel Cranfield Sackville, 1st Duke of Dorset, succeeded his father as Earl of Dorset and Middlesex in 1706. While he was dignified in appearance, 'he was in private the greatest lover of buffoonery and low company... he was never thought to have wanted a tendency to power, in whosever hands it was.'

The Darien Project, 1700
By the end of the 1690s, Scotland was jealous of England's developing colonies and it decided to create its own to give it a higher stake in the world market. It chose to colonise an area in the Gulf of Darién on the Isthmus of Panama, so an overland trade route could be opened between the Pacific and Atlantic oceans. A massive amount of Scottish money (between 25 and 50 per cent of the economy) was invested in the scheme.

The venture was called Caledonia but it was dogged by bad leadership and poor planning while disease decimated the colonists. A lack of trade undermined the validity of the Scottish scheme and the Darien project was abandoned when the Spanish besieged and blockaded the port in March 1700.

The abandonment of the colony seriously undermined the Scottish economy ruining many of its investors. Many of the Scottish landowners and merchants believed the only way to recover their money was to join with England and, hopefully, get a share of its successes. Some Scottish nobles asked England to wipe out their nation's debt in return for supporting a union between the two countries. They agreed, and wrote off nearly £400,000 as part of the 1707 Act of the Union.

The Union with Scotland, 1707
Scotland had remained an independent sovereign state with its own parliament and laws when the crowns united in March 1603. Anne announced it was 'very necessary' to conclude a union of England and Scotland following the introduction of the Act of Settlement. A joint Anglo-Scots commission failed to reach an agreement and Scotland introduced the Act of Security, which gave it the power to choose the next Scottish monarch if the Queen did not produce an heir. Anne refused to accept the Act until Scotland threatened to withdraw support for England's wars.

England introduced the Alien Act in 1705, which threatened to declare Scots aliens in England unless Scotland repealed the Act of Security or united with England. Scotland chose to unite and the Alien Act was dropped. The Acts of Union were agreed at the beginning of 1707 and England and Scotland were united into Great Britain, with a single parliament, on 1 May 1707.

Conclusions

There we have the story of 741 turbulent years in English history told through the eyes of the people who ran the kingdom on behalf of their kings or queens. It charts the many changes which started with William the Bastard of Normandy invading the Anglo-Saxon kingdom in 1066, over a broken promise. It ended with a nation called Great Britain which had emerged from the union between England, Wales, Ireland and Scotland in 1707 brought about by the failure of a Scottish colony in Central America.

The story started with invasion and conquest and it continued with unrelenting violence. Sometimes there was war between the king and his barons and sometimes it was against other countries. It has charted the conquering of Ireland and Wales and the acquisition and loss of territories in modern-day France. It has chronicled challenges to the monarch's power, like the twelfth century Anarchy, and early attempts to establish democracy for the chosen few, like the Barons' Wars.

More than a hundred years of war between England and France dominated the fourteenth and fifteenth centuries before England was plunged into a prolonged civil war between the warring factions of the Houses of York and Lancaster in the Wars of the Roses. Then there were the power struggles between the monarch and the Church in the sixteenth century, starting with Henry VIII creating a new Church of England and continuing with his children's different attitudes to religion.

There was another series of civil wars in the seventeenth century stemming from a difference of opinion over the governing of the kingdom in a struggle over how to rule the country; either by the monarch's absolute rule or through democratic discussion. But democracy had a strong grip on the country by the start of the eighteenth century and factions were content to decide matters in parliament rather than on the battlefield.

A monarch had to rely on strong, capable and loyal men to rule his kingdom on his behalf. It was far too big for him to keep visiting all the areas, especially when they also controlled a large part of modern France. He would either be busy in court or campaigning on the borders.

A king could buy loyalty if he carefully appointed the right men to be his earls. But newly appointed nobles were expected to manage their new acquisitions well, earning themselves and the crown revenue. A monarch could also hand out influential appointments, either political, administrative or military, to those who pleased him. But men were not always chosen for their ability, and a king often regretted choosing someone just because he was his favourite or because he was a yes-man. But a poor choice could cause resentment amongst the established families, especially if the newcomer used their new position to promote their family and friends.

Monarchs often relied on their favourites too much, rewarded them richly, to the disgust of the other nobles. Edward III made a poor choice in Piers Gaveston, Earl of Cornwall, while Elizabeth's choice of Robert Dudley, Earl of Leicester, upset many. James I entertained a string of favourites, each one pushed in front of him by the men trying to influence court.

Titles and appointments could also be confiscated if a noble did not do what was expected of him. They could also be cancelled if there was a change of monarch or if he changed his allegiance. They were often replaced by the worst punishment a noble could face, apart from death. That was an attainder, the cancellation of a title, and poverty, either temporary, for a generation, or permanent.

Some families lasted for many generations. Aubrey de Vere was created Earl of Oxford by Empress Matilda in 1141 for giving her support during the Anarchy. His namesake, the 20th Earl of Oxford, died in 1703 leaving no heirs, ending the unbroken line of the family after 550 years. But families could rise quickly into favour and then fall equally rapidly and spectacularly, none more so than the ambitious Thomas Boleyn. His family rose rapidly to great things in a short time as Henry VIII pursued his daughter Anne. But it ended quicker than it started with false accusations: the father was left with nothing, two of his children were executed, and his third was mother to the king's illegitimate child.

Whether the country was ruled by a monarch's absolute rule or if it was tempered by democracy was a long-running issue which sometimes flared into violence between the king and his subjects, especially if the monarch overtaxed his subjects to pay for foreign wars or introduced new laws to limit the power of his nobles. The Magna Carta in 1215, the Oxford Provisions in 1258, and the Lords Ordainers in 1310 are just three examples. Simon de Montfort, 6th Earl of Leicester, rallied support for his attempt to introduce democracy but it ended with the Baron's War in the 1260s and his gory death.

Plans to impose control on the king's unwise spending and diplomatic moves resulted in a split of opinion over how the country should be run; by absolute royal rule or democratic rule. It ended in a bloody Civil War in the 1640s and the only ever public execution of a monarch.

Family feuds played a big part in the uprisings and civil wars across the kingdom and they could start over anything. Territorial disputes, marriage issues, allegiances and the smallest slights of honour could escalate into bigger problems. Feuds were particularly prevalent in the border regions where tensions were often high. The famous example was the long-running rivalry between the Nevilles and the Percys along the Scottish borders. Several kings tried to keep the peace between these two powerful families, where a switch in loyalty could leave the north exposed to attack.

Monarchs often came into conflict with the Roman Catholic Church as they tried to assert control over the clergy. It must be remembered that the Church owned huge estates, raised large amounts of money for its own benefit and it influenced the people through its doctrines and ceremonies. There is no doubt about it, the crown and the church had to work hand in hand or there were problems.

The question over who wielded the power in great matters resulted in arguments over the rights and privileges of the Church. Henry I was excommunicated for attempting to undermine the power of the Church. The Archbishop of Canterbury, Thomas Beckett, was murdered when he opposed Henry II's Constitutions of Clarendon.

Going on crusade was a popular choice in the twelfth and thirteenth centuries. Some nobles decided to go on the long journey as atonement for their sins but others were ordered to go as a punishment. They faced travelling hundreds of miles, sometimes across hostile territory, to reach the Holy Land. They then faced more dangers as they fought the infidels in fearsome battles.

Religion in England came to a head during the reign of Henry VIII when there was a religious reformation sweeping across northern Europe. The king needed more money and his desire for a divorce led to the establishment of a new church, the Church of England, with Henry at its head. The new religion introduced a new fault line in the nobility as they had to choose between supporting their monarch or their established church. Many a baron struggled with their conscience and a few lost their lives because they chose the wrong side. The problems continued even after Elizabeth I introduced the compromise of the Anglican Church, as successive monarchs favoured Catholics or Protestants.

The era discussed in this book was, for the main part, a male dominated world. Men ruled, fought, taxed and died in the pursuit of their desires. There were few countesses in their own right because titles were passed through the male heirs. The few were sought-after brides who owned huge estates left to them by their deceased fathers or husbands. Countesses were rarely allowed to keep their inheritance for long because a king would marry them off to secure a man's loyalty. But some were so desirable that dishonourable nobles would use trickery and abduction to get their new bride and her inheritance.

Marrying for convenience rather than for love often brought its problems. Lustful husbands would seek pleasures with other women and their illegitimate children would cause problems of inheritance as often amongst the dukes and earls as it did amongst the kingdom's monarchs. While some long-suffering wives wanted to divorce their errant husbands, it was a man's prerogative and one which required the approval of the Church.

Throughout the period covered, the understanding of medical science was limited. Matters like infertility, miscarriage and infant deaths were seen as divine intervention rather than medical situations. Even so it did not stop the nobility trying for more children because each one held the promise of riches. Healthy sons could be used to marry wives who could bring a rich dowry while daughters could be used to form useful allegiances.

Noble children had a privileged life compared to that of the peasant classes but they rarely had a childhood. They were often married at early age and the child brides would be expected to be giving birth to strong sons and beautiful daughters as they entered their teenage years. It was quite common for nobles to be more loyal to their monarch than they were to their children, enjoying the rewards on offer rather than their offspring's happiness.

Several monarchs came to the throne when they were children, and the kingdom needed a regent until they came of age. The choice of regent was often a difficult one as the deceased monarch's close relatives struggled for control of the child. Two famous examples are that of Richard II and Edward VI. In the first it was the king's uncles who argued and in the second it was the young monarch's father, Henry VIII; he had chosen the Governor of the King's Person, executors of his will and a council. Richard III was more direct, arresting and then murdering his nephews so he could seize the crown. The young monarchs would often change policies as soon as they came of age and took control. The same problems occurred if a king became incapacitated through illness, as in the case of Henry IV. The argument over who would rule in his name was a major issue in the start of the Wars of the Roses.

The number of usurpations of the throne of England was high. For example, the Anarchy involving Matilda by Stephen, Richard II by Henry IV, Edward II by Edward III and James II by William. And these are just some of the successful ones, there were many more unsuccessful rebellions. All of them involved a group of England's nobles looking to either further their careers or get revenge against a spiteful or incompetent king. They faced another group of nobles who felt the same way about their man. More often than not, the monarch was little more than a figurehead in the revolt.

The number of premature deaths amongst England's monarchs was also high. For example, William II died in a hunting accident, young Edward V disappeared in the Tower with his brother, Richard III was killed at the Battle of Bosworth, and Charles I was executed. Nobles were either involved in their deaths, or were accused of being involved in them.

The same applied to heirs to the throne. They were prone to being imprisoned, executed or assassinated, whatever their age. An insecure king would go out of his way to track down all of his opponents, as was the case with Arthur and Eleanor, the Fair Maid of Brittany, at the beginning of the thirteenth century.

There were also a lot of failed attempts to change the way the country was run. The Epiphany Rising against Henry IV in 1400, the Southampton Plot against Henry V in 1415, the Gunpowder Plot against James I in 1605, and the Rye House Plot against Charles II in 1683 are just a few. Disgruntled nobles had a hand in all of them and they knew full well what would happen if they failed. Many a noble was imprisoned, exiled, tortured or executed for plotting against their king or queen.

Death was commonplace for everyone, especially during the early period. There was illness and disease to contend with but there were added dangers for the nobility. It was normal for a noble to lead his men into battle, which left him exposed to death in combat. But he would also face imprisonment or summary execution if he was taken prisoner.

Monarchs could execute their nobles at will if they thought they were conspiring against them. They usually stuck to the law when administering justice because few supported an unfair king, unless they were bribed to do so. But kings had it in their power to change the law or create a new one to suit their needs; Henry VIII was the master at using the law to his own benefit. Lawyers often used their knowledge of the law to give the monarch the decision they wanted. For example, Edward Seymour, 1st Duke of Somerset, was accused of felony for raising an unlicensed army when a charge of treason was dismissed. A different charge but the same outcome: execution.

But there were other ways of disposing of an unwanted noble. They could be declared insane and committed to prison where they could be dealt with at the king's pleasure, like Edward Plantagenet, 17th Earl of Warwick, who Henry VII had executed when Perkin Warbeck led a rebellion.

A noble could be accused of being a traitor and locked away where he could be offered the chance to change his opinions in exchange for his freedom. Philip Howard, 20th Earl of Arundel, was made a saint because he stuck to his Catholic religion rather than attend a Protestant service. Anyone held in the Tower dungeons knew they could face torture to extract the answer their king was looking for.

Once the death sentence had been passed, the king could choose how his prisoner would die. Would he face a swift, almost painless death or would he be made to endure a cruel, drawn-out affair? Beheading was the humane choice because it was quick, or at least that was the idea. If a poor executioner was employed or a blunt sword was used, the condemned man's end would be an unpleasant one.

Most nobles were beheaded on Tower Hill in the early days but a few were hung like common criminals at Tyburn where they were subjected to the howling mob. A traitor who was hung, drawn and quartered would experience an agonising end. He would be hung until nearly dead, then castrated and his guts torn out; once dead, his corpse was cut into pieces, his head presented to the king and displayed in a public place, and the parts of his body distributed to the four corners of the kingdom. Burning at the stake was the agonising death reserved for heretics and there were many when the kingdom struggled to come to terms with the switches in religion of the sixteenth century.

Sometimes nobles would be imprisoned or assassinated in the name of the king, to stop them making a challenge. Trumped-up or made-up charges were then invented, and cover-ups would take place to stop the king's name being associated with a mysterious death. For example, Richard II had Thomas of Woodstock, 1st Duke of Gloucester, murdered in Calais; William de la Pole, 1st Duke of Suffolk, was assassinated on Henry IV's orders; and Edward VI had Henry Holland, 3rd Duke of Exeter, drowned.

Of course the famous example of a mixture of the above methods is that of Richard III. He had his brother's marriage declared bigamous, his nephews' protectors executed on trumped-up charges, and his nephews imprisoned and murdered. All in pursuit of the coveted prize, the crown of England.

A king had to hope his subjects were blessed with the seven virtues: humility, kindness, virtue, patience, charity, diligence and sobriety. But the human frailties summarised as the seven deadly sins interfered in the running of a strong and stable kingdom. The monarch often found himself dealing with men who were driven by pride, greed, envy, wrath, sloth, gluttony and lust. All he could do was to reward the good, limit the powers of the bad, and execute the really bad.

All together the nobles of England were an eclectic mix of characters who needed careful handling if the monarch was to get the best out of them. They ranged from strong, loyal and brave men, through rebellious and unruly characters, to sex-mad drunks and gamblers. All the human weaknesses were displayed in the kingdom's nobility over the centuries, when rich rewards were promised for the right man and an agonizing end loomed for the wrong man.

Index